DICTIONARY OF PROVERBS

AND

QUOTATIONS

DICTIONARY OF PROVERBS

AND

QUOTATIONS

Bloomsbury Books
London

This edition published 1995 by Bloomsbury Books,
an imprint of Godfrey Cave Associates,
42 Bloomsbury Street, London, WC1B 3QJ.

ISBN 1 85471 695 6

Printed in UK

Contents

DICTIONARY OF PROVERBS

Contents

AGE, YOUTH
AND WISDOM

A child among men will soon be a man.

A creaking door hangs long on its hinges.

A fence lasts three years, a dog lasts three fences, a horse three dogs, and a man three horses.

A good life keeps off wrinkles.

A growing youth has a wolf in his belly.

A lazy youth, a lousy age.

A long life hath long miseries.

A man among children will be long a child.

A man as he manages himself, may die old at thirty or young at eighty.

A man at five may be a fool at fifteen.

A man at sixteen will prove a child at sixty.

A man often admits that his memory is at fault but never his judgement.

A new net won't catch an old bird.

A prudent youth is superior to a stupid old man.

A wild colt may become a sober old horse.

A worm is in the bud of youth and at the root of old age.

A young man negligent, an old man necessitous.

A young preacher, a new hell.

Action from youth, advice from middle age, prayers from the aged.

Affectation of wisdom often prevents us from becoming wise.

Age but tastes, youth devours.

Age is a sorry travelling companion.

All of us must be drunk once, youth is drunkenness without wine.

All would live long, but none would be old.

An idle youth, a needy age.

An old cat laps as much as a young kitten.

An old dog bites sore.

An old dog cannot alter its way of barking.

An old dog does not bark for nothing.

An old dog does not grow used to the collar.

An old dog will learn no tricks.

An old fox needs no craft.

An old lion is better than a young ass.

An old man is a bed full of bones.

An old man never wants a tale to tell.

An old man's saying's are seldom untrue.

An old man's shadow is better than a young man's sword.

An old ox ploughs a straight furrow.

An old ox will find shelter for himself.

An old physician and a young lawyer are the best.

An old poacher makes the best keeper.

An old soldier, an old fool.

An unseeded youth, a needy age.

As the boy, so the man.

As the old birds sing the young ones twitter.

As the old cock crows so the young ones learn.

As we journey through life let us live by the way.

Ask the mother if the child be like his father.

Bend the willow while it is young.

Better eat grey bread in youth than in your age.

Better poor, young, and wise, than rich, old and a fool.

Better to live well than to live long.

Better under the beard of the old man than the whip of the young.

Both folly and wisdom come upon us with years.

Boys will be boys.

Consider well and oft why thou comest into this world and how soon thou must go out of it.

Consult with the old and fence with the young.

Crabbed age and youth cannot live together.

Credulity is the man's weakness, but the child's strength.

Custom in infancy becomes nature in old age.

Don't teach your grandmother to suck eggs.

Every station in life has duties which are proper to it.

Few persons know how to be old.

Footprints in the sand of time are not made by sitting down.

Happy is he that knows his follies in his youth.

He is oft the wisest man who is not wise at all.

He is well onward in the way of wisdom, who can bear a reproof and mend by it.

He is young enough who has health, and he is rich enough who has no debts.

He lives long that lives till all are weary of him.

He lives long that lives well.

He lives longest that is awake most hours.

He that corrects not youth controls not age.

He that is not gallant at twenty, strong at thirty, rich at forty or experienced at fifty, will never be gallant, strong, rich or experienced.

He that would be long an old man must begin early to be one.

He who lives a long life must pass through much evil.

He who lives after nature shall never be poor; after opinion shall never be rich.

Heavy work in youth is quiet rest in old age.

If only youth had the knowledge; if only age had the strength.

If the old dog barks he gives counsel.

If the young knew, if the old man could, there is nothing but would be done.

If you lie upon roses while young, you'll lie upon thorns when old.

If you live enough before thirty you won't care to live at all after fifty.

If you play with boys you must take boy's play.

If youth knew what old age would crave,
  It would both get and save.

In childhood be modest, in youth temperate, in manhood just, in old age, prudent.

In the short life of man, no lost time can be afforded.

In youth beauty and wisdom is but rare.

Intemperate youth ends in an age imperfect and unsound.

It has been a great misfortune to many a one that he lived too long.

It is always the season for the old to learn.

It is as well now and then not to remember all we know.

It is difficult to grow old gracefully.

It is hard to put old heads on young shoulders.

It is less painful to learn in youth than to be ignorant in age.

It is not easy to straighten in the oak the crook that grew in the sapling.

It is the common failing of old men to attribute all wisdom to themselves.

Life begins at forty.

Life is half spent before one knows what life is.

Life is not measured by the time we live.

Life is short, yet sweet.

Life is too short to learn more than one business well.

Life that is too short for the happy is too long for the miserable.

Life's but a walking shadow.

Live not for time, but eternity.

Memory tempers prosperity, mitigates adversity and controls youth and delights old age.

Men are but children of a larger growth.

Men who live to be a hundred will not die at fifty.

Most old men are like old trees, past bearing themselves,
   will suffer no young plants to flourish beneath them.

No age agreeable but that of a wise man.

Never too old to learn.

No fool like an old fool

No man believes his own life will be short.

No man is born wise.

No man is so old but thinks he may live another day.

No man is the worse for knowing the worst of himself.

No one so old that he may not live a year, none so young
   that he may die today.

Of all the plagues none can compare with climbing boys.

Old age and treachery will always defeat youth and skill.

Old age brings companions with it.

Old age comes uncalled.

Old age, though despised, is coveted by all.

Old age itself is a disease.

Old age is a troublesome guest.

Old age is honourable.

Old boys have their playthings as well as young ones; the
   difference is only in price.

Old head and young hand.

Old men are twice children.

Old men for counsel, young men for war.

Old men who have loved young company have been of long life.

Old oxen have stiff horns.

Old oxen tread hard.

Old people see best in the distance.

Our time runs on like a stream, first falls the leaves and then the tree.

Reckless youth makes rueful old age.

Secure the three things, virtue, wealth and happiness, they will serve as a staff in old age.

Talents are best nurtured in solitude, but character in life's tempestuous sea.

That is pleasant to remember that which was hard to endure.

The aged in council, the young in action.

The bread of repentance we eat is often made of the wild oats we sow in our youth.

The follies of youth are food for repentance in old age.

The great man is he that does not lose his child's heart.

The great use of life is to spend it for something that out-lasts it.

The longest life is but a parcel of moments.

The old effect more by counsel than the young by war.

The old for want of ability and the young for want of knowledge let things be lost.

The old forget, the young don't know.

The old have death before their face, the young behind their back.

The old have every day something new.

The old man who dances furnishes the devil fine sport.

The old man who is loved is winter with flowers.

The old man's counsel is half deed.

The old ones sing, the young ones pipe.

The old see better behind than the young before.

The oldest man that ever lived died at last.

The only jewel you can carry beyond the grave is wisdom.

The only sure path to a tranquil life is through virtue.

The remembrance of a well spent life is sweet.

The reputation of a man depends on the first steps he takes in the world.

The warnings of age are the weapons of youth.

The way to live much is to live well betimes.

The web of your life is of a mingled yarn, good and ill together.

The young are slaves to novelty, the old to custom.

The young are not always with their bows bent.

The young man's wrath is like straw of fire,
But like red hot steel is the old man's ire.

There are more lamb skins than sheep skins.

There is a difference between living long and suffering long.

There's many a good tune played on an old fiddle.

There is a learning time in youth which suffered to escape and no foundation laid, seldom returns

They live too long who happiness outlive.

They who live longest will see most.

They who would be young when they are old must be old when they are young.

'Tis very certain the desire of life prolongs it.

To live long it is necessary to live slowly.

True wisdom is the price of happiness.

Wanton kittens make sober cats.

We are born crying, live complaining, and die disappointed.

We have all forgotten more than we remember.

We live not as we would but as we can.

We must not look for a golden life in an iron age.

We shall never be younger.

We pass our lives in doing what we ought not, and leaving undone what we ought to.

What the old man does is always correct.

What youth learns age does not forget.

When an old dog bites look out.

When men grow old they become more foolish and more wise.

When old age is evil youth can learn no good.

When the boy is growing he has a wolf in his belly.

Where the old are foolish the child learns folly.

Who follow not virtue in youth cannot fly sin in old age.

Who honours not age is unworthy of it.

Who is lazy in their youth must work in old age.

Who lives well sees afar off.

Who lives will see.

Who would be young in age, must in youth be sage.

Who would grow old with honour must begin early.

Whosoever masters not his own life may not be master of another's.

Wisdom adorns riches and shadows poverty.

Wisdom at proper times will forget.

Wisdom goes not always by years.

Wisdom in the mind is better than money in the hand.

Wisdom is a good purchase though we pay dear for it.

Wisdom is humble that he knows no more.

Wisdom is more to be envied than riches.

Wisdom is the least burdensome travelling pack.

Wisdom is the sunlight of the soul.

Wisdom rides on the ruins of folly.

Wisdom sometimes walks in clouted shoes.

Wisdom was the daughter of Knowledge by Reflection.

You are only as old as you feel.

You can't teach an old dog new tricks.

You cannot catch old birds with chaff.

You may break a colt, but not an old horse.

Young folk, silly folk, old folk, cold folk.

Young man soon give and soon forget affronts, old age is slow at both.

Young men are made wise, old men become so.

Young men should be learners when old men are actors.

Young men think old men are fools, and old men know young men to be so.

Young men's knocks old men feel.

Young people must be taught, old ones be honoured.

Young saint, old devil.

Youth and age will never agree.

Youth and white paper take any impression.

Youth comes but once in a lifetime.

Youth is a blunder, manhood a struggle, old age a regret.

Youth is a garland of roses, age is a crown of thorns.

Youth is full of pleasance, old age is full of care.

Youth is merry and holds no society with grief.

Youth is life's seed time.

Youth is the season of hope.

Youth looks forward and age backward.

Youth may stray but return at last.

Youth must be served.

Youth ne'er casts for peril.

Youth should be a saving's bank.

Youth will have it's swing.

APPEARANCE,
CONDUCT AND DRESS

A bad excuse is better than none.

A barking dog never bites.

A brain is worth little without a tongue.

A civil question deserves a civil answer.

A clean glove often hides a dirty hand.

A fair face may be a foul bargain.

A fair face may hide a foul heart.

A fair face will get its praise though the owner keep silent.

A gentleman should be honest in his actions and refined in his language.

A good anvil does not fear the hammer.

A good archer is not known by his arrow but by his aim.

A good horse is never of a bad colour.

A good face is a letter of recommendation.

A good name is a second inheritance.

A good name keeps its lustre in the dark.

A good word is as soon said as a bad one.

A grave and majestic outside is as it were the palace of the soul.

A hog in armour is still but a hog.

A leopard cannot change it's spots.

A liar ought to have a good memory.

A loud voice bespeaks a vulgar man.

A man is not known by his looks, nor is the sea measured with a bushel.

A man never speaks of himself without loss.

A man's character reaches town before his person.

A monkey remains a monkey though dressed in silk.

A proud look makes foul work in a fair face.

A quiet tongue shows a wise head.

A silent tongue and a true heart are the most admirable things on earth.

A smart coat is a good letter of introduction.

A sober man, a soft answer.

A still tongue makes a wise head.

A straight stick is crooked in the water.

Act honestly and go boldly.

23

Act so in the valley so you need never fear those who stand on the hill.

Actions speak louder than words.

Affected superiority mars good fellowship.

After the land's manner is mannerly.

Ale sellers should not be tale tellers.

All are not asleep who have their eyes shut.

All cats are grey in the dark.

All doors open to courtesy.

All that glitters is not gold.

Always appear what you are and a little below it.

An ape's an ape, a varlet's a varlet,
　Though he be dressed in silk or scarlet.

An art requires a whole man.

Appearances are deceitful.

As a man dresses so is he esteemed.

As the man so is his speech.

As you make your bed so must you lie on it.

As you sow, so you reap.

Ask advice of your equals, help of your superiors.

Ask me no questions and I'll tell you no lies.

Ask no questions and hear no lies.

Be not the trumpeter of your own praise.

Be silent or say something better than silence.

Be what you appear to be.

Bear and forebear.

Beauty and understanding seldom go together.

Beauty blemished once is forever lost.

Beauty comes not by forcing.

Beauty doth varnish age.

Beauty draws more than the oxen.

Beauty draws with a single hair.

Beauty is a frail advantage.

Beauty is in the eye of the beholder.

Beauty is no inheritance.

Beauty is but a blossom.

Beauty is but skin deep.

Beauty is the eye's food and the soul's sorrow.

Beauty is truth, truth beauty.

Beauty is worse than wine; it intoxicates both the holder and the beholder.

Beauty will buy no beef.

Beauty without modesty is infamous.

Beauty without virtue is a curse.

Better late than never.

Better to give than to receive.

Beware the wolf in sheep's clothing.

Brave actions never need a trumpet.

By nature all men are alike, but by education widely different.

By the stubble you may guess the grain.

Children should be seen and not heard.

Civility costs nothing.

Cleanliness is next to godliness.

Clothes make the man.

Compliments cost nothing, yet many pay dear for them.

Discretion is the better part of valour.

Do not always judge by appearances

Do not judge a book by it's cover.

Do not look a gift horse in the mouth.

Don't hide your light under a bushel.

Dress slowly when you are in a hurry.

Every picture tells a story.

Every rose has its thorn.

Fair play is a jewel.

Fine feathers make fine birds.

Fine linen often conceals a foul skin.

First impressions are the most lasting.

Give every man his due.

Good advice can be given, good name cannot be given.

Good looks buy nothing in the market.

Good manners are made up of petty sacrifices.

Goodness brightens beauty.

Handsome is as handsome does.

He cannot speak well that cannot hold his tongue

He gives double who gives unasked.

He looks as though butter would not melt in his mouth.

He that is proud of his clothes gets his reputation from his tailor.

He that is unkind to his own, will be unkind to others.

He that knows when to speak knows when to be silent too.

He who abuses others must not be particular about he answer he gets.

He who dresses in others' clothes will be undressed on the highway.

He who gives grudgingly shall be taught better by adversity.

He who has but one coat cannot lend it.

He who holds his tongue saves his head.

He who lives by the alter must serve by the alter.

He who says what he likes hears what he does not like.

If the cap fits wear it.

Imitation is the sincerest form of flattery.

In the land of the naked, people are ashamed of clothes.

In this world it is necessary that we help one another.

In your own country your name, in other countries your appearance.

It is a good tongue that speaks no ill.

It is an ill bird that fouls its own nest

It is not the fine but the course and ill-spun that breaks.

It is not the habit that makes the monk.

It is often better not to see an insult than to avenge it.

It is the quiet people who are dangerous.

It's the thought, not the action that counts.

Keep not two tongues in one mouth.

Let him mend his manners, they will be his own another day.

Let not your tongue cut your throat.

Long and lazy, little and loud, fat and fulsome, pretty and proud.

Manners and money make the gentleman.

Manners make the man.

Manners often make fortunes.

Meat is much, but manners is more.

Men seek less to be instructed than applauded.

Much is expected where much is given.

Near is my shirt, but nearer is my skin.

Nine tailors make the man.

No fine clothes can hide the clown.

No fire without smoke.

No smoke without fire.

Not every sort of wood is fit to make an arrow.

Nothing comes of nothing.

Novelty always appears handsome.

Offenders never pardon.

Old habits die hard.

One does not wash one's dirty linen in public.

One good turn deserves another.

One must be either hammer or anvil.

One never lost anything by politeness.

Other times, other manners.

Out of sight, out of mind.

Over the greatest beauty hangs the greatest pain.

Patience is a virtue.

People who live in glass houses should not throw stones.

Politeness is benevolence in small things.

Practice what you preach.

Pride goes before a fall.

Promises, like pie-crust, are made to be broken.

Proud looks lose hearts, but courteous words win them.

Punctuality and politeness are the inseparable companions of gentlemen.

Rich garments weep on unworthy shoulders.

Ruling one's anger well is not so good as preventing the anger.

Say not all you know, but believe all that you say.

See no evil, hear no evil, speak no evil.

Silence is golden.

Small is beautiful.

Spare to speak and spare to speed.

Still waters run deep.

Talk is cheap.

The archer that shoots badly has a lie ready.

The best manners are stained by the addition of pride.

The beetle is a beauty in the eyes of its mother.

The courteous learns his courtesy from the discourteous.

The cowl does not make the monk.

The eyes are the window of the soul.

The fairest rose at last is withered.

The golden covering does not make the ass a horse.

The grass is always greener on the other side.

The handsomest flower is not the sweetest.

The man in boots does not know the man in shoes.

The manner of speaking is as important as the matter.

The peacock hath fair feathers but foul feet.

The pot calls the kettle black.

The smith and his penny are both black.

The style is the man.

The tree is known by its fruit.

The white coat does not make the miller.

There are black sheep in every flock.

There are spots even on the sun.

There is a time and a place for everything.

There is no accounting for taste.

There is no making a good cloak of bad cloth.

There is no trusting to appearances.

Think first and then speak.

Thistles and thorns prick sore, but evil tongues prick more.

Too much humility is pride.

Two things a man should never be angry at; what he can
help and what he cannot.

Under a good cloak may be a bad man.

Under a shabby cloak may be a smart thinker.

Under the thorn grow the roses.

Virtue is it's own reward.

Virtue is the one and only nobility.

Vulgarity in manners defiles garments more than mud.

We may give advice but we cannot give conduct.

We seize the beautiful and reject the useful.

We should never be too proud to take advice even from the lowly.

What you see is what you get.

When angry, count ten; when very angry, a hundred.

When bowing, bow low.

When either side grows warm to argument the wisest man gives over first.

When in doubt, do nothing.

When in Rome, do as the Romans do.

When you have nothing to say, say nothing.

Where there is whispering there is lying.

Who answers for another pays.

Who answers suddenly knows little.

Who says little has little to answer for.

Whose heart is narrow his tongue is large.

You can't make a silk purse from a sow's ear.

You can't please everyone.

You can't put new wine in old bottles.

CRIME AND PUNISHMENT

A bad dog never sees the wolf.

A bad penny always comes back.

A bad tree does not yield young apples.

A crow is never the whiter for ever washing.

A fair booty makes a fair thief.

A fault confessed is half redressed.

A gold ring does not cure a felon.

A great crime is in a great man greater.

A hundred years of wrong do not make an hour of right.

A man who is his own lawyer has a fool for a client.

A mischievous dog must be tied short.

A monarch should be slow to punish, swift to reward.

A rotten egg cannot be spoiled.

A sinful heart makes a feeble hand.

A thief does not willingly see another carry a basket.

A thief is better than a lazy servant.

A thief knows a thief as a wolf knows a wolf.

A thief passes for a gentleman when stealing has made him rich.

A thief seldom grows rich by thieving.

A thief thinks every man steals.

A wolf is a wolf though it hath torn no sheep.

Accusing is proving when malice and force sit as judges.

Accusing the times is only accusing yourselves.

Advice after mischief is like medicine after death.

After one vice a greater follows.

Agree, for the law is costly.

All are not hanged who are condemned.

All are not thieves whom the dogs bark at.

All beginnings are hard, said the thief, and began by stealing the anvil.

All criminals turn preacher when under the gallows.

All fear but fear of heaven betrays a guilt.

All temptations are found in either hope or fear.

All vice infatuates and corrupts the judgement.

Although invisible there are always two witnesses present at our every action; God and our conscience.

An evil deed has a witness in the bosom.

An old physician and a young lawyer make the best counsel.

An old thief desires a new halter.

An open box tempts the thief.

Anger is to be avoided in inflicting punishment.

Anger punishes itself.

As good steal the horse as look over the hedge.

At an open chest the righteous sins.

Bad watch often feeds the wolf.

Better no law than law not enforced.

Better ten guilty escape than one innocent man suffer.

Better to be beaten than to be in bad company.

Better to do nothing than to do ill.

Birds of a feather flock together.

Bloody and deceitful men dig their own graves.

Caesar's wife must be above suspicion.

Catching is before hanging.

Charity covers a multitude of sins.

Cheats never prosper.

Commit a sin thrice and you will think it allowable.

Confession is good for the soul.

Conquer one besetting sin at a time.

Conscience makes cowards of us all.

Constant dropping wears away the stone.

Crime never pays.

Crimes may be secret, but not secure.

Criminals are punished that others may be amended.

Crooked by nature is never made straight by education.

Crooked iron may be straightened with a hammer.

Crows are never the whiter for washing themselves.

Curiosity often brings its own punishment.

Cut off the dog's tail he remains a dog.

Deceit and treachery make no man rich.

Deceit is in haste, but honesty can wait a fair leisure.

Devils must be driven out with devils.

Do as little as you can repent of.

Don't hear one and judge two.

Even doubtful accusations leave a stain behind them.

Every herring must hang by it's own gill.

Every land has its own law.

Every sin carries its own punishment.

Every tribe has its thief, every mountain its wolf.

Everyone takes his flogging in his own way.

Everyone's censure is first moulded in his own nature.

Evil comes to fall on him that goes to seek it.

Evil doers are evil dreaders.

Evil is soon done but slowly mended.

Examples of justice are more merciful than the unbounded exercise of pity.

Extreme justice is extreme injustice.

First a turnip, then a sheep, next a cow, and then the gallows.

Give a dog a bad name and hang him.

Give him enough rope and he will hang himself.

God help the sheep when the wolf is judge.

God permits the wicked, but not forever.

Gold is the devils fish-hook.

Good men are scarce.

Great thieves always have their sleeves full of gags.

Guilt has quick ears to a confession.

Guilt is always cowardly.

Guilt is always zealous.

Guilt sinks the brave to cowards.

Guilty men still judge others like them.

Guilty men still suspect what they deserve.

Habit in sinning takes away the sense of sin.

Half the truth is often the whole lie.

Hang him that have no shift and him that hath too many.

Hang the young thief and the old one will not steal.

Hanging is the worst use a man can be put to.

Hard cases make the law.

He acts the third crime that defends the first.

He confesses his guilt who flies from his trial.

He declares himself guilty who justifies himself before accusation.

He is a thief for he has taken a cup too many.

He is a thief indeed that robs a thief.

He keeps his road well enough who gets rid of bad company.

He sins as much who holds the bag as he who puts into it.

He that deals in dirt always has dirty fingers.

He that forgives gains the victory.

He that has an ill name is half hanged.

He that is disposed for mischief will never want occasion.

He that is embarked with the devil must sail with him.

He that is foolish in the fault, let him be wise in the punishment.

He that is innocent may well be confident.

He that lies down with dogs will get up with fleas.

He that shows his wealth to a thief is the cause of his own pillage.

He that slays shall be slain.

He that spares the wicked injures the good.

He that spares vice wrongs virtue.

He that wants to beat a dog is sure to find a stick.

He that will steal a pin will steal a better thing.

He who accuses too many accuses himself.

He who denies confesses all.

He who has a son grown up should not call another a thief.

He who is free from vice himself is the slower to suspect it in others.

He who lives wickedly lives in fear.

He who makes a law should keep it.

He who profits by a crime commits it.

He who sups with the devil should have a long spoon.

He's armed without that's innocent within.

Him who errs forgive once, but never twice.

Honesty is the best policy.

Honesty may be dear bought, but can never be ill penny-worth.

Hunger drives the wolf out of the wood.

Hunt with the wolves and be hunted with the wolves.

I am a man more sinned against than sinning.

I must be cruel only to be kind.

I'll trust him no farther than I can throw a millstone.

Idleness is the root of all evil.

If a man deceive me once, shame on him, if he deceives me twice shame on me.

If there were no receiver there would be no thief.

If you are born to be hanged then you will never be drowned.

If you can't be good, be careful.

If you cut down the woods you'll catch the thief.

If you would make a thief honest trust him.

Ignorance of the law is no excuse for breaking it.

Ill doth the devil deserve his servants.

Ill-gotten goods never thrive.

Ill laying up makes many thieves.

Ill weeds grow apace.

Ill-got, ill-spent.

In the land of sinners the unjust sit in judgement.

Innocence finds not so much protection as guilt.

Innocence is a wall of brass.

Innocence is no protection.

Innocence itself sometimes hath need of a mark.

Innocent actions carry their warrants with them.

It is an ill bird that fouls its own nest.

It is better to suffer wrong than do it.

It is cruelty to the innocent not to punish the guilty.

It is easier to hurt than to heal.

It is easy robbing when the dog is quietened.

It is easy to rob an orchard when none keeps it.

It is folly to expect justice from the unprincipled.

It is hard to steal where the host himself is a thief.

It is honourable to be accused by those who deserve to be accused.

It is less to suffer punishment than to deserve it.

It is more noble to pardon than to punish.

It is never too late to mend.

It is not enough to know how to steal, one must know how to conceal.

It is seldom that punishment, though lame of foot, has failed to overtake a villain.

It is the raised stick makes the dog obey.

It is wit to pick a lock and steal a horse, but wisdom to leave it alone.

Judge not that you be not judged.

Justice was never angry.

Keep yourself from opportunity and God will keep you from sin.

Know how to deceive, do not deceive.

Late repentance is seldom worth much.

Law cannot persuade where it cannot punish.

Law catches flies and lets hornets go free.

Law makers should not be law breakers

Laws go the way kings direct.

Laws grind the poor, and rich men rule the law.

Laws were made for rogues.

Laws were made to be broken.

Let justice be done or the heavens fall.

Let the punishment fit the crime.

Let them who deserve their punishment bear it patiently.

Little thieves are hanged by the neck, and great thieves by the purse.

Locks and keys are not made for honest fingers.

Look not at the thieves eating flesh, but look at them suffering punishment.

Man hath no greater enemy than himself.

Man punishes the action, but God the intention.

Many without punishment, none without sin.

Men are never so easily deceived as when they are trying to deceive others.

Money and friendship bribe justice.

Murder will out.

Necessity knows no law.

Needs must when the devil drives.

Never do evil that good may come of it.

New lords, new laws.

Nip sin in the bud.

No armour is proof against the gallows.

No crime is more infamous than the violation of the truth.

No deceit like the world's.

No man may be both accuser and judge.

No one likes justice brought home to his own door.

No one should be judge in his own case.

No villain like the conscientious villain.

Nothing is law that is not reason.

Nothing is profitable which is dishonest.

Old sin, new shame.

Old sins cast long shadows.

Once a rogue, always a rogue.

One crime has to be concealed by another.

One deceit brings on another.

One law for the rich and another for the poor.

One might as well be hanged for a sheep as a lamb.

One rotten apple in the barrel infects the rest.

One wrong step may give you great fall.

Opportunity makes the thief.

Our desires may undo us.

Plenty of words when the cause is lost.

Poverty is not a crime.

Prevention is better than cure.

Put a miller, a weaver, and a tailor in a bag and shake them, the first that comes out will be a thief.

Revenge is a kind of wild justice.

Revenge is sweet.

Riches without law are more dangerous than is poverty without law.

Save a thief from the gallows and he will cut your throat.

Set a thief to catch a thief.

Sin that is hidden is half forgotten.

Sooner or later the truth comes to light.

Strict law is often great injustice.

Successful crime is called virtue.

Swindling is the perfection of civilisation.

That which is evil is soon learnt.

The back door robs the house.

The breastplate of innocence is not always scandal proof.

The devil finds work for idle hands to do.

The devil looks after his own.

The devil makes his Christmas pies of lawyers' tongues and clerks' fingers.

The devil take the hindmost.

The devil's children have the devil's luck.

The first of all virtues is innocence; modesty the second.

The gallows takes its own.

The good fear no law; it is his safety and the bad man's awe.

The good hate to sin from love of virtue, the bad hate to sin from fear of punishment.

The greater the sinner, the greater the saint.

The guilty mind needs no accuser.

The guilt and not the gallows makes the shame.

The judge is condemned when the accused is acquitted.

The law devised, it's evasion contrived.

The law guards us from all evils but itself.

The law has a nose of wax; one can twist it as he will.

The law is not the same at morning and night.

The laws sometimes sleep but never die.

The monarch's errors are forbidden game.

The more laws the less justice.

The more laws, the more offenders.

The most cunning are the first caught.

The prince and even the people are responsible for the crimes they neglect to punish.

The stains that villainy leave behind no time will wash away.

The sting of a reproach bears the truth of it.

The surest panoply is innocence.

The thief becomes the gallows well.

The thief is frightened even by the mouse.

The thief proceeds from a needle to gold, and from gold to the gallows.

The thief steals until he comes to the gallows.

The tongue always returns to the sore tooth.

The triumphing of the wicked is short.

The truth is the best advocate.

The villain's censure is extorted praise.

The wages of sin is death.

The wicked ears are deaf to wisdom's call.

The wickedness of a few is the calamity of all.

The wise man seeks the lawyer early.

The wolf calls the fox robber.

The wolf must pay with his skin.

The wolf prays not in his own field.

The worst punishment of all is that in the court of his own conscience, no guilty man is acquitted.

The wrong doer never lacks a pretext.

There are good and bad everywhere.

There are more thieves than are hanged.

There is but one short step between lying and theft.

There is honour among thieves.

There is no crime without a precedent.

They hurt themselves that do wrong.

They that dance must pay the fiddler.

Thieves quarrel and thefts are discovered.

Those whom guilt stains it equals.

Those who sow injustice reap hate and vengeance.

Though justice has leaden feet it has leaden hands.

Though malice may darken truth it cannot put it out.

'Tis not the action but the intention that is good or bad.

To a bad character good doctrine avails nothing.

To accuse the wicked and defend the wretched is an honour.

To err is human, to forgive divine.

To know the law and do the right are two different things.

Too much cunning undoes.

Trust makes way for treachery.

Truth and oil always come to the surface.

Truth is mighty and will prevail.

Truth is straight but judges are crooked.

Truth may be suppressed but never strangled.

Truth never fears investigation.

Truth never perishes.

Truth stretches but never breaks.

Truth's cloak is often lined with lies.

Two wrongs do not make a right.

Vice is its own punishment and sometimes its own cure.

Vice is cherished and thrives by concealment.

Vice will stain the noblest race.

Virtue and vice cannot dwell under the same roof.

We are ever young enough to sin, never old enough to repent.

We easily forget crimes known only to ourselves.

We ought to weigh well what we can only once decide.

We should consult three things in all our actions; justice, honesty and utility.

What can innocence hope for, when such as sit her judges are corrupted.

What is just and right is the law of laws.

What is no sin is no shame.

When God means to punish a nation He deprives its rulers of wisdom.

When it thunders the thief becomes honest.

When men of talents are punished, authority is strengthened.

When the cat is away the mice will play.

When thieves fall out, honest men come by their own.

Where law ends tyranny begins.

Where the wolf gets one lamb he looks for another.

Where vice is vengeance follows.

While you trust to the dog the wolf slips into the sheepfold.

Who demands justice must administer justice.

Who does no ill can have no foe.

Who does not punish evil invites it.

Who has deceived thee as often as thyself.

Who is not afraid of his sins, sins double.

Who punishes one threatens a hundred.

Who will not be deceived must have as many eyes on his
head as hairs.

Woe be to him whose advocate becomes his accuser.

You are a fool to steal if you can't conceal.

You must not hang a man by his looks.

You'll dance at the end of a rope without teaching.

DEATH,
SUFFERING AND GRIEF

A day of sorrow is longer than a month of joy.

A dead man does not make war.

A dead man does not speak.

A dead man has neither friends or relations.

A dead mouse feels no cold.

A drowning man will clutch at a straw.

A living dog is better than a dead lion.

A man can die but once.

A man has learned much, who has learned to die.

A small tear relieves a great sorrow.

A sudden death is the best.

All death is sudden to the unprepared.

All men are born richer than they die.

All sorrows are bearable if there is bread.

Alone in counsel, alone in sorrow.

An honourable death is worth more than an inglorious life.

Another's suffering is but skin deep.

Any mind that is capable of real sorrow is capable of real good.

As a man lives so shall he die.

As soon as man is born he begins to die.

As soon dies the calf as the cow.

As soon goes the lamb's skin to market as the old cow.

As the tree falls so shall it lie.

Bad news travels fast.

Better once dead than all the time suffering in need.

Better two losses than one sorrow.

Blessed are the dead that the rain falls on.

Blessed is the misfortune that comes alone.

Call no man happy till he dies.

Come soon or late death's undetermined day,
   This mortal being only can decay.

Constant complaints never get pity.

Curses, like chickens will come home to roost.

Dead dogs don't bite.

Dead folks can't bite.

Dead men do not bite.

Dead men pay no surgeons.

Dead men tell no tales.

Death always comes too early or too late.

Death and life are in the power of the tongue.

Death and love are two wings which bear men from earth to heaven.

Death and marriage make term day.

Death defies the doctor.

Death does not blow a trumpet.

Death foreseen never comes.

Death has a thousand doors to let out life.

Death hath nothing terrible in it, but what life hath made so.

Death is a black camel that kneels at every man's gate.

Death is but what the haughty brave,
    The weak must bear, the wretch must crave.

Death is in the pot.

Death is never premature except to those who die without virtue.

Death is not the greatest of ills; it is worse to want to die, and not be able to.

Death is shameful in flight, glorious in victory.

Death is the great leveller.

Death keeps no calendar.

Death meets us everywhere.

Death opens the gate to good fame and extinguishes envy.

Death pays all debts.

Death rather frees us of ills than robs us of our goods.

Death is but a path that must be trod,
    If man would ever pass to God.

Death spares neither pope nor beggar.

Death spares neither man nor beast.

Death to the wolf is life to the lamb.

Death will hear of no excuse.

Deep swimmers and high climbers seldom die in their beds.

Desperate diseases must have desperate remedies.

Dig but deep enough, and under all earth runs water, under all life runs grief.

Do not speak ill of the dead, but deem them sacred who have gone into the immortal state.

Earth has no sorrow that heaven cannot heal.

Every cloud has a silver lining.

Every man must eat a peck of dust before he dies.

Every one can master a grief but he that has it.

Every one must pay his debt to nature.

Every substantial grief has twenty shadows, and most of them shadows of your own making.

Everything becomes intolerable to the man who is once subdued by grief.

Few have luck, all have death.

Good or bad we must all live.

Great griefs are mute.

Great griefs medicine the less.

Great pains cease us to forget the little ones.

Grey hairs are death's blossoms.

Grief diminishes when it has nothing to grow upon.

Grief is a stone that bears one down, but two bear it lightly.

Grief is satisfied and carried off by tears.

Grief is the agony of an instant; the indulgence of grief the blunder of a life.

Grief pent up will break the heart.

Hang sorrow, care will kill the cat.

He dies like a beast who has done no good while he lived.

He gains enough who loses sorrow.

He grieves more than is necessary who grieves before it is necessary.

He hath not lived that lives not after death.

He hauls at a long rope that expects another's death.

He is miserable indeed who must lock up his miseries.

He is miserable once who feels it, but twice who fears it before it comes.

He lives in fame who dies for virtue's cause.

He should wear iron shoes that bides his neighbour's death.

He that conceals his grief finds no remedy for it.

He that died half a year ago is as dead as Adam.

He that dies this year is quit of the next.

He that is uneasy at ever so little pain is never without some ache.

He that lives long suffers much.

He that lives most, dies most.

He that lives not well for one year sorrows it for seven.

He that lives on hope has but a slender diet.

He waits long that waits for another man's death.

He who cannot hold his peace will never live at ease.

He who fears death dies every time he thinks of it.

He who lives on hope dies on hunger.

He who loves sorrow will always find something to grieve over.

He who much has suffered much will know.

He who swims in sin will sink in sorrow.

Help you to salt, help you to sorrow.

Hope deferred makes a sick heart.

Hope for the best and prepare for the worst.

How wise in God to place death at the end of life.

If death be terrible the fault is not in death but thee.

If you want to be dead wash your head and go to bed.

Immoderate sorrow causes great mischief.

It is a great art to laugh at your own misfortunes.

It is a great journey to life's end.

It is as natural to die as to be born.

It is better to die once than to live always in the fear of death.

It is good to die before one has done anything deserving death.

It is good to see in the misfortunes of others what we should avoid.

It is hard even for the most miserable to die.

It is not work that kills but worry.

It is poor comfort for one who has broken his leg that another has broken his neck.

It is the lot of man to suffer.

It never rains but it pours.

Its ill waiting for dead men's shoes.

Keep thine eye fixed on the end of life.

Let pain deserved without complaint be borne.

Let the dead bury the dead.

Let us eat and drink for tomorrow we shall die.

Life ain't all beer and skittles.

Life and misery began together.

Life goes on.

Life is a road beset with roses and thorns.

Life is a state of warfare.

Life is labour, death is rest.

Life is not to be bought with heaps of gold.

Life would be too smooth if it had no rubs in it.

Light sorrows speak, great ones are dumb.

Make not two sorrows of one.

Many a one suffers for what he cannot help.

Men fear death as children go in the dark.

Misery acquaints a man with strange bedfellows.

Misery doth brave minds abate.

Misery is always unjust.

Misery loves company.

Misfortune does not always come to injure.

Misfortune is a good teacher.

Misfortunes never come singly.

Much of grief shows still some want of wit.

Never say die.

Never speak ill of the dead.

New grief awakens the old.

No day passes without some grief.

No man can be ignorant that he must die, nor be sure that he may not this very day.

No news is good news.

No priority among the dead.

No young man believes he shall ever die.

Nothing dries sooner than a tear.

Nothing is certain in this world but death and taxes.

Nothing is so bad that it might have been worse.

Of the great and of the dead, either speak well or say nothing.

Of thy sorrow be not too sad, of thy joy be not too glad.

Old men go to death, death comes to young men.

Old soldiers never die.

One funeral makes many.

Our griefs how swift, our remedies how slow.

Our own grief produces pity for another.

Pain makes even the innocent liars.

Pale death knocks at the cottage and the palace with an impartial hand.

Rejoice not in another's sorrow.

Sacred even to gods, is misery.

She grieves sincerely who grieves unseen.

Shrouds have no pockets.

Sin and sorrow are inseparable.

Six feet of earth makes all men equal.

So live and hope as if thou would die immediately.

So long as the sick man has life there is hope.

Sorrow concealed doth burn the heart to cinders.

Sorrow dwells on the confines of pleasure.

Sorrows remembered sweeten present joy.

Stone dead hat no fellow.

Suffer in order to know, toil in order to have.

Sufferings are lessons.

Tears are sometimes as weighty as words.

Tears benefit not the dead, they may injure the living.

Tears in mortal miseries are vain.

The actions of a dying man are void of disguise.

The best cure for sorrow is to pity somebody.

The bitter pill may have wholesome effects.

The bitterness of death must be tasted by him who is to appreciate the sweetness of deliverance.

The bridge between joy and sorrow is not long.

The darkest hour is just before the dawn.

The dead and absent have no friends.

The dead are soon forgotten.

The dead govern the living.

The dead man is unenvied.

The dead open the eyes of the living.

The evening praises the day, death the life.

The fewer his years the fewer his tears.

The first breath is the beginning of death.

The good die young.

The greatest business of life is to prepare for death.

The grief of the heir is only masked laughter.

The holidays of joy are the vigils of sorrow.

The miseries of the virtuous are the scandal of the good.

The only cure for grief is action.

The road of death must be travelled by us all.

The sharper the storm, the sooner its over.

The sorrow men have for others hangs upon a hair.

The sublimest grief will eat at last.

The sun and death are two things we cannot stare in the face.

The tears of the night equal the smiles of the day.

There is a remedy for everything except death.

There is no greater misfortune than not to be able to bear misfortune.

There is no pain so great that time will not soften.

There is no remembrance which time does not obliterate, nor pain which death does not put an end to.

They that live longest must die at last.

They truly mourn that mourn without a witness.

Those who have known grief seldom seem sad.

They who live in a worry invite death in a hurry.

Three may keep a secret if two of them are dead.

Time and thinking tame the strongest grief.

Time goes, death comes.

Time is a great healer.

To grief there is a limit, not so to fear.

To live in the hearts we leave behind us is not to die.

Too late to grieve when the chance is past.

Two in distress make sorrow less.

Until death there is no knowing what may befall.

We die as we live.

We must live by the quick, not by the dead.

We must suffer much or die young.

We shall lie all alike in our graves.

When misery is highest, help is nearest.

When one is dead it is for a long time.

When sorrow is asleep wake it not.

When you die even your tomb shall be comfortable.

When you die your trumpeter will be buried.

Where a man feels pain he lays his hand.

Wherever we meet misery we owe pity.

While there is life there is hope.

Who dies in youth and vigour dies best.

Who has no plagues makes himself some.

Who often changes, suffers.

Who thinks often of death does nothing worthy of life.

Whom the Gods love die young.

You can only die once.

You cannot shift an old tree without it dying.

ENTERPRISE
AND COMMERCE

A carpenter is known by his chips.

A good beginning is half the work.

A good head and industrious hand are worth gold in any land.

A handful of trade is a handful of gold.

A journey of a thousand miles begins with a single step.

A man can do no more than he can.

A man of words and not of deeds is like a garden full of weeds.

A man without a smiling face must not open a shop.

A ploughman on his legs is higher than a gentleman on his knees.

A poor workman blames his tools.

A weak foundation destroys the work.

A work ill done must be done twice.

A work well begun is half done.

Absence of occupation is not rest.

Adversity makes men, prosperity monsters.

Adversity overcome is the highest glory.

All work and no play makes Jack a dull boy.

Ambition has no rest.

Ambition is no cure for love.

An oak is not felled at one stroke.

Attempt not or accomplish.

Attempt nothing beyond your strength.

Be not a baker if your head be of butter.

Begin in time to finish without hurry.

Better direct well than work hard.

Better sit idle than work for nothing.

Blind ambition quite mistakes her road.

Boldness in business is the first, second, and third thing.

Business before pleasure.

Business is the salt of life.

Business makes a man as well as tries him.

Business neglected is business lost.

Business sweetens pleasure, and labour sweetens rest.

Buy in the cheapest market and sell in the dearest.

By the hands of many a great work is made light.

By the work we know the workman.

By work you get money, by talk you get knowledge.

Cheap things are not good, good things are not cheap.

Climb not too high lest the fall be the greater.

Commerce loves freedom.

Creditors have better memories than debtors.

Defer not till tomorrow what may be done today.

Diligent work makes a skilful workman.

Do business, be not a slave to it.

Do not neglect your own field and plough your neighbours.

Do the head work before the hand work.

Don't have too many irons in the fire or some will be sure to burn.

Drive thy business, let not that drive thee.

Early to bed and early to rise, makes a man healthy, wealthy and wise.

Every man as his business lies.

Every man does his own business best.

Every man is the architect of his own fortune.

Every trade has its ways.

Everybody's business is nobody's business.

Faith will move mountains.

First come, first served.

Follow the river and you will find the sea.

Fortune favours the brave.

Fortune knocks at least once on every man's door.

From small beginnings come great things.

Fuel is not sold in a forest, nor fish on a lake.

God helps them that help themselves.

Good material is half the work.

Good works will never save you but you cannot be saved without them.

Great gain makes work easy.

He is a poor workman who cannot talk of work.

He that comes first to the hill may sit where he will.

He that heweth above his height may have a chip in his eye.

He that is ashamed of his calling ever lives shamefully in it.

He that labours is tempted by one devil and he that is idle by a thousand.

He that thinks his business below him will always be above his business.

He never wrought a good day's work that went about grumbling about it.

He who does not advance recedes.

He who hesitates is lost.

He who toils with pain will eat with pleasure.

He who wills the end, wills the means.

If a thing is worth doing it is worth doing well.

If at first you don't succeed; try, try again.

If you don't make mistakes you'll never make anything.

If you want a thing done properly, do it yourself.

In all labour there is profit.

In for a penny, in for a pound.

Industry is fortune's right hand, and frugality her left.

Industry pays debts but despair increases them.

It is better to travel hopefully than to arrive.

It is easier said than done.

It is for want of application rather than of means that men fail of success.

It is lost labour to sow where there is no soil.

It is more noble to make yourself great than to be born so.

It is the first step that is difficult.

It's all in the day's work.

Jack of all trades and master of none.

Keep thy shop and thy shop will keep thee.

Labour has a bitter root but a sweet taste.

Life gives nothing to man without great labour.

Make hay while the sun shines.

Man works from sun to sun, a woman's work is never done.

Many a man labours for the day he may never live to see.

Many hands make light work.

Mighty work must be done with few words.

Mind no business but your own.

Necessity is the mother of invention.

Necessity never made a good bargain.

Never cross a bridge until you come to it.

Never pay your workman beforehand.

Never send a boy to do a man's job.

No gain without pain.

Not to oversee workmen is to leave your purse open.

Nothing is achieved without toil.

Nothing succeeds like success

Nothing ventured, nothing gained.

One door never shuts but another opens.

Pity and compassion spoil business.

Punctuality is the soul of business.

Put a stout heart to a steep hill.

Reward sweetens labour.

Rome was not built in a day.

Seek and ye shall find.

Slow work produces fine goods.

Sour work, sweet sleep.

Strike while the iron is hot.

Success has many fathers while failure is an orphan.

Tall oaks from little acorns grow.

The buyer has need of a hundred eyes, the seller but of one.

The customer is always right.

The difficult is done at once, the impossible takes a little longer.

The end must justify the means.

The higher the monkey climbs the more he shows his tail.

The labourer is worthy of his hire.

The longest road is the shortest way home.

The result tests the work.

The time is never lost that is devoted to work.

The work praises the workman.

There are many rare abilities in the world that fortune never brings to light.

There is always room at the top.

There is no eel so small it does not expect to become a whale.

There is no such thing as a free lunch.

They conquer who believe they can.

Think of ease, but work on.

Thy hand is never the worse for doing thy own work.

To make a man of yourself you must toil.

To the brave and faithful nothing is difficult.

Toil is prayer.

Too many cooks spoil the broth.

What is a workman without tools.

Whatever has been attained is attainable.

When toil ceases the people suffer.

Where bees are, there is honey.

Where there is a will there is a way.

Where there is muck there is money.

Who begins too much accomplishes little.

Who hath a good trade through all waters may wade.

Work first and then rest.

Work makes the workman.

Work produces virtue, and virtue honour.

Workmen are easier found than masters.

You can't win them all.

You cannot get blood from a stone.

You cannot make bricks without straw.

You must speculate to accumulate.

You never know what you can do until you try.

FAMILY
AND FRIENDS

A babe in the house is a well spring of pleasure.

A babe is a mother's anchor, she cannot swing far from her moorings.

A babe is an angel whose wings decrease as his legs increase.

A broken friendship may be soldered but will never be sound.

A brother's sufferings claim a brother's pity.

A bustling mother makes a slothful daughter.

A child may have too much of his mother's blessing.

A child's back must be bent early.

A clear bargain, a dear friend.

A courageous enemy is better than a cowardly friend.

A fair weather friend changes with the wind.

A faithful friend is the true image of the deity.

A false friend and a shadow attend only when the sun shines.

A false friend has honey in his mouth, gall in his heart.

A false friend is worse than an open enemy.

A father is a treasure, a brother a comfort, but a friend is both.

A father lives after the death of his son.

A father loves his children in hating their faults.

A father maintains ten children better than ten children one father.

A father's blessing cannot be drowned in water nor consumed by fire.

A father's love for all others is air.

A favourite has no friends.

A foe to God was never true friend to man.

A fond mother produces mischief.

A friend and look to thyself.

A friend as far as conscience allows.

A friend at one's back is a safe bridge.

A friend cannot be known at the market.

A friend cannot be known in prosperity nor an enemy hidden in adversity.

A friend in need is a friend in deed.

A friend in the market is better than money in the chest.

A friend is best found in adversity.

A friend is never known until needed.

A friend is not known till he is lost.

A friend is not so soon found as lost.

A friend is to be taken with his faults.

A friend loves at all times, and a brother is born for adversity.

A friend; one soul, two bodies.

A friend should bear a friend's infirmities.

A friend that you buy with presents will be bought from you.

A friend to everybody is a friend to nobody.

A friend without faults will never be found.

A friend's dinner is soon dressed.

A friend's faults should be known but not abhorred.

A friend's frown is better than a fool's smile.

A good-natured friend is often only an enemy in disguise.

A good friend is better than silver or gold.

A good friend is my nearest relation.

A good friend never offends.

A good master of the house must be first to bed and first out.

A good mother does not hear the music of the dance when her children cry.

A good wife and health is a man's best friend.

A good wife makes a good husband.

A hedge between keeps friendships green.

A lame mule and a stupid son have to endure everything.

A landmark is well placed between two brothers fields.

A little absence does much good.

A lost friendship is an enmity won.

A man, a dog, and a horse never tire of each other's company.

A man is known by the company he keeps.

A man may see his friend need but will not see him bleed.

A man without a friend is only half a man.

A man would not be alone even in paradise.

A mother is a mother all the days of her life, a father is a father 'til he gets a new wife.

A mother's heart is always with her children.

A mother's love changes never.

A mother's love is best of all.

A near neighbour is better than a distant cousin.

A ready way to lose a friend is to lend him money.

A reconciled friend is half an enemy.

A rich friend is a treasure.

A small family is soon provided for.

A son pays his father's debts, but a father will not recognise his son's.

A son-in-law's friendship is a winter's sun.

A sure friend is known in a doubtful case.

A table friend is changeable.

A thousand friend are few, one foe many.

A trouble shared is a trouble halved.

A true friend does sometimes venture to be offensive.

A true friend is above all things capital.

A true friend is forever a friend.

A wise son makes a glad father, but a foolish son is the heaviness of his mother.

Absence doth but hold off a friend to make one see him more clearly.

Absent or dead still let a friend be dear.

Admonish your friends in private, praise them in public.

All are not friends who speak one fair.

An Englishman's home is his castle.

An ill father desires not an ill son.

An old friend is better than two new ones.

An old mother in the house is a hedge.

An unpeaceable man hath no neighbour.

An untried friend is like an uncracked nut.

As the field, so the crops; as the father so the sons.

As the mother so the daughter.

At first babes feed on the mother's bosom, but always on her heart.

At weddings and funerals friends are discovered from kinsfolk.

Avoid a friend who covers you with his wings and destroys you with his beak.

Be a friend to thyself and others will be so too.

Be blind to the failings of your friends but never to their vices.

Before you make a friend eat a peck of salt with him.

Behold thy friend and of thyself the pattern see.

Better a good cow than a cow of good kind.

Better foes than hollow friends.

Better have a friend in the marketplace than money in your coffer.

Better have a friend on the road than gold or silver in your purse.

Better lose a jest than a friend.

Better is a neighbour that is near than a brother that is far off.

Better the child cry than the mother sigh.

Between two brothers two witnesses and a notary.

Birds of a feather flock together.

Blood is thicker than water.

Blood will tell.

Bought friends are not friends in deed.

By requiting one friend we invite many.

Ceremony is the cloak of friendship.

Charity begins at home.

Chasten thy son while there is hope.

Children are certain cares.

Children are poor men's riches.

Children sweeten labours, but they make misfortunes more bitter.

Children tell in the highway what they hear by the fireside.

Children when little make parents fools, when great mad.

Choose a wife rather by your ear than by your eye.

Come live with me and you shall know me.

Daughters are easy to rear but difficult to marry.

Daughters can never take too much care of their fathers.

Disparity of fortune is the bane of friendship.

Even as the father was so shall the son be.

Even reckoning keeps long friends.

Every mother's child is handsome.

Every one can keep house better than her mother till she tries.

Everything goes by favour and cousinship.

Faithful are the wounds of a friend.

Fall sick and you will find who your friend is and who is not.

Familiarity breeds contempt.

Fate chooses our relatives, we choose our friends.

Fathers in reclaiming a child should outwit him and seldom beat him.

Fish and guests stink after three days.

Forget not the mother that fondled you at the breast.

Fresh fish and poor friends soon grow ill favoured.

Friends agree best at a distance.

Friends and mules fail us at hard passes.

Friends are born not made.

Friends are far from the man who is unfortunate.

Friends are like fiddle strings, they must not be screwed too tight.

Friends are thieves of time.

Friends got without desert are lost without cause.

Friends may meet, but mountains never greet.

Friends need no formal invitation.

Friends tie their purses with cobweb strings.

Friendship always benefits; love sometimes injures.

Friendship is a sheltering tree.

Friendship is love with understanding.

Friendship is not bought at the fair.

Friendship is the perfection of love.

Friendship is the wine of life.

Friendship should be unpicked not rent.

Friendships multiply joys and divide griefs.

From clogs to clogs is only three generations.

From shirtsleeves to shirtsleeves in three generations.

From the father comes honour, from the mother, comfort.

Give me a child for the first seven years and you may do what you like with him afterwards.

Give to a pig when it grunts and to a child when it cries, and you will have a fine pig and a bad child.

Go slowly to the entertainments of thy friends and quickly to their misfortunes.

God could not be everywhere, therefore he made mothers.

God keep me from my friends, from my enemies I will keep myself.

Good company makes short miles.

Greatness of name in the father oft-times overwhelms the son.

Happy is he that is happy in his children.

Happy is he whose friends were born before him.

He does not sing his father's song.

He has made a younger brother of him.

He is a good friend who speaks well of us behind our backs.

He is my friend that grinds at my mill.

He is no friend that eats his own by himself, and mine with me.

He makes no friend who never made a foe.

He never was a friend who ceased to be so.

He that has a wife has a master.

He that has no children knows not what love is.

He that bring up his son to nothing breeds a thief.

He that has no fools, knaves or beggars in his family was begot by a flash of lightning.

He that is absent will not be the heir.

He that obliges me in a strange country makes himself my brother.

He that seeks to have many friends never has any.

He that would have many friends should try a few of them.

He to whom God gave no sons the devil gives nephews.

He who cannot counterfeit a friend, can never be a dangerous enemy.

He who for his own sake would expose a friend deserves not to have any.

He who has a good nest finds good friends.

He who has a thousand friends has not a friend to spare, he who has one enemy shall meet him everywhere.

He who has daughters to marry let him give them silk to spin.

He who picks up the staff of his father with respect will not beat his dog.

He who takes the child by the hand takes the mother by the heart.

His mother an onion, his father garlic, himself comes out a conserve of roses.

Home is home, though it's never so homely.

Home is where the heart is.

If you want enemies excel others, if you want friends let others excel you.

In time of prosperity friends will be plenty,
In time of adversity not one among twenty.

Instinctive, unlike rational affection, has no favourite.

It costs something to support a family, however small.

It is a good friend that is always giving though it be never so little.

It is a wise child that knows its own father.

It is better to be the best of a low family than the worst of a noble one.

It is good to have friends everywhere.

It is good to have friends in high places.

It is more disgraceful to suspect our friends than to be deceived by them.

It is not the anger of the father but his silence that the well-born son dreads.

It takes three generations to make a gentleman.

Keep your own fish-guts for your own sea-maws.

Leave your son a good reputation and employment.

Lend your money and lose your friend.

Life without a friend is death without a witness.

Like breeds like.

Like father like son.

Like mother like daughter.

Like will to like.

Long absence changes friends.

Long absent soon forgotten.

May God not prosper our friends that they forget us.

Mother's love is ever in its spring.

Mother's truth keeps constant youth.

My friend is he that helps me in time of need.

My friend's enemy is often my best friend.

My son is my son till he gets him a wife, but my daughter's my daughter all the days of her life

No advice like a fathers.

No ape but swears he has the handsomest children.

No better friend than the man himself.

No mother is so wicked but she desires to have good children.

None of us like the crying of another one's baby.

Nothing can be sweeter than friendship.

Nothing so dangerous as an ignorant friend.

Of brothers-in-law and red dogs few are good.

Old friends and new reckoning.

Old friends and old wine are best.

Old tunes are sweetest and old friends are surest.

Once a buffoon, never the good father of a family.

One good turn deserves another.

One seldom finds white ravens and true friends.

One tear of a mother can blot out a thousand complaints against her.

Our domestic affections are the most salutary basis of all good government.

Own brothers keep careful accounts.

Patched up friendship seldom becomes whole again.

Praise the child and make love to the mother.

Save us from our friends.

She spins a good web that brings up her son well.

So yourself be good, a fig for your grandfather.

Spare the rod and spoil the child.

Sudden friendship, sure repentance.

Suffering for a friend doubles friendship.

The apple never falls far from the tree.

The best of friends must part.

The brother had rather see the sister rich than make her so.

The child is father to the man.

The company makes the feast.

The family that prays together, stays together.

The father a saint, the son a devil.

The father in praising his son extols himself.

The father sighs more at the death of one son than at the birth of many.

The father to the bough, the son to the plough.

The father's virtue is the child's best inheritance.

The fire burns brightest on one's own hearth.

The friendship of the great is fraternity with lions.

The greatest blessing is a true friend.

The hand that rocks the cradle rules the world.

The husband's mother is the wife's devil.

The joys of parents are secret, and so are their griefs and fears.

The more acquaintances the more danger.

The mother knows best whether the child be like the father.

The mother of a coward does not often weep.

The mother of a timid son never weeps.

The mother reckons well, but the child reckons better.

The mother's breath is always sweet.

The mother-in-law must be entreated and the pot must be let stand.

The only reward of virtue is virtue; the only way to have a friend is to be one.

The ornament of the house is the friends who frequent it.

The portrait of the father is but a picture to the stranger, to the son a book which points out his duties.

The shoemaker's son will always go barefoot.

The son disgraces himself when he blames the father.

The son that yawns at his father's oft repeated stories will weep little at his death.

The tardy son reaps not with his father.

The ungrateful son is a wart on his father's face; to leave it is a blemish, to cut it off is a pain.

The vulgar estimate friends by the advantage to be derived from them.

The wrath of brothers is the wrath of devils.

The younger brother hath the more wit.

The younger brother is the ancient gentleman.

There can be no friendship where there is no freedom.

True friendship is imperishable.

Upon my family at home depends my character abroad.

Walnuts and pears you plant for your heirs.

We carry our neighbour's failings in sight; we throw our own over our shoulders.

We think our fathers fools, so wise we grow,
Our wiser sons will think us so.

Wife and children are bills of charges.

What is sucked in with the mother's milk runs out in the shroud.

When a friend asks there is no tomorrow.

When good cheer is lacking, our friends will be packing.

When the blind lead the blind they both shall fall in the ditch.

When there are two friends to one purse, the one sings, the other weeps.

When two fall out the third wins.

Where can one be happier than in the bosom of his family.

Where there are friends there are riches.

Who chatters to you will chatter of you.

Who has gold can choose his son-in-law.

Who has no son has no satisfaction.

Who makes friends of all keeps none.

Whom we love best, to them we can say least.

Whom will he help that does not help his mother.

Without a friend the world is a wilderness.

Without hearts it is no home.

Write down the advice of him that loves you though you like it not at present.

You may thank God your father was born before you.

You scratch my back and I'll scratch yours.

You should know a man seven years before you stir his fire.

FOOD AND DRINK

A black plum is as sweet as a white.

A day without bread is a long day indeed.

A drunkard's purse is a bottle.

A drunken man may soon be made to dance.

A full stomach studies unwillingly.

A good eater must be a good man.

A man hath often more trouble to get food than to digest it.

A man that has had his fill is no eater.

A meal without wine is like a day without sunshine.

A rotten egg cannot be spoiled.

A sharp stomach makes a short devotion.

After dinner rest awhile, after supper walk awhile

After sweet meat comes sour sauce.

Ale sellers should not be tale tellers.

All is fish that comes to the net.

All is grist that comes to the mill.

All meat is not the same in every man's mouth.

Always rise from the table with an appetite and you will never sit down without one.

An army marches on its stomach.

An old dram drinker is the devil's decoy.

As a man eats so he works.

As you bake so shall ye brew.

Better a dinner of herbs than a stalled ox where hate is.

Better half an egg than an empty shell.

Better weak beer than an empty cask.

Bread is the staff of life.

Bread of a day, ale of a month, and wine of a year.

Butter spoils no meat and moderation no cause.

Cheese and bread make the cheek red.

Cheese is gold in the morning, silver at noon and lead at night.

Drink and drouth come not always together.

Drink little that ye may drink long.

Drink in the morning staring, and in the evening sparing.

Drink nothing without seeing it, sign nothing without reading it.

Drink upon salad costs doctor a ducat, drink upon eggs costs him two.

Drink washes off the daub and discovers the man.

Drink wine and have the gout, drink nothing and have it too.

Drink wine and let the water go to the mill.

Drinking kindness is drunken friendship.

Drunkenness does not produce faults; it uncovers them.

Drunkenness is a bewitching devil, a pleasant poison and a sweet sin.

Drunkenness is a pair of spectacles to see the devil and all his works.

Drunkenness is an egg from which all vices are hatched.

Drunkenness is nothing but voluntary madness.

Drunkenness turns a man out of himself and leaves a beast in his room.

Drunkenness makes some men fools, some beasts and some devils.

Drunken folk seldom take harm.

Eat a bit before you drink.

Eat at pleasure, drink by measure.

Eat bread that is light and cheese by weight.

Eat peas with the king and cherries with the beggar.

Eaten bread is soon forgotten.

Eating and drinking make the stomach full but the purse empty.

Every animal but man keeps to one dish.

Every cook praises his own broth.

Fiddlers, dogs and fleas come to a feast uncalled.

First catch your hare and then cook it.

Fresh pork and new wine, kill a man before his time.

God sends meat, but the devil sends cooks.

Good ale is meat, drink and cloth.

Good drink drives out bad thoughts.

Good wine is milk for the aged.

Good wine makes a bad head and a long story.

Good wine makes good blood.

Good wine praises itself.

Good wine ruins the purse and bad the stomach.

He that banquets every day never makes a good meal.

He that eats and saves sets his table twice.

He that eats most porridge shall have most meat.

He thinks of everything who wants of bread.

He who has drunk will drink.

He who likes drinking is always talking of wine.

Hunger is the best sauce.

Hungry men think the cook lazy.

In the looking-glass we see the form, in wine the heart.

Inflaming wine dulls the noble heart.

It is an ill cook that cannot lick his own fingers.

It is the stomach that bears the feet.

Let the drunkard alone and he will fall of himself.

Man cannot live by bread alone.

Man is what he eats.

Many a good drop of broth is made in an old pot.

Of what use is the golden cup if the wine in it be sour

Of wine the middle, of oil the top and of honey the bottom
   is best.

Often drunk and seldom sober falls like the leaves in
   October.

Old wood to burn, old wine to drink.

One does not eat acorns when he has peaches.

Only what I drink is mine.

Passion makes a man a beast, but wine makes him worse.

Salt spilt is never all gathered.

Send not for a hatchet with which to break open the egg.

Since the wine is drawn it must be drunk.

Small choice in rotten apples.

Small stomachs, light heels.

Sour grapes can never make sweet wine.

Spilt wine is worse than water.

Starve together, eat together.

– Stolen bread stirs the appetite.

Stranger's meat is the greatest treat.

Sweet is the apple when the keeper is away.

Sweet wine makes sour vinegar.

Sweets to the sweet.

The appetite comes with the eating.

The best cure for drunkenness is while sober to see a drunken man.

The counsels that are given in wine, Will do no good to thee or thine.

The drunkard is discovered by his praise of wine.

The drunken man's joy is often the sober man's sorrow.

The drunken mouth reveals the heart's secrets.

The eggs do not teach the hen.

The first draught a man drinks ought to be for thirst, the second for nourishment, the third for pleasure, and the fourth for madness.

The nearer the bone the sweeter the meat.

The proof of the pudding is in the eating.

The smaller the drink the cooler the blood and the clearer the head.

The stew that boils much loses its flavour.

The stomach is a shopkeeper that gives no credit.

The stomach is easier filled than the eye.

The stomach rules the head.

The way to a man's heart is through his stomach.

The well fed man does not believe in hunger.

The wise drunkard is a sober fool.

There are more old drunkards than old doctors.

There is no such witness as a good measure of wine.

There is no sweet without sour.

They that drink longest live longest.

Thick wine is better than clear water.

Thirst makes wine out of water.

Thoughts when sober, said when drunk.

Thousands drink themselves to death before one dies of thirst.

To good eating belongs good drinking.

To the hungry no bread is bad.

Too many cooks spoil the broth.

Truth and folly dwell in the wine cask.

Water is the strongest drink; it drives mills.

What is in the heart of the sober man is on the tongue of the drunken man.

What is sauce for the goose is sauce for the gander.

What soberness conceals drunkenness reveals.

What the sober man thinks the drunkard tells.

What you do when drunk you must pay for when sober.

What's sauce for the goose is sauce for the gander.

When the stomach is full the heart is glad.

Where the best wine is grown the worst is drank.

Where there is milk in the can for one there is milk in the can for two.

While the pot boils friendship blooms.

Who eats and leaves has another good meal.

Who eats his dinner alone must saddle his horse alone.

Wine in the bottle will not quench the thirst.

Wine will not keep in a foul vessel.

You can't have your cake and eat it.

You can't make an omelette without breaking eggs.

You must take the fat with the lean.

You never miss your water until your well runs dry.

You spoil a good dish with ill sauce.

FOOLS AND FOLLY

A barber learns to shave by shaving fools.

A braying ass eats little hay.

A cucumber being offered a poor man he refused it because it was crooked.

A fair promise makes a fool merry.

A flatterer is the shadow of a fool.

A fool always comes short of his reckoning.

A fool always finds a greater fool than himself.

A fool always finds a greater fool to admire him.

A fool and his money are soon parted.

A fool at forty is a fool indeed.

A fool bolts a door with a boiled carrot.

A fool brings a staff to beat his own head.

A fool can dance without a fiddle.

A fool cannot be silent.

A fool cut down the oak to plant a thistle.

A fool demands much, but he is a greater that gives it.

A fool digs a well by the river.

A fool expects that larks will fall ready roasted into his own mouth.

A fool expects to find water at the first stroke of his spade.

A fool fights with his own shadow.

A fool fishes in the air and hunts in the sea.

A fool fouls the stream and expects it to be pure.

A fool has given a hen for an egg.

A fool if he holds his tongue passes for wise.

A fool is always meditating how he can begin his life, a wise man how he can end it.

A fool is better than an obstinate man.

A fool is one who gives, a greater one who will not take.

A fool is the wise man's ladder.

A fool killed the goose that laid the golden egg.

A fool laughs when others laugh.

A fool may chance to say a wise thing.

A fool may make money but it takes a wise man to spend it.

A fool must now and then be right by chance.

A fool never admires himself so much as when he has committed a folly.

A fool only wins the first game.

A fool pulled down the house for the sake of the mortar.

A fool put the cart before the horse.

A fool put water into a basket.

A fool sees not the same tree that a wise man sees.

A fool thinks nothing right but what he does himself.

A fool wants his cloak on a rainy day.

A fool when he hath spoken hath done all.

A fool who speaks the truth is better than a hundred liars.

A fool will be foiled.

A fool will laugh when he is drowning.

A fool's bolt is soon shot.

A fool's heart dances on his lips.

A fool's tongue is long enough to cut his own throat.

A lazy boy and a warm bed are hard to part.

A madman and a fool are no witnesses.

A man is a stark fool all the time he is angry.

A man never appreciates ashes until he slips on the ice.

A man's folly is his worst foe and his discretion his best friend.

A man's folly ought to be his greatest secret.

A nod for a wise man and a rod for a fool.

A pointless saying is a fool's doing.

A rolling stone gathers no moss.

A vacant mind is open to all suggestions, as a hollow mountain returns all sounds.

A wager is a fool's argument.

A wise man associating with the vicious becomes an idiot, a dog travelling with good men becomes a rational being.

A wise man begins in the end and a fool ends in the beginning.

A wise man may look ridiculous in the company of fools.

A wise man thinks all that he says, a fool says all that he thinks.

A wise man will not reprove a fool.

A wise man's thoughts walk within him, a fool's without him.

Advice to a fool goes in one ear and out the other.

All asses do not go on four feet.

All but fools know fear sometimes.

All fails that fools think.

All the fools are not dead yet.

An ass does not hit himself twice against the same stone.

An ass is but an ass though laden with gold.

An ass let him be who brays at an ass.

An ass will deny more in an hour than a hundred philosophers will prove in a hundred years.

An easy fool is a knave's tool.

Anger begins with folly and ends in repentance.

Anger may glance into the breast of a wise man, but rests only in the bosom of fools.

Ashes always fly back in the face of him that throws them.

Ask a silly question and get a silly answer.

Avarice is both knave and fool.

Better a witty fool than a foolish wit.

Better to weep with the wise man than to laugh with the fool.

Better with the wise in prison than the fools in paradise.

Between two stools one falls to the ground.

Big head, little wit.

Buffoonery and scurrility are the corruption of wit, as knavery is of wisdom.

Careless shepherds make many a feast for the wolf.

Change of weather is the discourse of fools.

Children and fools are prophets.

Children and fools have merry lives.

Children and fools should not see half done work.

Children and fools tell the truth.

Do not ask which is the right way from a blind man.

Do not bite the hand that feeds you.

Drunkards have a fool's tongue and a knave's heart.

Each wise man has a fool for his brother.

Empty vessels make the most sound.

Even a fool can bet a good hand at poker.

Even an ass will not fall twice in the same quicksand.

Every ass thinks himself worthy to stand with the king's horses.

Every fool is pleased with his bauble.

Every fool will be meddling.

Every potter praises his own pot and the more if it be cracked.

Experience keeps a dear school; but fools will learn in no other.

Experience is the mistress of fools.

Flattery is the food of fools.

Folly and learning oft dwell together.

Folly as well as wisdom is justified by it's children.

Fool's names, like fool's faces are often seen in public places.

Fools and madmen ought not to be left in their own company.

Fools are free the whole world over.

Fools are known by looking wise.

Fools ask questions that wise men cannot answer.

Fools build houses and wise men live in them.

Fools for luck.

Fools invent fashions and wise men follow them.

Fools rush in where angels fear to tread.

Fools set stools for wise men to stumble at.

For want of a horseshoe nail a kingdom was lost.

Forbid a fool a thing and that he'll do.

Fortune favours fools.

From the fool and the drunkard you may learn the truth.

Halfwitted folk speak much and say little.

He calls for the shoeing horn to help on his gloves.

He catches the wind with a net.

He chastises the dead.

He draws water with a sieve.

He gives grass to the lion and meat to the horse.

He gives straw to his dog and bones to his ass.

He hath some wit but a great fool hath the guidance of it.

He hides the sun with a sieve.

He is a fool who cannot be angry, but he is a wise man who will not.

He is a fool that praises himself and a madman that speaks ill of himself.

He is a fool who buys an ox to have good cream.

He is building a bridge over the sea.

He is fool enough himself who will bray against another ass.

He is making clothes for fishes.

He is making ropes of sand.

He is not a wise man who cannot play the fool on occasion.

He looks for his ass and sits upon his back.

He seeks water in the sea.

He seeks wool on an ass.

He takes a spear to kill a fly.

He takes oil to extinguish the fire.

He that blows in the fire will get sparks in his eyes.

He that is a wise man by day is no fool by night.

He that makes himself an ass must not take it ill if men ride on him.

He that slanders is a fool.

He who is born a fool is never cured.

He who is of no use to himself is of no use to anyone.

He who won't be advised can't be helped.

He who would make a fool of himself will find many to help him.

Heaven protects children, sailors and drunken men.

If fools wore white caps we would seem a flock of geese.

If folly were a pain there would be groaning in every house.

If one, two, three say you are an ass then put on a bridle.

If the fool have a hump no one notices; if the wise man has a pimple everyone talks about it.

If there were no fools there would be no wise men.

If thou play the fool, stay for the fellow.

If we will have the kindness of others we must endure their follies.

If you want to get into the bog, ask five fools the way to the woods.

It is a cunning part to play the fool well.

It is better to associate with the half fool than with the half wise.

It is better to be saved with the fool than to perish with the wise.

It is better to please a fool than to anger him.

It is folly to drown on dry land.

It is folly to fear what we cannot avoid.

It is folly to sing twice to a deaf man.

It is well to profit by the folly of others.

It needs a cunning hand to shave a fool's head.

It's no use crying over spilt milk.

Knaves and fools divide the world.

Learned fools are the greatest of all fools.

Light minds are pleased with trifles.

Little minds like weak liquors are soonest soured.

Love of wit made no man rich.

Make your affairs known in the market place and one will call them black and another white.

Man learns to be wise by the folly of others.

Many that are wits in jest are fools in earnest.

Men may live fools, but fools they cannot die

Men talk wisely but live foolishly.

Mere wishes are silly fishes.

Mingle a little folly with your wisdom.

More people know Tom Fool than Tom Fool knows.

Much laughter, little wit.

Natural folly is bad enough, but learned folly is intolerable.

No creature smarts so little as a fool.

No fools so insufferable as those who affect to be wits.

No one is a fool always; everyone sometimes.

No show without punch.

Nobody is so wise but has a little folly to spare.

Nobody is twice a fool.

None but fiddlers and fools sing in front of their meat.

None but a fool distasteful truth will tell.

None is so wise but the fool overtakes him.

None so blind as those who won't see.

Nothing passes between asses but kicks.

Nothing so bold as a blind man.

Oftimes to please fools the wise men err.

One fool is enough in a house.

One fool praises another.

One should either be born a king or a fool.

Penny wise and pound foolish.

Praise a fool and you may make him useful.

Pride is the never failing vice of fools.

Proposing without performing is mere folly.

Send a fool to market and a fool he will return.

Silent fools may pass for wise.

Such as are careless of themselves can hardly be mindful of others.

The ass does not know the worth of his tail until he has lost it.

The ass eating oats dreams of thistles

The ass of a king is still but an ass.

The desire for the superfluous is folly for it hath no bounds.

The false modesty of fools will conceal ulcers rather than have them cured.

The fear of the Lord is the beginning of knowledge but fools despise wisdom and instruction.

The feast passes and the fool remains.

The first day of April you may send a fool whither you will.

The first degree of folly is to think one's self wise, the next to tell others so, the third to despise all council.

The fish always stinks from the head downwards.

The follies of the fathers are no warning to the children.

The folly of one man is the fortune of another.

The fool cuts himself with his own knife.

The fool discerns the faults of others and forgets his own.

The fool doth think that he is wise, the wise man knows himself to be a fool.

The fool hunts for misfortune.

The fool runs away while his house is burning.

The fool speaks only folly.

The fool wanders, the wise man travels.

The fool wonders, the wise man asks.

The fool's pleasure costs him dear.

The foolish alchemist sought to make gold of iron and made iron of gold.

The greatest of all fools is he who is wise to soon.

The least foolish is accounted wise.

The malady that is most incurable is folly.

The more riches the fool hath, the greater fool he is.

The most exquisite folly is made of wisdom too tightly spun.

The older a fool the worse he is.

The praise of a fool is censure in disguise.

The shadow of a lord is the cap for a fool.

The shortest follies are the best.

The wise and the fool have their fellow.

The wise can learn of fools.

The wise make jests and the weak repeat them.

The wise man draws more advantage from his enemies than the fool from his friends.

The wise man when he holds his tongue says more than the fool when he speaks.

The wise must endure fools.

The wise seek wisdom, the fool has found it.

The wise too jealous are, fools too secure.

There are no foolish trades, there are only foolish people.

There is a fool at every feast.

There is no art can make a fool wise.

There is no fool like an old fool.

There is no knife cuts keener than a fool turned doctor.

There is no one so wise that wine does not make him a
   fool.

There is nothing blackens like the ink of fools.

There must be fools in the world.

They can do least who boast loudest.

Throw dirt enough and some will stick.

Throw not your axe so far you can't get it back.

To ask an elm tree for pears.

To be employed in useless things is to be half idle.

To counsel and disregard his own safety is folly.

To dig a well to put out a house on fire.

To dig a well with a needle.

To every fool his cap.

To promise and give nothing is comfort to a fool.

To reprove a fool is but lost labour.

To throw pearls before swine.

Trust not thy finger in a fool's mouth.

Truth and folly dwell in the wine cask.

Two fools in one house are too many.

Valiant fools were made by nature for the wise to work with.

We cannot all be wise.

We have all been fools in our time.

What is bred in the bone won't out in the flesh.

When a man becomes angry his reason rides out.

When the cat's away the mice will play.

When the moon is in the full, then the wit is in the wane

Where ignorance is bliss 'tis folly to be wise.

Where you see a jester a fool is not far off.

Who is in great haste should not ride an ass.

Whoever falls sick of folly is long in getting cured.

Whom the Gods would destroy, they first make mad.

Wine and women make fools of everybody.

Wise men change their minds, fools never.

Wise men have mouths in their hearts, fools their hearts in their mouths.

Wise men learn from the mistakes of others, fools from their own.

Wise men learn more from fools than fools learn from wise men.

Wise men make proverbs and fools repeat them.

Wise men propose and fools determine.

Wishes can never fill the sack.

Wishes were ever fools.

Wishes won't wash dishes.

Wit and wisdom are rarely seen together.

Wit does not take the place of knowledge.

Wit is folly unless a wise man has the keeping of it.

Wit without wisdom cuts other men's meat and its own fingers.

Worthless is the advice of fools.

You can take a horse to water but you can't make him drink.

HEALTH
AND HAPPINESS

A blithe heart makes a blooming visage.

A change is as good as a rest.

A cool mouth and warm feet live long.

A good heart overcomes evil fortune.

A good wife and health are a man's best wealth.

A happy heart is better than a full purse.

A happy life consists in virtue.

A joyous heart spins the hemp.

A man too busy to look after his health is like a mechanic too busy to look after his tools.

A merry fellow was never yet a sensible man.

A merry heart doth good like a medicine.

A merry host makes merry guests.

A pennyworth of mirth is worth a pound of sorrow.

All happiness is in the mind.

All our sweetest hours fly fastest.

All the joys in the world cannot take one grey hair out of our heads.

All who joy would win, must share it; happiness was born a twin.

Always merry is seldom rich.

An apple a day keeps the doctor away.

As he who has his health is young, so he who owes nothing is rich.

As long lives the merry heart as the sad.

Be always as merry as you can, foe no one delights in a sorrowful man.

Be happy when you can for you are a long time dead.

Be merry and wise.

Better lose a supper than have a hundred physicians.

By the side of sickness health becomes sweet.

Cheerful company shortens the miles.

Cheerfulness and goodwill make the labour light.

Cold hand, warm heart.

Content yourself with your own skin.

Continual cheerfulness is a sign of wisdom.

Do not jest if you cannot bear a jest.

Every life has its joy; every joy its law.

Everyone takes his pleasure where he finds it.

Feed a cold and starve a fever.

Good health is above wealth.

Happiness invites envy.

Happy he who can live in peace.

Happy he who can take warning from the mishap of others.

Happy is he that is content.

Happy is he that is happy in his children.

Happy is he that knows the folly of his youth.

Happy is he that serves the happy.

Happy is he whose friends were born before him.

Happy is the man who does all the good he talks of.

Happy is the man who keeps out of strife.

Happy men have happy friends.

Happy men have many friends.

He is happy who knows not himself to be otherwise.

He is happy who knows his good fortune.

He is not happy who knows it not.

He is truly happy who makes others happy.

He laughs best who laughs last.

He that goes to bed thirsty rises healthy.

He that is of merry heart hath a continual feast.

He that sits with his back to a draft sits with his face to the coffin.

He who has not health has nothing.

He who is happy is rich enough.

He who laughs last laughs longest.

He who never was sick dies the first.

Health and cheerfulness mutually beget each other.

Health and understanding are the two great blessings of life.

Health is happiness.

Health is not valued till sickness comes.

Health is the vital principle of bliss.

If you can be well without health, you may be happy without virtue.

If your joys cannot be long, so neither can your sorrows.

In the time of mirth take heed.

It is a fortunate head that never ached.

It is a poor heart that never rejoices.

Joy and sorrow are next door neighbours.

Joy and sorrow usually succeed each other.

Joy is the tender shadow which sorrow casts.

Joy surfeited turns to sorrow.

Joy which we cannot share with others is only half enjoyed.

Joys are not the property of the rich alone.

Keep your feet dry and your head cool and for the rest live like a beast.

Laugh and the world laughs with you, weep and you weep alone.

Laughter is the best medicine.

Let them laugh that win.

Life is not mere existence but the enjoyment of health.

Living well is the best revenge we can take on our enemies.

Men go laughing to heaven.

Mirth and mischief are two things.

Mirth and motion prolong life.

Mirth cannot move a soul in agony.

Mirth is the medicine of life; it cures its ills and calms its strifes.

Neither gold nor grandeur can render us happy.

No cure, no pay.

No estate can make him rich that has a bad heart.

No happiness without holiness.

No joy like Heaven's.

No man can be called happy before his death.

No man can be happy without a friend, nor be sure of his friend till he is unhappy.

No man is happy unless he believes he is.

Not to wish to recover is a mortal symptom.

Obedience is the mother of happiness.

One hour of sleep before midnight is worth two after.

Spare diet and no trouble keep a man in good health.

Strong folks have strong maladies.

Study sickness while you are well.

Sudden joy kills sooner than excessive grief.

That is but slippery happiness that fortune can give and fortune can give away.

The best things in life are free.

The man that is happy in all things is more rare than the phoenix.

The memory of happiness makes misery woeful.

The more the merrier.

The wise with hope support the pains of life.

There is no happiness without virtue.

'Tis not good to be too happy too young.

'Tis only happiness can keep us young.

To be content with little is true happiness.

To be of use in the world is the only way to be happy.

To make one man happy you may calculate on making ten others miserable.

To rise at five, dine at nine, sup at five, go to bed at nine makes a man live to ninety-nine.

To the well man every day is a feast day.

True happiness is to no place confined, but still is found in a contented mind.

Variety is the spice of life.

Virtue and happiness are mother and daughter.

We are never so happy or fortunate as we think ourselves.

We are usually the best men when in the worst health.

We should publish our joys and conceal our griefs.

When joy is in the parlour, sorrow is in the passage.

When you are well keep as you are.

With mirth and laughter let the wrinkles come.

Without health life is not life, life is useless.

KNOWLEDGE
AND LEARNING

A book that remains shut is but a block.

A book's a book though there is nothing in it.

A flow of words is no proof of wisdom.

A gem unwrought is a useless thing, so a man unlearned is a senseless being.

A golden key can open any door.

A good book praises itself.

A great book is a great evil.

A handful of good life is better than seven years of learning.

A learned man can only be appreciated by another learned man.

A library is a repository of medicine for the mind.

A little knowledge is a dangerous thing.

A man becomes learned by asking questions.

A man can know nothing of mankind without knowing something of himself.

A man cannot leave a better legacy to the world than a well educated family.

A man is not known until he comes to honour.

A man knows no more to any purpose than he practices.

A man profits more by the sight of an idiot than by the orations of the learned.

A man who is wise and learned, but without virtue, shall be despised.

A mind quite vacant is a mind quite distressed.

A profound thinker always thinks he is superficial.

A single conversation across the table with a wise man is better than ten years study of books.

A student usually has three maladies: poverty, itch and pride.

A teacher is better than two books.

A thinking man is always striking out something new.

A thousand probabilities do not make one truth.

A well prepared mind hopes in adversity, and fears in prosperity.

A wise man hath more ballast than sail.

A wise man is never less alone than when he is alone.

A word to the wise is enough.

Action is the proper fruit of knowledge.

Action must be founded on knowledge.

All is not true that is told.

All our knowledge is ourselves to know

All roads lead to Rome.

All we know is nothing is nothing can be known.

Art and knowledge bring bread and honour.

Art is long and life is short.

Be wisely worldly but not worldly wise.

Believe nothing of what you hear and half of what you see.

Better suffer for truth than prosper by falsehood.

Books are for company, the best friends and counsellors.

Books can never teach the use of books.

Books will speak plain when counsellors blanch.

Do not learn to do that from which there is no advantage.

Each one brings his understanding to market.

Education is the poor man's haven.

Education polishes good natures and corrects the bad ones.

Every good scholar is not a good schoolmaster.

Experience is the best teacher.

Experience is the father of wisdom.

Fact is stranger than fiction.

Facts are stubborn things.

Fine words butter no parsnips.

Genius is an infinite capacity for taking pains.

God deliver me from the man of one book.

Government of the will is better than increase of knowledge.

Great minds think alike.

Half our knowledge we must snatch, not take.

Half the world knows not how the other half lives.

Have thy study full of books rather than thy purse full of money.

He is sufficiently learned that knows how to do well, and has power enough to refrain from evil.

He is the happiest who knows nothing.

He knows enough who knows how to live and keep his own council.

He knows which side of his bread is buttered.

He teaches ill that teaches all.

He teaches me to be good that does me good.

He that follows truth too near will have dirt kicked in his face.

He that imagines he hath knowledge enough hath none.

He that knows himself knows others.

He that knows least commonly presumes most.

He that knows little soon repeats it.

He that teaches himself has a fool for a master.

He that travels far knows much.

He that would know what shall be must consider what hath been.

He that would learn to pray let him go to sea.

He who can, does, he who cannot, teaches.

He who has an art has everywhere a part.

He who has learned unlearns with difficulty.

He who increases knowledge increases sorrow.

He who knows but little tells it quickly.

He who knows himself best, esteems himself least.

He who knows little is confident in everything.

He who knows nothing never doubts.

He who thinks he knows most knows least.

He who understands most is other men's master.

Hidden knowledge differs little from ignorance.

History repeats itself.

I envy no man who knows more than myself but pity them that know less.

If thou love learning thou shalt be learned.

It is easy to be wise after the event.

It is for want of thinking that most men are undone.

It is good to learn at other men's cost.

It is never too late to learn.

It is not permitted to know all things.

It is not the quantity but the quality of knowledge that is valuable.

It is the mind that ennobles, not he blood.

It is the mind that makes the body rich.

It is vain to fish without a hook or learn to read without a book.

It is well for one to know more than he says.

It requires a long time to know anyone.

Know thyself.

Knowledge begins a gentleman but it is knowledge that completes him.

Knowledge comes but wisdom lingers.

Knowledge directs practice and practice increases knowledge.

Knowledge finds its price.

Knowledge is a second light and hath bright eyes.

Knowledge is a treasure but practice is the key to it.

Knowledge is folly, except grace guide it.

Knowledge is no burden.

Knowledge is power.

Knowledge is proud that he knows so much.

Knowledge is silver among the poor, gold among the nobles, and a jewel among princes.

Knowledge is the foundation of eloquence.

Knowledge makes one laugh but wealth makes one dance.

Knowledge must be gained by ourselves.

Knowledge without education is but armed injustice.

Knowledge without practice makes but half an artist.

Learn from your mistakes.

Learn not and know not.

Learn some useful art that you may be independent of the caprice of fortune.

Learn the luxury of doing good.

Learn to labour and wait.

Learning is a sceptre to some, a bauble to others.

Learning is an ornament in prosperity, a refuge in adversity, and a provision in old age.

Learning is better than house and land.

Learning is the eye of the mind.

Learning makes a good man better and a bad man worse..

Learning makes a man fit companion for himself.

Learning procures respect to good fortune and helps the bad.

Learning refines and elevates the mind.

Life without learning bears the stamp of death.

Little things please little minds.

Many a true word is spoken in jest.

Nature abhors a vacuum.

No book is so bad that something may be learned from it.

No man is so wise that he cannot become wiser.

No man knows until he hath tasted both fortunes.

No man learns but by pain or shame.

No man was ever wise by chance.

Not to know what has been transacted in former times is to continue always a child.

Nothing so much worth as a mind well educated.

One learns by failing.

One part of knowledge consists in being ignorant of such things as are not worthy of knowing.

One picture is worth a thousand words.

One should make a study of pastime.

Patience surpasses learning.

Practice makes perfect.

Profess not the knowledge thou hast not.

Say as men say, but think to yourself.

Science is organised knowledge.

Search all things, hold fast that which is true.

Seeing is believing.

Something is learned every time a book is opened.

Soon learnt, soon forgotten.

Study makes learned men but not always pious and wise.

Study to be useful

Take heed of many, the advice of few.

Take heed of the words of the wise.

Teaching others teaches yourself.

The best blood by learning is refined.

The exception proves the rule.

The first step to self-knowledge is self-distrust.

The fountain of wisdom flows through books.

The greatest learning is to be seen in the greatest plainness.

The intellect engages us in the pursuit of truth, the passions impel us to action.

The learned man has always riches in himself.

The least foolish is wise.

The meaning is best known to the speaker.

The mind is the man.

The more a man knows the more he is inclined to be modest.

The more understanding the fewer words.

The most learned are not the wisest.

The older one grows the more one learns.

The only jewel which will not decay is knowledge.

The pen is mightier than the sword.

The rust of the mind is the blight of genius.

The seeds of knowledge may be planted in solitude but must be cultivated in public.

The tutors of youth have an ascendancy over the stars of their nativity.

The wise man does not hang his knowledge on a hook.

There are two sides to every question.

There are two sides to every story.

There is always a first time.

There is more learning than knowledge in the world.

There is no education like adversity.

There is no royal road to learning.

Think much, speak little and write less.

Think with the wise but talk with the vulgar.

Thinking is not knowing.

Thinking is very far from knowing.

Through being too knowing the fox lost his tail.

To be conscious you are ignorant is a great step towards knowledge.

To know all is to forgive all.

To know how many beans make five.

To know one perfectly one must live in the same house as him.

To know one's self is true progress.

To know the disease is the commencement of the cure.

To know where the shoe pinches.

To know which way the wind blows.

Travel broadens the mind.

Truth lies at the bottom of a well.

Truth will out.

Two heads are better than one.

What you don't know can't hurt you.

When house and land are gone and spent, the learning is most excellent.

Where ignorance is bliss 'tis folly to be wise.

Who has never done thinking never begins doing.

Who knows forgives most.

Who knows most believes least.

Who teaches often learns himself.

Without knowledge there is no sin.

Word by word the great books are made.

You cannot teach your grandmother to suck eggs.

You may pay more for your schooling than your learning is worth.

Your knowing a thing is nothing unless another knows you know it.

Zeal without knowledge is fire without light.

LOVE
AND MARRIAGE

A bonny bride is soon dressed.

A boy's love is water in the sieve.

A brilliant daughter makes a brittle wife.

A cold lover is a faithless friend.

A dark man is a jewel in a fair woman's eye.

A deaf husband and a blind wife are always a happy couple.

A fence between makes love more keen.

A good Jack makes a good Jill.

A good son makes a good husband.

A good wife and health are a man's best wealth.

A good wife makes a good husband.

A great dowry is a bed full of brambles.

A growing moon and a flowing tide are lucky times to marry in.

A kiss of the mouth often touches not the heart.

A lover's soul lives in the soul of his mistress.

A maiden with many wooers often chooses the worst.

A man has a choice to begin love, but not to end it.

A man without a wife is a man without a care.

A man without a wife, a house without a roof.

A pretty face is half a dowry.

A rich bride goes young to the church.

A sweet and innocent compliance is the cement of love.

Absence makes the heart grow fonder.

Affinity in hearts is the nearest kindred.

All are fools or lovers first or last.

All mankind love a lover.

All's fair in love and war.

Always in love never married.

Always a bridesmaid, never a bride.

Among thorns grow roses.

An expensive wife makes a pensive husband.

An oyster may be crossed in love.

As is the lover so is the beloved.

Be loving and you will never want for love.

Beauties without fortune have sweethearts plenty but husbands none at all.

Better be an old man's darling than a young man's slave.

Better one house spoiled than two.

Cold cools the love that kindled too hot.

Deep lies the heart's language.

Esteem and love were never to be sold.

Every heart hath its own ache.

Every lover is a soldier.

Faint heart never won fair lady.

Fanned fire and forced love never did well yet.

Far from the eyes, far from the heart.

Fire in the heart sends smoke into the head.

Follow love and it will flee, flee love and it will follow thee.

For love of the nurse many kiss the child.

For love the wolf eats the sheep.

For the lover, travel and patience.

For the sake of the knight, the lady kisses the squire.

Forced love does not last.

Generally we love ourselves more than we hate others.

Glasses and lasses are brittle wares.

Gold and love affairs are hard to hide.

Hanging and wiving go by destiny.

Happy's the wooing that's not long in doing.

He loves thee well who makes thee weep.

He loves well who chastises well.

He loves well who never forgets.

He that has luck leads the bride to church.

He that hath love in his heart hath spurs in his heels.

He that is an enemy of the bride does not speak well of the wedding.

He that will thrive must first ask the wife.

He who dances well goes from wedding to wedding.

He who takes a wife takes a master.

He who would not be indolent let him fall in love.

He who would the daughter win, with the mother must begin.

Hearts alone buy hearts.

Hell hath no fury like a woman scorned.

Honey catches more flies than vinegar.

Honour in love is silence.

Hot love and hasty vengeance.

If you can kiss the mistress, never kiss the maid.

If you would be happy for a week take a wife.

It is best to be off with the old love before you are on with the new.

It is hard to wife and thrive both in the same year.

It is loving too much to die of love.

It takes two to tango.

Kissing goes by favour.

Let him not be a lover who has no courage.

Love abounds in honey and poison.

Love all, trust a few, be false to none.

Love and a cough cannot be hid.

Love and faith are seen in works.

Love and light cannot be hid.

Love and pride stalk bedlam.

Love asks faith and faith asks firmness.

Love begets love.

Love begins at home.

Love but laughs at lover's perjury.

Love can make any place look agreeable.

Love can neither be bought nor sold; its only price is love.

Love ceases to be a pleasure when it ceases to be a secret.

Love comes by looking.

Love comes in at the window and out by the door.

Love conquers all things, let us yield to love.

Love conquers all.

Love delights in praise.

Love does much, but money does more.

Love does wonders but money makes marriage.

Love expels jealousy.

Love fears no danger.

Love grows with obstacles.

Love has no law.

Love is a sweet tyrant because the lover endures his torments willingly.

Love is a thing full of anxious fears.

Love is as strong as death, jealousy as cruel as the grave.

Love is as strong as death, many waters cannot quench love, neither can the floods drown it.

Love is better than fame.

Love is blind.

Love is never without jealousy.

Love is not to be found in the market.

Love is the soul of genius.

Love is the touchstone of virtue.

Love is the wisdom of the fool and the folly of the wise.

Love is without prudence and anger without counsels.

Love knows hidden paths.

Love knows no measure.

Love laughs at locksmiths.

Love levels all inequalities.

Love lies in cottages as well as courts.

Love makes all hearts gentle.

Love makes labour light.

Love makes one fit for any work.

Love makes the world go round.

Love makes time pass away, and time makes love pass away.

Love must be attracted by beauty of mind and body.

Love rules his kingdom without a sword.

Love sees no faults.

Love sought is good, but given unsought is better.

Love teaches asses to dance.

Love warms more than a thousand fires.

Love will find the way.

Love without return is like a question without an answer.

Love yields no employment.

Love's anger is fuel to love.

Love's humility is love's pride.

Love's plant must be watered with tears and tended with care.

Love's the noblest frailty of the mind.

Love, knavery, and necessity make men good orators.

Love, thieves and fear make ghosts.

Lovers are fools.

Lovers break not hours unless to come before their time.

Lovers ever run before the clock.

Lovers live by love as larks live by leeks.

Lovers remember everything.

Lovers think others blind.

Lucky at cards, unlucky in love.

Man loves but once.

Marriage has it's pains, but a bachelor's life has no pleasures.

Marriage is a lottery.

Marriages are made in heaven.

Marry and grow tame.

Marry first and love will follow.

Marry in haste and repent in leisure.

Marry in lent, live to repent.

Marry in May, rue for aye.

Marry with your match.

Men are April when they woo, December when they wed.

Never choose your women or your linen by candlelight.

Never marry for money, but marry where money is.

New loves drive out the old.

No folly to being in love.

No God above gets all man's love.

No jealousy, no love.

No love without bread and wine.

No man is a match for a woman until he is married.

No rose without a thorn, no love without a rival.

None but the brave deserve the fair.

Old love does not rust.

Old lover, young fool.

One always returns to one's first love.

One cannot love and be wise.

One grows used to love and to fire.

One wedding brings another.

Out of the fullness of the heart love speaks.

Perfect love never settled in a high head.

Pity is akin to love.

Prettiness makes no pottage.

See for your love and buy for your money.

She that is born a beauty is half married.

She who loves an ugly man thinks him handsome.

The bravest are the tenderest, the loving are the daring.

The conversation of lovers is inexhaustible.

The course of true love never did run smooth.

The faded rose no suitor knows.

The grey mare is the better horse.

The heart has its reasons, of which reason knows nothing.

The husband is always the last to know.

The lover in the husband may be lost.

The oaths of one that loves a woman are not to be believed.

The only victory over love is flight.

The prostrate lover when he lowest lies, but stoops to conquer, but kneels to rise.

The quarrel of lovers is the renewal of love.

The sight of lovers feed those in love.

The soul is not where it lives but where it loves.

The truth of truths is love.

The two greatest stimulants are love and debt.

The way to a man's heart is through his stomach.

The weeping bride makes a laughing wife.

There are as good fish in the sea as ever came out of it.

There are no reasons that explain love, but a thousand that explain marriage.

There goes more to marriage than four bare legs
in a bed.

There is more pleasure in loving than in being loved.

There is no handsome woman on the wedding day except
the bride.

'Tis better to have loved and lost than never to have loved
at all.

To woo is a pleasure in young men, a fault in old.

Unkissed; unkind.

We never know how much we loved till what we loved
was lost.

Wedlock is a padlock.

What comes from the heart goes to the heart.

When poverty comes in at the door, love flies out
the window.

When two partners are of one mind, clay is into gold refined.

When you go to the dance take heed who you take
by the hand.

Where there is great love there is great pain.

Where there is no love all faults are seen.

Where there is not equality there can be no perfect love.

Where we do not respect we soon cease to love.

Who would be loved must love.

Whom we love best to them we can say least.

Works and not words are the proof of love.

POVERTY
AND WEALTH

A beggar can never be bankrupt.

A beggar is never out of his road.

A beggar's purse is bottomless.

A beggar's wallet empty is heavier than a full one.

A clown enriched knows neither relation or friend.

A fallen rich man may make a good master, but not an enriched poor man.

A great fortune is a great slavery.

A hungry man is an angry man.

A lamb is as dear to a poor man as an ox to the rich.

A light purse makes a heavy heart.

A little house well filled, a little land well tilled, and a little wife well willed are great riches.

A man that keeps riches and enjoys them not, is like an ass that carries gold and eats thistles.

A man who is proud of his money rarely has anything else to be proud of.

A man without money is like a bow without an arrow.

A man without money is like a ship without sails.

A miser grows rich by seeming poor, an extravagant man grows poor by seeming rich.

A moneyless man goes quick through the market.

A north wind has no corn and a poor man no friend.

A penny is sometimes better spent than spared.

A poor man has not many marks for fortune to shoot at.

A poor man is hungry after eating.

A poor man wants something, a covetous man all things.

A poor man's debt makes a great noise.

A poor man's joy has much alloy.

A poor man's shilling is but a penny.

A proud mind and a poor purse are ill met.

A proud pauper and a rich miser are contemptible things.

A ragged sack holds no grain, a poor man is not taken into counsel.

A rich child often sits in a poor mother's lap.

A rich man is either a rogue or a rogue's heir.

A rich man is never ugly in the eyes of a girl.

A rich man knows not his friends.

A rich man without understanding is a sheep with golden wool.

A rich man's foolish sayings pass for wise ones.

A rich mouthful, a heavy groan.

A thousand pounds and a bottle of hay are just the same at doomsday.

All ask if a man be rich, none if he be good.

All powerful money gives birth and beauty.

All strive to give to the rich man.

As long as there are some poorer than you, praise God even if you are unshod.

As water runs towards the shore, so does money towards the rich man's hand.

At the door of the rich are many friends, at the door of the poor none.

Bad money always comes back.

Be considerate towards the poor.

Before the rich man is willing to give, the poor man dies.

Beggars and borrowers cannot be choosers.

Better beg than steal.

Better die a beggar than live a beggar.

Better rich in God than rich in gold.

Blessed be nothing when the tax gatherer comes around.

But few prize money before honour.

Do not lend your money to a great man.

Don't borrow from a poor man.

Every one is kin to the rich man.

Every poor man is counted a fool.

Fair money can cover much that's foul.

For one rich man that is content there are a hundred who are not.

For poor people, small coin.

Give and spend, and God will send.

Give me neither poverty or riches.

Giving much to the poor doth increase a man's store.

God help the poor for the rich can help themselves.

God help the poor, the rich can beg.

God helps them that help themselves.

God makes and apparel shapes, but it is money that makes the man.

God sends us of our own when the rich men go to dinner.

Hat in hand goes through the land.

Have you goods, have you none, lose heart and all is gone.

He alone is rich who makes proper use of his riches.

He bears poverty very ill who is ashamed of it.

He has riches enough who need neither borrow nor flatter.

He is not fit for riches who is afraid to use them.

He is not poor that hath not much, but he that craves much.

He is not rich who is not satisfied.

He is poor indeed that can promise nothing.

He is rich enough who does not want.

He is rich enough who has true friends.

He is rich enough who owes nothing.

He is richest who is content with least, for content is the wealth of a nation.

He is too poor to buy a rope to hang himself.

He is truly rich who desires nothing and he is truly poor who covets all.

He that does not save his pennies will never have pounds.

He that goes a borrowing goes a sorrowing.

He that goes barefoot must not plant thorns.

He that has nothing to spare must not keep a dog.

He that hath no money in his pot, let him have it in his mouth.

He that hath no money in his purse should have fair words on his lips.

He that hath no money shall need no purse.

He that hath nothing is not contented.

He that hath plenty of goods shall have more.

He that hath lost his credit is dead to the world.

He that hoards up money takes pains for other men.

He that is fallen cannot help him that is down.

He that is known to have no money has neither friends nor credit.

He that labours and thrives spins gold.

He that lies on the ground can fall no further.

He that makes haste to be rich, shall not be innocent.

He that never fails never grows rich.

He that shows his money shows his judgement.

He that wants money is accounted among those that want wit.

He that wants to be rich in a year comes to the gallows in half a year.

He that will not stoop for a pin shall never be worth a pound.

He who despises small things seldom grows rich.

He who devours the substance of the poor, will find at length a bone to choke him.

He who is rich can have no vice and he that is poor can have no virtue.

He who knows how to beg may leave his money at home.

He who pays the piper may call the tune.

He who stoppeth his ear at the cry of the poor, shall cry himself and not be heard.

He who throws away money with his hands, will seek it with his feet.

Health and money go far.

I never knew a silent rich man.

If money be not thy servant it will be thy master.

If poor, act with caution.

If rich be not elated, if poor be not dejected.

If riches were granted even beggars would become rich.

If you had as little money as manners you'd be the poorest of all your kin.

If you have money take your seat,
If you have none take to your feet.

If you make money your god, 'twill plague you like the devil.

Is it not sheer madness to live poor to die rich.

It is a miserable sight to see a poor man proud and a rich man avaricious.

It is a rare miracle for money to lack a master.

It is better to be poor and well than rich and ill.

It is better to be poor with honour than rich with shame.

It is not without a purpose when a rich man greets a poor man with kindness.

It would make a man scratch where he doth not itch to see a man live poor to die rich.

Men often seem rich to become rich.

Mention money and the world is silent.

Moderate riches will carry you, if you have more you must carry them.

Money amassed either serves or rules us.

Money answers all things.

Money borrowed is soon sorrowed.

Money burns many.

Money does all.

Money does not get hanged.

Money in purse will always be in fashion.

Money in whatever hands will confer power.

Money is a good servant but a bad master.

Money is a sword that can cut even the Gordian knot.

Money is a universal language speaking any tongue.

Money is lost only for the want of money.

Money is money's brother.

Money is needed both by monk and dervish.

Money is power.

Money is the best bait to fish for man with.

Money is the fruit of evil as often as the root of it.

Money is the god of the world.

Money is the measure of all things.

Money is the only power that all mankind bow down before.

Money is the picklock that never fails.

Money is the root of all evil.

Money is the sinews of love as well as war.

Money is the soul of business.

Money is the very life and blood of mortals.

Money is wise, it knows it's own way.

Money lent, an enemy made.

Money makes dogs dance.

Money rules the world.

Money taken, freedom forsaken.

Money talks.

Money turns bad into good.

Money will make the pot boil though the devil pour water on the fire.

Money wins the battle, not the long arm.

Much wisdom is lost in poor men's mouths.

Much wisdom is smothered in a poor man's head.

Much wit is lost in a poor man's purse.

My money is little, my heart without strife.

Need conquers pride.

Neither a borrower nor a lender be.

No good man ever becomes suddenly rich.

No one is poor but he who thinks himself so.

No one so hard upon the poor as the pauper who has got into power.

No one so liberal as he who has nothing to give.

None have all and none have nothing.

Not he who has little, but he who wishes for more is poor.

Not possession but use is the only riches.

Nothing have, nothing crave.

Once poor, my friend, still poor you must remain, The rich alone have all the means of gain.

One day a beggar the next a thief.

One never gets more than the money's worth of anything.

Poor and content is rich and rich enough.

Poor folk's wisdom goes for little.

Poor folks say "thank you" for a little.

Poor men do penance for rich men's sins.

Poor men seek meat for their stomachs, rich men stomachs for their meat.

Poor men's tables are soon spread.

Poor men's words have little weight.

Poor without debt is better than a prince.

Poor, what he can; rich, what he will.

Poor men's money and cowards' weapons are often flourished.

Poverty breeds strife.

Poverty is a good all men hate.

Poverty is no sin, but it is terribly inconvenient.

Poverty makes a man mean.

Pride breakfasted with plenty, dined with poverty, supped with infamy.

Public money is like holy water; everyone helps himself to it.

Put not your trust in money but your money in trust.

Rather a man without money, than money without a man.

Rather be a hog than an ignorant rich man.

Rich for yourself, poor for your friend.

Rich in gold, rich in care.

Rich men and fortunate men have need of much prudence.

Rich men are slaves condemned to the mines.

Rich men feel misfortunes that pass over
poor men's heads.

Rich men have no faults.

Rich men seem happy, great and wise, all which the good
man only is.

Rich men's spots are covered with money.

Rich people are everywhere at home.

Riches abuse them who know not how to use them.

Riches and cares are inseparable.

Riches and favour go before wisdom and art.

Riches and virtue do not always keep each
other company.

Riches are always restless; it is only to poverty the gods
give content.

Riches are but the baggage of fortune.

Riches are first to be sought for, after wealth virtue.

Riches are like muck which stinks in a heap but spread
abroad makes the earth fruitful.

Riches are often abused but never refused.

Riches breed care, poverty is safe.

Riches cause arrogance, poverty meekness.

Riches come better after poverty than poverty after riches.

Riches hath made more men covetous, than covetousness hath made men rich.

Riches hath their embarrassments.

Riches have wings.

Riches never come even by chance to him whose destiny it is to be poor.

Riches only adorn the house, but virtue adorns the person.

Riches serve the wise man but command the fool.

Riches take peace from the soul but rarely if ever confer it.

Riches well got and well used are a blessing.

Riches will bear out folly.

Riches without understanding, a body without a soul.

Take care of the pennies and the pounds will look after themselves.

That costs dear which is bought with begging.

That man is not poor who has the use of things necessary.

That which is stamped a penny will never be a pound.

The abuse of riches is worse than the want of them.

The art is not in making money but in keeping it.

The cottage is a palace to the poor.

The dainties of the great are the tears of the poor.

The devil wipes his tail with the poor man's pride.

The foolish saying of the rich man pass laws in society.

The impartial earth is open to the poor as well as the sons of kings.

The miser and the pig are of no use till dead.

The miser is always poor.

The money paid, the work delayed.

The money you refuse will never do you good.

The only good a miser does is to prove the little happiness there is to be found in wealth.

The pleasures of the mighty are the terrors of the poor.

The poor are rich when they are satisfied.

The poor can live in one house together when two kings cannot in a kingdom.

The poor cannot, the rich will not.

The poor is always put to the worst.

The poor live secure.

The poor man eats at double cost.

The poor man must keep his word, and the rich when it suits him.

The poor man seeks for food, the rich man for appetite.

The poor man turns his cake and another comes and takes it away.

The poor man wants much, the miser everything.

The poor man's budget is full of schemes.

The poor man's coin always grows thin.

The poor man's honour is worth more than the
rich man's gold.

The poor man's penny unjustly obtained is a coal of fire in
the rich man's purse.

The poor man's wisdom is as useless as a palace in
the wilderness.

The poor must dance as the rich pipe.

The poor pay for all.

The poor pour, and the rich drink the wine.

The poor rich man is emphatically poor.

The poor sing free throughout the world.

The poor sit in Paradise on the first benches.

The poor trying to imitate the powerful perish.

The poor you always have with you.

The poorhouses are filled with the most honest people.

The pride of the rich makes the labours of the poor.

The rich are trustees under God for the poor.

The rich can only eat with one mouth.

The rich man carries nothing away with him but his
shroud.

The rich man is often poorer than the beggar.

The rich need not beg a welcome.

The rich never need for kindred.

The rich rule over the poor and the borrower is servant to the lender.

The rich think poor men have no souls.

The riches of the miser fall into the hands of the spendthrift.

The sign invites you but your money must get you out.

The smell of money is good, come whence it may.

The thirst for money brings all the sins into the world.

The whole world is the house of the rich and they may live in whatever apartment they please.

The wise discourses of a poor man go for nothing.

The wolf is sometimes satisfied, the miser never.

There are many things that may not be uttered by men in threadbare coats.

There are none so poor they cannot help, and none so rich as not to need help.

There be as many miseries beyond riches as on this side of them.

There is God's poor and the devil's poor, the first from providence, the other from vice.

There is no revenging yourself on a rich man.

Those who believe money can do everything are frequently prepared to do everything for money.

To be rich one must have a relation at home with the devil.

To beg of the miser is to dig a hole in the sea.

To condemn the poor because of their poverty is to affront God's providence.

To disregard money on suitable occasions is often a great profit.

To have nothing is to have rich eyes and poor hands.

Touch not another man's money, for the most honest never added to it.

We give the rich, and take from the poor.

What the poor are to the poor none knows but themselves and God.

When honour grew mercenary, money grew honourable.

When money speaks, truth keeps silent.

When riches increase, the body decreases.

When the poor become rich they sink the village.

Where nothing is nothing can be had.

Where there's money there's the devil, But where there's none a greater evil.

Where there's muck, there's money.

Wherever a poor man is, there is his destiny.

Who closes his ear to the poor, Peter will not hear when he knocks.

Who has nothing fears nothing.

Who is not ashamed to beg is soon not ashamed to steal.

Who is wealthy and free is rich.

Who nothing have shall nothing save.

Who readily borrows, readily lies.

Who will become rich must cast his soul behind the money-chest.

Who will become rich must have great care and little conscience.

With money you would not know yourself, without money nobody would know you.

Withhold not the wages of the poor.

Without money, without fear.

Would you know the value of money go borrow some.

You will see more ruined than saved by ill-gotten money.

POWER
AND CONFLICT

A brave man will yield to a brave man.

A brave man's country is wherever he chooses his abode.

A bully is always a coward.

A cake eaten in peace is worth two in trouble.

A cat may look at a King.

A certain peace is to be preferred to an expected victory.

A chain is no stronger than it's weakest link.

A crown is no cure for the headache.

A foreign war is preferable to one at home.

A gallant man needs no drums to rouse him.

A good cause makes a stout heart and a strong arm.

A good prince does not cut out freedom's tongue.

A house divided against itself cannot stand.

A king is never powerful that hath not power on the sea.

A patriot is a fool in any age.

A poor freedom is better than a rich slavery.

A proud soldier is fellow to the king.

A short sword for a brave man.

A stick is a peacemaker.

A tyrant's breath is another's death.

A war, even when most victorious, is a national misfortune.

Absolute power corrupts absolutely.

All are brave when the enemy flies.

All are not free who mock their chains.

All are not princes that ride with the emperor.

All men can't be masters.

Ambition is the last infirmity of noble minds.

Ambition is the soldier's virtue.

Ambition is torment enough for an enemy.

Ambition knows no gorge but the grave.

An ill man in office is a mischief to the public.

An office that does not give the holder enough to eat is not worth two beans.

An oppressive government is more to be feared than a tiger.

Argument makes three enemies to one friend.

Argument seldom convinces anyone against
their inclination.

As princes fiddle, subjects must dance.

At the wars do as they do at the wars.

Attack is the best form of defence.

Before the time great courage, when at the point great fear.

Better a lean peace than a fat victory.

Better a master be feared than despised.

Better be a free bird than a captive king.

Better free in a foreign land than a slave at home.

Big fish eat little fish.

Black ambition stains a public cause.

Blood will have blood.

Bribes will enter without knocking.

By wisdom peace, by peace plenty.

Common-sense is the growth of all countries.

Conspiracies no sooner should be formed than executed.

Corporations have neither bodies to be punished, nor souls
to be damned.

Councils of war never fight.

Courage in danger is half the battle.

Courage in war is safer than cowardice.

Courage, conduct and perseverance conquer all before them.

Cursed is he that doth his office craftily, corruptly or maliciously.

Diamonds cut diamonds.

Divide and rule.

Do as would be done by.

Dog does not eat dog.

Eagles don't catch flies.

Even the worm will turn

Even war is better than a wretched peace.

Every dog will have its day.

Every man for himself.

Every man has his price.

Every man is master in his own house.

Every one has his master.

Everybody loves a lord.

Everyone is emperor on his own ground.

Fight fire with fire.

Forewarned is forearmed.

From prudence peace, from peace abundance.

Give me liberty or give me death.

Good fences make good neighbours.

Good kings never make war but for the sake of peace.

Great office, great care.

Happy is the country that has no history.

He hath a great office, he must need thrive.

He is most powerful that governs himself.

He must be strong indeed who takes the club from Hercules.

He that commands well shall be obeyed well.

He that hath a fellow ruler hath an over-ruler.

He that is hated by his subjects cannot be king.

He that makes a good war makes a good peace.

He that makes himself a sheep shall be eaten by the wolf.

He that put on a public gown must put off the private person.

He that stands may fall.

He that will out wit the fox must rise before him.

He who cannot command himself, it is folly to think to command others.

He who demands does not command.

He who fights and runs away may live to fight another day.

He who has land hath war.

He who pays the piper may call the tune.

He who stands high is seen from afar.

He who would rule, must hear and be deaf, see and be blind.

If peace cannot be maintained with honour it is no longer peace.

If you can't beat them, join them.

If you can't stand the heat, get out of the kitchen.

Impartial vigour and example are the best means of governing.

In a false quarrel there is no true valour.

In the land of the blind the one-eyed man is king

In time of war the devil makes more room in hell.

In war according to war.

In war reputation is strength.

It is a bad war from which no one returns.

It is much safer to obey than rule.

It is skill not strength that governs a ship.

It is the raised stick makes the dog obey.

It is thou must honour the office and not the office thee.

It takes two to make a quarrel.

Kings love the treason, but not the traitor.

Kings ought to be kings in all things.

Little is done where many command.

Mad wars destroy in one year the works of many years of peace.

Many are called but few are chosen.

Many return from the war who cannot give an account of the battle.

Might is right.

Money is power.

New brooms sweep clean.

No affections and a great brain; these are the men to command the world.

No government can be long secure without a formidable opposition.

No man can serve two masters.

No office so humble but is better than nothing.

No one can have peace longer than his neighbour pleases.

No prince is poor that hath rich subjects.

No ruler good save God.

Of a master who never forgives, the orders are seldom disobeyed.

Of all wars peace ought to be the end.

Office tests the man.

Office without pay makes thieves.

Old politicians chew on wisdom past.

One hand washes the other.

One man with courage makes a majority.

One man's loss is another man's gain.

One peace is better than ten victories.

One sword keeps another in the scabbard.

One volunteer is worth two pressed men.

Only one can be emperor.

Oppression causes rebellion.

Oppression will make a wise man mad.

Our master is our enemy.

Peace flourishes when reason rules.

Peace in the village is better than war in the city.

Peace is the father of friendship.

Peace with a cudgel in hand is war.

Peace without truth is poison.

Power goes before talent.

Power on my head or the raven on my corpse.

Power tends to corrupt, and absolute power
    corrupts absolutely.

Power weakens the wicked.

Rebellion to tyrants is obedience to God.

Reform that you may prosper.

Rewards and punishment are the basis of a good government.

See, listen, and be silent, and you will live in peace.

Set thine house in order.

Small strokes fell great oaks.

Such is the government, such is the people

Talk of the war but do not go to it.

The ballot is stronger than the bullet.

The best government is that which governs least

The bigger they are the harder they fall.

The cause finds arms.

The choice of the people is the surest and best title to reign over them.

The fear of war is worse than the war itself.

The first duty of a soldier is obedience.

The greatest king must at last go to bed with a shovel.

The greatest of all evils is a weak government.

The hearts of the people are the only legitimate foundations of empire.

The king can do no wrong.

The king's favour is no inheritance.

The mob has many heads but no brains.

The office shows the man.

The race is not to the swift, nor the battle to the strong.

The right divine to govern wrong.

The subjects' love is the king's best guard.

The surest way to avoid a war is not to fear it.

The sword keeps the peace of the land.

The time of the prince belongs to the people.

The trap to the high born is ambition.

The tree of liberty grows only when watered by the blood of tyrants.

The unbought loyalty of men is the cheap defence of nations.

The voice of the people is the voice of God.

The weakest go to the wall.

The word of a king ought to be as binding as the oath of a subject.

The world without peace is the soldier's pay.

There are no miracles in politics.

There is a great force hidden in a sweet command.

There is no little enemy.

There is no worse heresy than that the office sanctifies the holder.

There is nothing humbler than ambition when it is about to climb.

There was never a good war nor a bad peace.

They conquer who believe they can.

They that buy an office must sell something.

They that govern most make least noise.

Those who cannot govern themselves must be governed.

'Tis sweet to die for one's country.

To command many will cost much.

To grow proud in office is the nature of man.

To preserve friendship one must build walls.

To take ambition from a soldier is to rob him of his spurs.

To the victor the spoils.

Troy was not taken in a day.

Two captains sink the ship.

Tyranny is far the worst treason.

United we stand, divided we fall.

War gives no opportunity for repeating a mistake.

War is a proceeding that ruins those who succeed.

War makes robbers and peace hangs them.

What belongs to the master is forbidden to the slave.

When all you have is a hammer everything looks like a nail.

When Greek meets Greek then comes the tug of war.

When power puts in its plea the laws are silent.

When the helm is gone the ship will soon be wrecked.

When the ship is sunk everyone knows she might have been saved.

When two play one must lose.

When war is raging the laws are dumb.

Where money and counsel are wanting it is better not to make war.

Where the cause is just the small conquers the great.

Who builds on the mob builds on sand.

Who fills an office must learn to bear reproach and blame.

Who loves peace serves God.

Who obtains an office surreptitiously like a wolf will administer it like a fox.

Who shall keep the keepers?

Whosoever draws his sword against the prince must throw the scabbard away.

Why keep a dog and bark yourself.

Without a shepherd sheep are not a flock.

You must ask your neighbour if you shall live in peace.

You must not be more royalist than the King.

PRUDENCE, CAUTION
AND EXCESS

A barley-corn is better than a diamond to a cockerel.

A belly full of gluttony will never study willingly.

A bird in the hand is worth two in the bush.

A bird never flew on one wing.

A bit in the morning is better than nothing all day.

A burnt child fears fire.

A closed mouth catches no flies.

A coconut shell full of water is an ocean to an ant.

A covetous man is good to none, but worse to himself.

A covetous man makes a halfpenny of a farthing and a liberal man makes sixpence of it.

A covetous man makes no friend.

A danger foreseen is half avoided.

A fine cage won't feed the bird.

A full belly neither fights nor flies well.

A glutton is never generous.

A good "take heed" will surely speed.

A grain of prudence is worth a pound of craft.

A jest driven too far often brings home hate.

A little pot is soon hot.

A little too late is much too late.

A man cannot whistle and drink at the same time.

A man never appreciates ashes until he slips on the ice.

A man of pleasure is a man of grief.

A miss is as good as a mile.

A modest dog seldom grows fat.

A nod is as good as a wink to a blind horse.

A penny saved is a penny got.

A place for everything and everything in it's place.

A promise is a debt.

A prudent haste is wisdom's leisure.

A prudent man does not make the goat his gardener.

A prudent man procures in summer the sleigh and in winter the wagon.

A prudent question is one half of wisdom.

A short cut is often a losing cut.

A stitch in time saves nine.

A watched pot never boils.

Abstinence and fasting cure many a complaint.

Abstinence is the best medicine.

Abstinence is the mother of competence.

Abundance begets indifference.

After one that earns comes one that wastes.

All comes right to him that can wait.

All covet, all lose.

All things belong to the prudent.

Always rise from the table with an appetite and you will never sit down without one.

Always to be sparing is always to be in want.

Anyone who has to ask the cost cannot afford it.

At an auction keep your mouth shut.

Be just before you are generous.

Be slow in choosing, but slower in changing.

Better a good cow than a cow of good kind.

Better be envied than pitied.

Better gain in mud than lose in gold.

Better late than never.

Better on a sound boat than a leaky ship.

Better poor on land than rich at sea.

Better return half way than lose yourself.

Better safe than sorry.

Better sit still than rise up and fall.

Better spare at the brim than at the bottom.

Better spared than ill spent.

Better the devil you know than the devil you know not.

Better three hours too soon than a minute too late.

Better to be convinced by words than by blows.

Better twice measured than once wrong.

Big mouthfuls often choke.

Burning the candle at both ends.

Cast no dirt in the well that gives you water.

Colts by falling and lads by losing grow prudent.

Covet nothing over much.

Covetous men are neither clothed, fed nor respected.

Covetous men live drudges to die wretches.

Covetousness as well as prodigality brings a man to
a morsel of bread.

Covetousness brings nothing home.

Covetousness is never satisfied until its mouth is
full of dirt.

Covetousness is the father of unsatisfied desires.

Covetousness starves other vices.

Curiosity killed the cat.

Cut your coat according to your cloth.

Delays are dangerous.

Desires are nourished by delays.

Different strokes for different folks.

Dig a well before you are thirsty.

Do not cry out before you are hurt.

Do not give your measure to anyone but your tailor.

Do not go from one extreme to the other.

Do not hang all on one nail.

Do not meet troubles halfway.

Do not pass sentence before hearing the evidence.

Do not run too fast after gain.

Do not sail too near to the wind.

Do not strip before bedtime.

Do not take hold of a nettle, but if you do grasp it tight.

Do not wade where you cannot see the bottom.

Don't believe in the saint unless he works miracles.

Don't build castles in the air.

Don't climb the hill until you get to it.

Don't count your chickens before they are hatched.

Don't cry herrings till they are in the net.

Don't curse the crocodile's mother before you cross the river.

Don't cut off your nose to spite your face.

Don't fly until your wings are feathered.

Don't go near the water until you have learned to swim.

Don't halloo until you are out of the woods.

Don't leave the high road for a short cut.

Don't put all your eggs in one basket.

Don't put your finger in too tight a ring.

Don't sell the bearskin until you have killed the bear.

Don't sing your triumph before you have conquered.

Don't snap you fingers at the dog before you are out of the village.

Don't spoil the ship for a halfpenny worth of tar

Don't throw away your old shoes until you have got new ones.

Don't throw out the baby with the bath-water

Don't throw out your dirty water until you have got clean.

Drive gently over the stones.

Each person for his own skin.

Easy does it.

Enough is a feast, too much vanity.

Enough is as good as a feast to one that is not a beast.

Enough is as good as a feast.

Enough is better than a sack full.

Enough to keep the wolf from the door.

Every excess becomes a vice.

Every man draws the water to his own mill.

Every sparrow to its ear of wheat.

Everyone is bound to live within their means.

Everyone rakes the fire under his own pot.

Everything in excess is adverse to nature.

Excess of wine neither keeps secrets nor performs promises.

Extremes meet.

Fair and softly goes the day.

Fire is a good servant but a bad master.

First things first.

Frugality is a great revenue.

Frugality when all is spent comes too late.

Full bottles and glasses make swearers and asses.

Give and take is fair play.

Go further and fare worse.

Go to bed without supper and you will rise without debt.

Good at a distance is better than evil at hand.

Good and quickly seldom meet.

Good weight and measure is Heaven's treasure.

Good-nature without prudence is foolishness.

Govern your passions, otherwise they will govern you.

Grasp no more than thy hand will hold.

Greed and the eye can no man fill.

Greedy folks have long arms.

Gut no fish before you catch them.

Haste makes waste.

Haste often brings shame.

Hasty climbers have sudden falls.

He is the nearest to God that has the fewest wants.

He that desires but little has no need of much.

He that gets forgets, but he that wants thinks on.

He that grasps at all loses all.

He that runs in the dark may well stumble.

He that spares something today will have something to spare tomorrow.

He that has a glass roof should not throw stones at his neighbours.

He that is hasty fishes in an empty pond.

He that sows thorns shall never reap grapes.

He who spends more than he should, shall not have to spare when he would.

Health consists with temperance alone.

His eye is bigger than his belly.

Hurry no man's cattle.

If it is not broken, don't fix it.

If men will have no care for the future, they will soon have sorrow for the present.

If you can't be good, be careful.

If you play with fire expect to get burned.

If you pursue two hares both will get away from you.

If you would be well served, serve yourself.

It is an ill wind that blows nobody good.

It is best to be on the safe side.

It is hard to both have and want.

It is ill speaking between a full man and a fasting.

It is safest sailing within reach of the shore.

It is the last straw that breaks the camel's back.

It is the principle rule of life not to be too much addicted to one thing.

It is too late to spare when the pocket is bare.

It is too late too shut the stable door after the horse has bolted.

Keep a thing seven years and you will always find a use for it.

Keep no more cats than will catch mice.

Keep the common road and thou art safe.

Keep the feast to feast to feast day.

Least said is soonest mended.

Less is more.

Let sleeping dogs lie.

Let well alone.

Let your purse be your master.

Live not to eat but eat to live.

Live within your harvest.

Look before you leap.

Make a virtue of necessity.

Make it do, or do without.

Measure a thousand times and cut once.

Measure is a merry mean.

Measure is a treasure.

Meat and mass never hindered man.

Milk the cow but don't pull off the udder.

Moderate measures succeed best.

Moderation in all things.

More men are drowned in the bowl than in the sea.

More than enough is too much.

More than we use is more than we want.

Much meat, much maladies.

Much on earth, but little in heaven.

Much would have more.

Necessity seeks bread where it is to be found.

Never answer a question until it is asked.

Never mention rope in the house of a man who has been
hanged.

Nothing to excess.

Of two evils choose the less.

Once bitten, twice shy.

One hand for oneself and another for the ship.

One man's meat is another man's poison.

One pin for your mouth and two for your purse.

One step at a time.

Penny wise and pound foolish.

People who live in glass houses should not
throw stones.

Please your eye and plague your heart.

Praise the sea but keep on land.

Produce much, consume little, labour diligently, speak cautiously.

Prudence supplies the want of every good.

Puff not against the wind.

Pull down your hat on the weak side.

Pull gently at a weak rope.

Regulate thy own passions and bear those of others.

Rule lust, temper the tongue, and bridle the belly.

Scatter with one hand gather with two.

Self is the first object of charity.

Self preservation is the first law of nature.

Send not to market for trouble.

Set your sail according to the wind.

Slowly but surely.

Softly, softly, catchee monkey.

Spare well and have to spend.

Spare your breath to cool your pottage.

Stretch your arm no further than your sleeve will reach.

Stretch your legs according to your coverlet.

Sweep before your own door.

Take care of the pence and the pounds will take care of themselves.

Take it easy and live long are brothers.

Take the middle of the way and thou wilt not fall.

The beaten road is the safest.

The bounty of nature is too little for the greedy man.

The gentle calf sucks all the cows.

The half is better than the whole.

The last drop makes the cup run over.

The less said the better.

The more a man denies himself, the more will he receive from heaven.

The more you get the more you want.

The more you stir the more it stinks.

The most prudent yield to the strongest.

The noblest task is to command one's self.

The pitcher will go to the well once too often.

The prudent still have fortune on their side.

The road to hell is paved with good intentions.

The table robs more than the thief.

There is always some trouble mixed up with the greatest pleasure.

There is many a slip 'twixt the cup and the lip.

There is safety in numbers.

Thousands drink themselves to death before one dies of thirst.

Three removes are as bad as a fire.

Thrift is a great revenue.

Too many sacks are the death of the ass.

Too much bed makes a dull head.

Too much of a good thing is a bad thing.

Too much water drowned the miller.

Too much wax burns the church.

Try before you trust.

Try the ice before you venture on it.

Two captains sink the ship.

Two watermelons cannot be held under one arm.

Waste not, want not.

What is done hastily is not done well.

What is enough is never little.

What is got over the devil's back is spent under his belly.

What the eye doesn't see the heart doesn't grieve over.

What you have, hold.

What you've never had you never miss.

What's done cannot be undone.

When all is consumed repentance comes too late.

Where necessity pinches, boldness is prudence.

Who hastens too much often leaves behind.

Who sows thorns should not go barefoot.

Whose carriage is greediness, his companion is beggary.

Wilful waste makes woeful want.

You can have too much of a good thing.

You cannot run with the hare and hunt with the hounds.

You cannot sail as you would but as the wind blows.

You must learn to walk before you can run.

You must shift your sail with the wind.

Time, Season
and Weather

A bad day never had a good night.

A bolt does not always fall when it thunders.

A bushel of March dust on the leaves is worth
a king's ransom.

A cherry year, a merry year, a plumb year, a dumb year.

A cold April bread and wine.

A cold April the barn will fill.

A day to come shows longer than a year that's gone.

A dripping June sets all in tune.

A flow will have an ebb.

A foul morn may turn to a fine day.

A green Yule means a fat churchyard.

A hundred years hence we shall all be bald.

A hundred years is not much but never is a long time.

A red sky at night, shepherd's delight,
A red sky at morning, shepherd's warning.

A snow year is a rich year.

A thousand years hence the river shall run as it did.

A wet August never brings dearth.

A windy March and a rainy April, make a beautiful May.

A swarm in May is worth a load of hay, a swarm in June is worth a silver spoon, but a swarm in July is not worth a fly.

After a storm comes the calm.

After clouds a clear sun.

After winter spring will come.

All good things must come to an end.

All the months in the year curse a fair February.

All the treasures of the earth would not bring back one lost moment.

All times when old are good.

All's well that ends well.

An evening red and a morning grey, is a sign of a fine day.

April and May are the key to the year.

April cling good for nothing.

April flood carries away the frog and her brood.

April showers bring forth May flowers.

As good have no time as make no good use of it.

As the day lengthens so the cold strengthens.

Calm weather in June sets corn in tune.

Cold weather and crafty knaves come out of the north.

Coming events cast their shadow before.

Each day is the scholar of yesterday.

Each passing year robs us of something.

Enjoy today for tomorrow the first grey hair may come.

Every day brings a new light.

Every day hath its night, every weal its woe.

Every day in thy life is a day in thy history.

Every day is not a holiday.

Every scrap of a wise man's time is worth saving.

Every tomorrow brings its bread.

Everything has a time.

Everything has its time and that time must be watched.

Everything is of every year.

Everything may be bought except day and night.

Fair weather cometh out of the north.

February makes a bridge and March breaks it.

From tomorrow to tomorrow time goes a long journey.

He never broke his hour who kept his day.

He that has most time has none to lose.

He that has time and looks for more, loses time.

He that passes a winter's day escapes his enemy.

He who falls today may rise tomorrow.

He who gains time gains everything.

Hope springs eternal.

Hour by hour time departs.

If Candlemass day be sunny and bright, winter will have
   another flight; if Candlemass day be cloudy with rain,
   winter is gone and won't come again.

If in February there be no rain, neither good for
   hay nor rain.

If St. Paul's day be fair and clear, it will betide
   a happy year.

If the weather is fine put on your cloak; if it rains
   do as you please.

If things look badly today, they may look better tomorrow.

If today will not, tomorrow may.

In fair weather prepare for foul.

In the wane of the moon a cloudy morning bodes a
   fair afternoon.

In time the savage bull doth bear the yolk.

It is a long lane that has no turning.

It is all one a hundred years hence.

It is easy to be wise after the event.

It is good to be in good time, you know not
how long it will last.

It is not spring until you can put you foot upon
twelve daisies.

It is time enough to set when the oven comes
to the dough.

It is time to yolk when the cart comes to the oxen.

It may be a fire but tomorrow it will be ashes.

It never thunders but it rains.

Lightning never strikes twice.

Long foretold, long last, short notice, soon past.

Lost time is never found again, and what we call time
enough always proves little enough.

Make hay while the sun shines.

Make the night night, and the day day, and you will live
pleasantly.

Man cannot buy time.

Many seek good nights and lose good days.

March borrows three days of April and they will be ill.

March comes in like a lion and out like a lamb.

March grass never did good.

March wind and May sun makes clothes white
and maids dun.

March winds and April showers bring forth May flowers.

May borrows ten days from March to kill off cattle
and old people.

May chickens come cheeping.

Never defer to tomorrow that which you can do today.

Never is a long time.

Never mind the weather, so the wind don't blow.

No day but has its evening.

No day is wholly productive of evil.

No day should pass without something being done.

No man can call back yesterday.

No man can tether time nor tide.

No time like the present.

No weather is ill, if the wind be still.

No-one has ever seen tomorrow.

No-one waits for yesterday.

On the first of March the crows begin to search.

Once in ten years a man hath need of another.

One hour today is worth two tomorrow.

One of these days is none of these days.

One swallow does not make a summer.

One today is worth two tomorrows.

One year borrows another year's food.

Open your door to a fine day, but make yourself ready for a foul one.

Other times, other folks.

Other times, other manners.

Pleasant hours fly past.

Praise a fine day at night.

Rain before seven, fine before eleven

Rain comes after sunshine, and after a dark cloud, a clear sky.

Saint Swithun's day, if thou be fair, for forty days it will remain; Saint Swithun's day, if thou bring rain, for forty days it will remain.

Seize the present day, giving no credit to the succeeding ones.

September blow soft, 'til the fruits in the loft.

So many mists in March, so many frosts in May.

Straw tells which way the wind blows.

Sufficient unto the day is the evil thereof.

Take time by the forelock.

Take time to be quick.

Take time when time is, for time will away.

The best preacher is time.

The better the day the better the deed.

The crutch of time does more than the club of Hercules.

The day has eyes, the night has ears.

The day is never so holy that the pot refuses to boil.

The day is short and the work is much.

The day sees the workmanship of the night and laughs.

The day that you do a good thing there will be
seven new moons.

The days follow each other and are not alike.

The full moon brings fair weather.

The good time comes but once.

The greatest expense we can be at is that of our time.

The heavens are just, and time suppresses time.

The ill year comes in swimming.

The longest day must have an end.

The mill cannot grind with the water that is past.

The more snow the more healthy the season.

The past is for wisdom, the present for action, but for joy
the future.

The time to come is no more ours than the time past.

The sharper the storm the sooner it's over.

The sun loses nothing by shining into a puddle.

The year has a wide mouth and a big belly.

There is a time for all things.

There is a time to fish and a time to dry nets.

There is a time to jest and a time when jests are unreasonable.

There is no appeal from time past.

There is no better counsellor than time.

There is no day without its night.

There is no day without sorrow.

There is no hand to catch time.

There is nothing more precious than time.

There is nothing new under the sun.

Time and hour are not to be tied with a rope.

Time and hour run through the longest day.

Time at last sets all things even.

Time brings everything to those that can wait for it.

Time brings roses.

Time covers and discovers everything.

Time devours all things.

Time discovers everything.

Time dresses the greatest wounds.

Time enough is little enough.

Time fleeth away without delay.

Time heals all wounds.

Time is a file that wears and makes no noise.

Time is a river without banks.

Time is a true friend to sorrow.

Time is an unpaid advocate.

Time is anger's medicine.

Time is God's and ours.

Time is money.

Time is precious but truth is more precious than time.

Time is the great innovator.

Time is the herald of truth.

Time is the rider that breaks youth.

Time makes hay.

Time misspent is not lived but lost.

Time moves slowly to him whose employment it is to watch its flight.

Time passes like the wind.

Time past never returns, a moment lost is lost forever.

Time reveals all things.

Time rolls his ceaseless course.

Time stays not at he fool's leisure.

Time stoops to no man's lure.

Time subdues all things.

Time tries all.

Time works wonders.

Time, motion and wine cause sleep.

Times change and me with time.

To a child all weather is cold.

To him that does everything in its proper time one day is worth three.

To save time is to lengthen life.

Today is yesterday's pupil.

Today must borrow nothing of tomorrow.

Today's egg is better than tomorrow's hen.

Tomorrow is another day.

Tomorrow never comes.

Tomorrow is fresh fields and pastures new.

Tomorrow never comes.

Tomorrow's remedy will not ward off the evil of today.

Tomorrow's sun to thee may never rise.

Use not today what tomorrow may want.

We take no note of time but from its loss.

What a day may bring a day may take away.

What greater crime than loss of time.

What is my turn today, may be thine tomorrow.

What is new cannot be true.

What is wrong today won't be right tomorrow.

What lay hidden under the snow cometh to light at last.

What reason and endeavour cannot bring about
   time often will.

What will be will be.

What's done cannot be undone.

When it rains in August it rains honey and wine.

When it rains in February it will be temperate all the year.

When the wind is in the west
   The weather is at the best.

Who has no time yet waits for time, comes to a time
   of repentance.

Winter eats what summer provides.

Winter finds out what summer lays up.

Winter is summer's heir.

Winter never rots in the sky.

Winter thunder makes summer wonder.

Winter weather and women's thoughts change oft.

Years and sins are always more than owned.

You saddle today and ride out tomorrow.

DICTIONARY OF QUOTATIONS

DICTIONARY OF QUOTATIONS

Contents

CHILDREN AND CHILDHOOD

Jane Austen
On every formal visit a child ought to be of the party, by
way of provision for discourse.
  Sense and Sensibility

Sir J(ames) M(atthew) Barrie
When the first baby laughed for the first time, the laugh
broke into a thousand pieces and they all went skipping
about, and that was the beginning of the fairies.
  Peter Pan

Every time a child says "I don't believe in fairies," there
is a little fairy somewhere that falls down dead.
  Ibid

Ambrose (Gwinett) Bierce
The fact that boys are allowed to exist at all is evidence
of a remarkable Christian forbearance among men.
  San Francisco News Letter 1869

George Gordon (Noel), 6th Lord Byron
A little curly-headed good-for-nothing,
And mischief-making monkey from his birth.
  Don Juan

Lewis Carroll [Charles Lutwidge Dodgson]
Child of the pure unclouded brow
And dreaming eyes of wonder!
Through the Looking-Glass and What Alice Found There

Sir Winston (Leonard Spencer) Churchill
There is no finer investment for any community than
putting milk into babies.
Radio broadcast, 1943

R(ichard) H(enry) Dana
Better to be driven out from among men than to be
disliked of children.
The Idle Man: Domestic Life

George Eliot [Mary Ann Evans]
Childhood has no forebodings.
Mill on the Floss

Thomas Fuller
Children are poor men's riches.
Gnomologia

(Henry) Graham Greene
There is always one moment in childhood when the door
opens and lets the future in.
The Power and the Glory

Charles Lamb
Boys are capital fellows in their own way, among their
mates; but they are unwholesome companions for grown
people.
The Old and the New Schoolmaster

Henry Wadsworth Longfellow
Ye are better than all the ballads
That ever were sung or said;
For ye are living poems,
And all the rest are dead.
  Children

A boy's will is the wind's will,
And the thoughts of youth are long, long thoughts.
  My Lost Youth

Sir John Lubbock, 1st Baron Avebury
It is customary, but I think it is a mistake, to speak of
happy childhood. Children are often over-anxious and
acutely sensitive. Man ought to be man and master of his
fate; but children are at the mercy of those around them.
  The Pleasures of Life

John Masefield
He who gives a child a treat
Makes joy-bells ring in Heaven's street,
And he who gives a child a home
Builds palaces in Kingdom come.
  The Everlasting Mercy

John Milton
  The childhood shows the man
As morning shows the day.
  Paradise Regained

Christopher Morley
The greatest poem ever known
Is one all poets have outgrown:

The poetry, innate, untold,
Of being only four years old.
To a Child

Jean Jacques Rousseau

Lacking all sense of right and wrong, a child can do nothing that is morally evil, or that merits either punishment or reproof.
Emile

John Ruskin

Give a little love to a child, and you get a great deal back.
The Crown of Wild Olive

Antoine de Saint-Exupéry

Grown-ups never understand anything for themselves, and it is tiresome for children to be always and forever explaining things to them.
The Little Prince

Sir Walter Scott

Just at the age 'twixt boy and youth,
When thought is speech, and speech is truth.
Marmion

William Shakespeare

And then the whining schoolboy, with his satchel
And shining morning face, creeping like snail
Unwillingly to school.
As You Like It 2

George Bernard Shaw

Youth is a wonderful thing. What a crime to waste it on children.

Muriel Spark

One's prime is elusive. You little girls, when you grow up, must be on the alert to recognize your prime at whatever time of your life it may occur.

The Prime of Miss Jean Brodie

Robert Louis Stevenson

A child should always say what's true,
And speak when he is spoken to,
And behave mannerly at table:
At least as far as he is able.

A Child's Garden of Verses

Harriet (Elizabeth) Beecher Stowe

"Do you know who made you?"

"Nobody, as I knows on," said the child, with a short laugh…"I 'spect I grow'd. Don't think nobody ever made me."

Uncle Tom's Cabin

Jonathan Swift

I have been assured by a very knowing American of my acquaintance in London, that a young healthy child well nursed is at a year old a most delicious, nourishing, and wholesome food, whether stewed, roasted, baked, or boiled, and I make no doubt that it will equally serve in a fricassee, or a ragout.

A Modest Proposal for preventing the Children of Ireland
from being a Burden to their Parents or Country

William Makepeace Thackeray

When you think that the eyes of your childhood dried at the sight of a piece of gingerbread, and that a plum-cake

was a compensation for the agony of parting with your mamma and sisters; O my friend and brother, you need not be too confident of your own fine feelings.
Vanity Fair

Francis Thompson

Know you what it is to be a child?…It is to believe in love, to believe in loveliness, to believe in belief; it is to be so little that the elves can reach to whisper in your ear; it is to turn pumpkins into coaches, and mice into horses, lownesss into loftiness, and nothing into everything, for each child has its fairy godmother in its own soul.
Shelley

Count Leo (Nikolaevich) Tolstoy

Children are a torment and nothing more.
The Kreutzer Sonata

William Wordsworth

The child is the father of the man.
My Heart Leaps Up

Heaven lies about us in our infancy!
Shades of the prison house begin to close
　　Upon the growing boy.
Intimations of Immortality

Sweet childish days, that were as long
As twenty days are now.
To a Butterfly

YOUTH AND AGE

Henry (Brooks) Adams
Young men have a passion for regarding their elders as
senile.
   The Education of Henry Adams

Henri Frédéric Amiel
To know how to grow old is the masterwork of wisdom, and
one of the most difficult chapters in the great art of living.
   Journal, 21 Sept. 1874

Aristophanes
Old men are children for a second time.
   Clouds

Guillaume de Salluste, Seigneur du Bartas
Who well lives, long lives: for this age of ours
Should not be numbered by years, days and hours.
   Divine Weeks and Works: Fourth Day

Bernard M(annes) Baruch
To me, old age is always fifteen years older than I am.

H(erbert) E(rnest) Bates
An old man looks permanent, as if he had been born an
old man.
   Death in Spring

John Berryman

I always wanted to be old, I wanted to say
I haven't read that for fifteen years.
His Toy, His Dream, His Rest

The Bible

Rejoice, O young man, in thy youth; and let thy heart
cheer thee in the days of thy youth.
Ecclesiastes 11

When I was a child, I spake as a child, I understood as a
child, I thought as a child: but when I became a man, I
put away childish things.
1 Corinthians 13

Ambrose (Gwinett) Bierce

Age: that period of life in which we compound for the
vices that we still cherish by reviling those that we have
no longer the enterprise to commit.
The Devil's Dictionary

Longevity: Uncommon extension of the fear of death.
Ibid

(Robert) Laurence Binyon

They shall grow not old, as we that are left grow old:
Age shall not weary them, nor the years condemn.
Poems for the Fallen

Rupert Chawner Brooke

They love the Good; they worship Truth;
They laugh uproariously in youth;
(And when they get to feeling old,
They up and shoot themselves, I'm told.)
'The Old Vicarage, Grantchester'

Samuel Butler
There's many a good tune played on an old fiddle.
The Way of All Flesh

George Gordon (Noel), 6th Lord Byron
There is an order
Of mortals on the earth, who do become
Old in their youth, and die ere middle age.
Manfred

Years steal
Fire from the mind as vigour from the limb;
And Life's enchanted cup but sparkles near the brim.
Ibid

Lewis Carroll [Charles Lutwidge Dodgson]
"You are old, Father William," the young man said,
"And your hair has become very white;
And yet you incessantly stand on your head—
Do you think, at your age, it is right?"
Alice's Adventures in Wonderland

Sir Winston (Leonard Spencer) Churchill
Twenty to twenty-five! These are the years! Don't be
content with things as they are. "The earth is yours and
the fullness thereof." Enter upon your inheritance, accept
your responsibilities.
Roving Commission: My Early Life

Bejamin Disraeli, 1st Earl of Beaconsfield
Youth is a blunder; manhood a struggle; old age a regret.
Coningsby

The Youth of a Nation are the Trustees of Posterity.
Sybil

John Dryden
Men are but children of a larger growth.
All for Love

George Eliot [Mary Ann Evans]
If youth is the season of hope, it is often so only in the sense that our elders are hopeful about us.
Middlemarch

Henri Estienne
Si jeunesse savoit; si viellesse pouvoit.
If only youth had the knowledge; if only age had the strength.
Les Prémices

Benjamin Franklin
At twenty years of age the will reigns; at thirty the wit; at forty the judgment.
Poor Richard's Almanac 1741

All would live long; but none would be old.
Ibid 1749

Gavarni [Sulplice Guillaume ("Paul") Chevalier]
Les enfants terribles.
The embarassing young.
Title of a series of prints

Joel Chandler Harris
I am in the prime of senility.
Attributed, 1906

Seymour Hicks
You will recognize, my boy, the first sign of old age: it is when you go out into the streets of London and realize for

the first time how young the policemen look.
They Were Singing by C. Pulling

Washington Irving
Whenever a man's friends begin to compliment him
about looking young, he may be sure that they think he is
growing old.
Bracebridge Hall

Dr Samuel Johnson
Towering in the confidence of twenty-one.
Boswell's *Life of Johnson*

Charles Kingsley
When all the world is young, lad
And all the trees are green;
And every goose a swan, lad
And every lass a queen.
The Water Babies

Rudyard Kipling
And the measure of our torment is the measure of our
youth.
Gentlemen Rankers

Michel Eyquem de Montaigne
Old age puts more wrinkles in our minds than on our
faces.
Essays

Juan Montalvo
Old age is an island surrounded by death.
On Beauty

Thomas Moore
What though youth gave love and roses,
Age still leaves us friends and wine.
National Airs: Spring and Autumn

Benito Mussolini
Youth is a malady of which one becomes cured a little
every day.
On his 50th birthday

Stephen Phillips
A man not old, but mellow, like good wine.
Ulysses

Alexander Pope
You've play'd and lov'd, and ate and drank, your fill.
Walk sober off, before a sprightlier age
Comes tittering on, and shoves you from the stage.
Imitations of Horace: Epistles

Saki [Hector Hugh Munro]
The young have aspirations that never come to pass, the
old have reminiscences of what never happened.
Reginald at the Carlton

Seneca
Old age is an incurable disease.
Epistulae ad Lucilium

William Shakespeare
Your lordship, though not clean past your youth, hath yet
some smack of age in you, some relish of the saltiness of time.
King Henry IV Part II

Have you not a moist eye, a dry hand, a yellow cheek, a

white beard, an increasing belly? Is not your voice
broken, your hand short, your chin double, your wit
single, and every part about you blasted with antiquity,
and will you yet call yourself young?
Ibid

Thou wilt fall backward when thou comest to age
For you and I are past our dancing days.
Romeo and Juliet 1

Therefore my age is as a lusty winter
Frosty, but kindly.
As You Like It 2

Then come kiss me, sweet and twenty,
Youth's a stuff will not endure.
Twelfth Night 2

Crabbed age and youth cannot live together:
Youth is full of pleasance, age is full of care.
The Passionate Pilgrim

Age, I do abhor thee, youth, I do adore thee.
Ibid

George Bernard Shaw
Every man over forty is a scoundrel.
Man and Superman: Maxims for Revolutionists

Youth, which is forgiven everything, forgives itself
nothing: age, which forgives itself anything, is forgiven
nothing.
Ibid

It's all that the young can do for the old, to shock them
and keep them up to date.
Fanny's First Play

(Lloyd) Logan Pearsall Smith
The denunciation of the young is a necessary part of the hygiene of older people, and greatly assists the circulation of their blood.
All Trivia

Sydney Smith
That sign of old age, extolling the past at the expense of the present.
Lady Holland's *Memoir of the Rev. Sydney Smith*

Sir Richard Steele
There are so few who can grow old with a good grace.
The Spectator, 1711

Robert Louis Stevenson
Youth is the time to go flashing from one end of the world to the other both in mind and body; to try the manners of different nations; to hear the chimes at midnight; to see sunrise in town and country; to be converted at a revival; to circumnavigate the metaphysics, write halting verses, run a mile to see a fire, and wait all day long in the theatre to applaud "Hernani".
Virginibus Puerisque

Jonathan Swift
No wise man ever wished to be younger.
Thoughts on Various Subjects, Moral and Diverting

Horace Walpole, 4th Earl of Oxford
Old age is no such uncomfortable thing if one gives oneself up to it with a good grace, and don't drag it about

"to midnight dances and the public show."
  Letter, 1774

Walt Whitman

Youth, large, lusty, loving—youth full of grace, force, fascination,
Do you know that Old Age may come after you with equal grace, force, fascination?
  Youth, Day, Old Age and Night

Oscar (Fingall O'Flahertie Wills) Wilde

The old believe everything: the middle-aged suspect everything: the young know everything.
  Phrases and Philosophies for the Use of the Young Chameleon

Thomas Woodrow Wilson

Generally young men are regarded as radicals. This is a popular misconception. The most conservative persons I ever met are college undergraduates.
  Address, 1905

MIDDLE AGE

Franklin P. Adams
Years ago we discovered the exact point the dead centre
of middle age. It occurs when you are too young to take
up golf and too old to rush up to the net.
  Nods and Becks

Anonymous
You've reached middle age when all you exercise is
caution.

Robert Benchley
A man of forty today has nothing to worry him but falling
hair, inability to button the top button, failing vision,
shortness of breath, a tendency of the collar to shut off all
breathing, trembling of the kidneys to what ever tune the
orchestra is playing, and a general sense of giddiness when
the matter of rent is brought up. Forty is Life's Golden Age.
  In *Bartlett's Unfamiliar Quotations*

Edward Ernest Bowen
Forty years on, growing older and older,
  Shorter in wind, as in memory long,
Feeble of foot, and rheumatic of shoulder,
  What will it help you that once you were strong?
  Forty Years On (Harrow School song)

George Gordon (Noel), 6th Lord Byron

Of all the barbarous middle ages, that
  Which is most barbarous is the middle age
Of man; it is—I really scarce know what;
  But when we hover between fool and sage.
  Don Juan

Nathaniel Cotton

He who at fifty is a fool
Is far too stubborn grown for school.
  Slander

Elmer Davis

When a middle-aged man says in a moment of weariness
that he is half dead, he is telling the truth.
  By Elmer Davis, 'On not being Dead, as Reported'

Daniel Defoe

Middle Age is youth without its levity,
And Age without decay.

John Dryden

I am resolved to grow fat, and look young till forty!
  Secret Love, or The Maiden Queen

F(rancis) Scott (Key) Fitzgerald

Thirty–the promise of a decade of loneliness, a thinning
list of single men to know, a thinning briefcase of enthu-
siasm, thinning hair.
  The Great Gatsby

It is in the thirties that we want friends. In the forties we
know they won't save us any more than love did.
  Notebooks

Johann Wolfgang von Goethe
Once a man's thirty, he's already old,
He is indeed as good as dead.
It's best to kill him right away.
   Faust

Bob Hope [Leslie Townes Hope]
Middle age is when your age starts to show around the middle.
   Attributed

R(udolph) C(hambers) Lehmann
A boy may still detest age,
   But as for me I know
A man has reached his best age
   At forty-two or so.
   Middle Age

Don(ald Robert Perry) Marquis
Of middle age the best that can be said is that a middle-aged person has likely learned how to have a little fun in spite of his troubles.
   The Almost Perfect State

Sir Arthur Wing Pinero
From forty till fifty a man is at heart either a stoic or a satyr.
   The Second Mrs Tanqueray

Jonathan Swift
I swear she's no chicken; she's on the wrong side of thirty, if she be a day.
   Polite Conversation

Sophie Tucker
Life begins at forty.
  Song title

E(lwyn) B(rooks) White
In a man's middle years there is scarcely a part of the
body he would hesitate to turn over to the proper
authorities.
  The Second Tree from the Corner

Edward Young
  Be wise with speed;
A fool at forty is a fool indeed.
  Love of Fame

DEATH, DYING AND GRIEF

Woody Allen [Allen Stewart Konigsberg]
On the plus side, death is one of the few things that can
be done as easily as lying down.
  Getting Even

Death is an acquired trait.
  Woody Allen and His Comedy by E. Lax

Kingsley Amis
Death has got something to be said for it:
There's no need to get out of bed for it.
  'Delivery Guaranteed'

Anaxandrides
It is good to die before one has done anything deserving
death.
  Fragment

Francis Bacon
I have often thought upon death, and I find it the least of
all evils.
  An Essay on Death

I do not believe that any man fears to be dead, but only
the stroke of death.
  Ibid

Honoré de Balzac
What does farewell mean, if not death? But will death itself be a farewell?
   Louis Lambert

Sir J(ames) M(atthew) Barrie
To die will be an awfully big adventure.
   Peter Pan

The Bible
For dust thou art, and unto dust shalt thou return.
   Genesis 3

Death is swallowed up in victory. O death, where is thy sting? O grave, where is thy victory.
   Ibid

And I looked, and behold a pale horse: and his name that sat on him was Death.
   Revelation 6

In the midst of life we are in death.
   The Book of Common Prayer: Burial of the Dead

We therefore commit his body to the ground; earth to earth, ashes to ashes, dust to dust; in sure and certain hope of the Resurrection to eternal life.
   Ibid

Man, that is born of a woman, hath but a short time to live.
   Ibid

John Bright
The Angel of Death has been abroad throughout the land; you may almost hear the beating of his wings.
   House of Commons speech, 1855

Thomas Brown
A leap into the dark.
  Letters from the Dead

Robert Browning
What is he buzzing in my ears?
  "Now that I come to die,
Do I view the world as a vale of tears?"
  Ah, reverend sir, not I!
  Confessions

Robert Burns
O Death! the poor man's dearest friend,
The kindest and the best!
  Man was Made to Mourn

Samuel Butler
It costs a lot of money to die comfortably.
  Note Books

George Gordon (Noel), 6th Lord Byron
'Tis vain to struggle—let me perish young.
  Stanzas to the Po

Old man! 'tis not so difficult to die.
  Manfred

Death in the front, Destruction in the rear!
  Childe Harold's Pilgrimage

Gaius Julius Caesar
Nothing is easier than to blame the dead.
  The Gallic War

Marcus Tullius Cicero
No man can be ignorant that he must die, nor be sure that he may not this very day.
De Senectute

Dante Alighieri
All hope abandon, ye who enter!
The Divine Comedy: Inferno

Charles Dickens
Grief never mended no broken bones, and as good people's wery scarce, what I says is, make the most on 'em.
Sketches by Boz: Gin Shops

It is a far, far better thing that I do, than I have ever done; it is a far, far better rest that I go to, than I have ever known.
A Tale of Two Cities

Benjamin Disraeli, 1st Earl of Beaconsfield
Grief is the agony of an instant; the indulgence of grief the blunder of a life.
Vivian Grey

Those who have known grief seldom seem sad.
Endymion

John Donne
Any man's death diminishes me, because I am involved in mankind; and therefore never send to know for whom the bell tolls; it tolls for thee.
Devotions upon Emergent Occasions

Ralph Waldo Emerson
Goodbye, proud world! I'm going home;

Thou art not my friend, and I'm not thine.
Poems: Goodbye

Henry Fielding

It hath been often said, that it is not death, but dying
which is terrible.
Amelia

Benjamin Franklin

The body of Benjamin Franklin, Printer, (like the cover of
an old book, its contents torn out and stripped of its
lettering and gilding), lies here, food for worms; but the
work shall not be lost, for it will (as he believed) appear
once more in a new and more elegant edition, revised and
corrected by the Author.
Epitaph on himself, 1728

Thomas Gray

Far from the madding crowd's ignoble strife.
Elegy Written in a Country Churchyard

Horace [Quintus Horatius Flaccus]

Pale Death, with impartial foot, strikes at poor men's
hovels and the towers of kings.
Odes

A(lfred) E(dward) Housman

And silence sounds no worse than cheers
After death has stopped the ears.
A Shropshire Lad: To an Athlete Dying Young

The man that runs away
Lives to die another day.
Ibid: The Day of Battle

Aldous (Leonard) Huxley
Death…It's the only thing we haven't succeeded in
completely vulgarizing.
 Eyeless in Gaza

Ignore death until the last moment; then when it can't be
ignored any longer have yourself squirted full of morphia
and shuffle off in a coma.
 Time Must Have A Stop

Thomas Jefferson
I enjoy good health: I am happy in what is around me, yet
I assure you I am ripe for leaving all this year, this day,
this hour.
 Letter, 1816

Dr Samuel Johnson
It matters not how a man dies, but how he lives.
 Boswell's *Life of Johnson*

Jean de La Bruyère
A long illness between life and death makes death a
comfort both to those who die and to those who remain.
 Caractères

Jean de La Fontaine
La mort ne surprend point le sage,
Il est toujours prêt à partir.
Death does not surprise the wise man, he is always ready
to leave.
 Fables: La Mort et le Mourant

George Henry Lewes
The only cure for grief is action.
The Spanish Drama

Georg Christoph Lichtenberg
I am always grieved when a man of real talent dies. The world needs such men more than Heaven does.
Aphorismen

Henry Wadsworth Longfellow
There is no grief like the grief which does not speak.
Hyperion

Thomas Babington Macaulay, 1st Baron Macaulay
There are not ten people in the world whose deaths would spoil my dinner, but there are one or two whose deaths would break my heart.
Letter to Hannah Macaulay, 1833

Mary Tudor
When I am dead and opened, you shall find "Calais" lying in my heart.
Holinshed's *Chronicles*

W(illiam) Somerset Maugham
Dying is the most hellishly boresome experience in the world! Particularly when it entails dying of "natural causes".
The Two Worlds of Somerset Maugham

Menander
Whom the gods love dies young.
Moyostikhoi

H(enry) L(ouis) Mencken
Of all escape mechanisms, death is the most efficient.
  A Book of Burlesques

John Milton
Of Man's first disobedience, and the fruit
Of that forbidden tree, whose mortal taste
Brought death into the world, and all our woe.
  Paradise Lost

John Muir
On no subject are our ideas more warped and pitiable
than on death...Let children walk with nature...and they
will learn that death is stingless indeed, and as beautiful
as life, and that the grave has no victory, for it never
fights. All is divine harmony.
  A Thousand-Mile Walk to the Gulf

Vladimir Nabokov
Life is a great surprise. I do not see why death should not
be an even greater one.
  Pale Fire

Dorothy (Rothschild) Parker
How could they tell?
[On being told of the death of President Calvin
Coolidge.]
  Attributed, 1933

Cesare Pavese
Many men on the point of an edifying death would be
furious if they were suddenly restored to life.

235

Samuel Pepys

I went out to Charing Cross, to see Major-General Harrison hanged, drawn and quartered; which was done there, he looking as cheerful as any man could do in that condition.

Diary, 13 Oct. 1660

Sylvia Plath

Dying
Is an art, like everything else.
I do it exceptionally well.

Lady Lazarus

Alexander Pope

But thousands die, without or this or that,
Die, and endow a college or a cat.

Moral Essays

Marcel Proust

Happiness is beneficial for the body, but it is grief that develops the powers of the mind.

Remembrance of Things Past

Jean Jacques Rousseau

All men are afraid of dying, this is the great law of sentient beings, without which the entire human species would soon be destroyed.

Julie, or the New Eloise

Nicholas Rowe

Death is the privilege of human nature,
And life without it were not worth our taking.

The Fair Penitent

Saki [Hector Hugh Munro]
Waldo is one of those people who would be enormously
improved by death.
  Beasts and Super-Beasts: The Feast of Nemesis

Alan Seeger
I have a rendezvous with Death
At some disputed barricade,
At midnight in some flaming town.
  I Have a Rendezvous with Death

William Shakespeare
A man can die but once.
  King Henry IV, Part II 3

Set honour in one eye and death i' the other,
And I will look on both indifferently.
  Julius Caesar 1

When beggars die, there are no comets seen;
The heavens themselves blaze forth the death of princes.
  Ibid 2

Cowards die many times before their deaths;
The valiant never taste of death but once.
  Ibid

Why, he that cuts off twenty years of life
Cuts off so many years of fearing death.
  Ibid 3

To be or not to be: that is the question:
Whether 'tis nobler in the mind to suffer
The slings and arrows of outrageous fortune,

Or to take arms against a sea of troubles,
And by opposing end them? To die: to sleep.
  Hamlet 3

  If I must die
I will encounter darkness as a bride,
And hug it in mine arms.
  Measure for Measure 3

  Nothing in his life
Became him like the leaving it; he died
As one that had been studied in his death
To throw away the dearest thing he ow'd,
As 'twere a careless trifle.
  Macbeth 1

Tomorrow, and tomorrow, and tomorrow,
Creeps in this petty pace from day to day,
To the last syllable of recorded time;
And all our yesterdays have lighted fools
The way to dusty death. Out, out, brief candle!
  Macbeth 5

The stroke of death is as a lover's pinch
Which hurts, and is desired.
  Antony and Cleopatra 5

He that dies pays all debts.
  The Tempest 3

"Stevie" (Florence Margaret) Smith
I was much too far out all my life
And not waving but drowning.
  Not Waving but Drowning

Edmund Spenser
Sleep after toil, port after stormy seas,
Ease after war, death after life, does greatly please.
   The Faerie Queene

Stanislaus Leszczynski
He who fears death dies every time he thinks of it.
   Oeuvres du philosophe bienfaisant

Robert Louis Stevenson
Under the wide and starry sky,
Dig the grave and let me lie.
   Requiem

Suetonius [Gaius Suetonius Tranquillus]
Ave, Imperator, morituri te salutant.
Hail, Caesar, those about to die salute thee.
   Life of Claudius

Jonathan Swift
I shall be like that tree, I shall die at the top.
   Memoirs of Jonathan Swift by Sir Walter Scott

Alfred, Lord Tennyson
Half a league, half a league,
   Half a league onward,
All in the valley of Death
Rode the six hundred.
   The Charge of the Light Brigade

Their's not to make reply,
Their's not to reason why,
Their's but to do and die:
   Ibid

Dylan Thomas

Do not go gentle into that good night,
Old age should burn and rave at close of day;
Rage, rage against the dying of the light.
   Do Not Go Gentle

Mark Twain [Samuel Langhorne Clemens]

All say, "How hard it is that we have to die"—a strange
complaint to come from the mouths of people who have
had to live.
   Pudd'nhead Wilson

The reports of my death are greatly exaggerated.
   Cable to Associated Press from Europe

John Webster

I saw him now going the way of all flesh.
   Westward Hoe

Death hath ten thousand several doors
For men to take their exit.
   The Duchess of Malfi

Oscar (Fingall O'Flahertie Wills) Wilde

A thing is not necessarily true because a man dies for it.
   Sebastian Melmoth

One can survive anything nowadays except death.
   A Woman of No Importance

William Wordsworth

   There is
One great society alone on earth;
The noble Living and the noble Dead.
   The Prelude

LAST WORDS

Joseph Addison
I have sent for you that you may see how a Christian can die.

Alexander the Great
I die by the help of too many physicians.

Henry Ward Beecher
Now comes the mystery.

Ludwig van Beethoven
I shall hear in heaven.

Anne Boleyn
The executioner is, I believe, very expert, and my neck is very slender.

James Drummond Burns
I have been dying for twenty years, now I am going to live.

Elizabeth I
All my possessions for a moment of time.

Gaius Julius Caesar
Et tu, Brute!
You too, Brutus!

Charles II

Don't let poor Nelly starve. [His mistress, Nell Gwynne.]
He had been, he said, a most unconscionable time dying,
but he hoped that they would excuse it.
   Macauley's *History of England*

Oliver Cromwell

It is not my design to drink or to sleep, but my design to
make what haste I can to be gone.

Georges Jacques Danton

Be sure you show my head to the mob. It will be a long
time ere they see its like.
   At his execution

George Eastman

My work is done. Why wait?
   His suicide note

Kathleen Ferrier

Now I'll have *eine kleine* pause.

Charles James Fox

I die happy.

George IV

Wally, what is this? It is death, my boy: they have
deceived me.
   To his page, Sir Walthen Waller

St Gregory VII

I have loved justice and hated iniquity: therefore I die in
exile.

Henry VIII
All is lost. Monks, monks, monks!

O. Henry [William Sydney Porter]
Turn up the lights—I don't want to go home in the dark.
  Quoting a popular song by Harry H. Williams

Thomas Hobbes
I am about to take my last voyage, a great leap in the
dark.

"Stonewall" (Thomas Jonathan) Jackson
Let us cross the river, and rest under the trees.

John Keats
I feel the flowers growing over me.

Cotton Mather
Is this dying? Is this all? Is this what I feared when I
prayed against a hard death? Oh, I can bear this! I can
bear it!

Sir Thomas More
I pray you, I pray you, Mr Lieutenant, see me up safe,
and for my coming down let me shift for myself.
  At his execution

Henry John Temple, 3rd Viscount Palmerston
Die, my dear doctor, that's the last thing I shall do!
  Attributed

Anna Pavlova
Get my Swan costume ready.

William Pitt the Younger
I think I could eat one of Bellamy's veal pies.

Sir Walter Raleigh
So the heart be right, it is no matter which way the head
lieth.
At his execution

Theodore Roosevelt
Put out the light.

Henry David Thoreau
I leave this world without a regret.

Sir Henry Vane
Death is but a little word, but 'tis a great work to die.
On the scaffold

Voltaire [François Marie Arouet]
Do let me die in peace.

Oscar (Fingall O'Flahertie Wills) Wilde
I expect I shall have to die beyond my means.
Taking a glass of champagne on his deathbed

HAPPINESS AND SORROW

Aeschylus
Who, save the gods, can be happy all life long?
Agamemnon

Jane Austen
Perfect happiness, even in memory, is not common.
Emma

William Blake
The busy bee has no time for sorrow.
The Marriage of Heaven and Hell: Proverbs of Hell

Ancius Manlius Severinus Boethius
Nothing is miserable unless you think it so; conversely,
every lot is happy if you are content with it.
Consolationis Philosophiæ

Sir Thomas Browne
To enjoy true happiness we must travel into a very far
country, and even out of ourselves.
Christian Morals

Robert Browning
Make us happy and you make us good.
The Ring and the Book

George Gordon (Noel), 6th Lord Byron

There comes
For ever something between us and what
We deem our happiness.
Sardanapalus

Charles Caleb Colton

He that thinks himself the happiest man, really is so.
Lacon

Dante Alighieri

Nessun maggior dolore,
Che ricordarsi del tempo felice
Nella miseria.
No greater sorrow than to recall in our misery the time
when we were happy.
The Divine Comedy: Inferno

Ralph Waldo Emerson

To fill the hour—that is happiness.
Essays, First Series: Experience

Edward FitzGerald

Here with a Loaf of Bread beneath the Bough,
A Flask of Wine, a Book of Verse—and Thou
Beside me singing in the Wilderness—
And Wilderness is Paradise enow.
The Rubaiyat of Omar Khayyam

Thomas Fuller

When sorrow is asleep, wake it not.
Gnomologia

Théophile Gautier
Happiness is white and pink.
   Caprices et zigzags

Robert B(rowning) Hamilton
I walked a mile with Sorrow
   And ne'er a word said she;
But, oh, the things I learned from her
   When Sorrow walked with me.
   Along the Road

Nathaniel Hawthorne
Happiness in this world, when it comes, comes inciden-
tally. Make it the object of pursuit, and it leads us a wild-
goose chase, and is never attained. Follow some other
object, and very possibly we may find that we have
caught happiness without dreaming of it.
   American Notebooks

William Hazlitt
I have wanted only one thing to keep me happy, but
wanting that have wanted everything.
   Winterslow: My First Acquaintance with Poets

Thomas Hood
So sorrow is shared by being poured
From one vessel into another.
   Miss Kilmansegg: Her Misery

"Kin" (Frank McKinney) Hubbard
It's pretty hard to tell what does bring happiness; poverty
and wealth have both failed.
   Abe Martin's Broadcast

Victor Hugo

The misery of a child is interesting to a mother, the
misery of a young man is interesting to a young woman,
the misery of an old man is interesting to nobody.
   Les Misérables

Aldous (Leonard) Huxley

Happiness is like coke—something you get as a by-
product in the process of making something else.
   Point Counter Point

Thomas Jefferson

He is happiest of whom the world says least, good or
bad.
   Letter to John Adams, 1786

François, Duc de La Rochefoucauld

We are more interested in making others believe we are
happy than in trying to be happy ourselves.
   Maxims

The happiness or unhappiness of men depends no less
upon their dispositions than on their fortunes.
   Ibid

We are never so happy, nor so unhappy, as we think we are.
   Ibid

Henry Wadsworth Longfellow

Believe me, every man has his secret sorrows, which the
world knows not; and oftentimes we call a man cold
when he is only sad.
   Hyperion

Into each life some rain must fall,
Some days must be dark and dreary.
   The Rainy Day

John Stuart Mill
Ask yourself whether you are happy, and you cease to be
so.
   Autobiography

Unquestionably, it is possible to do without happiness; it
is done involuntarily by nineteen-twentieths of mankind.
   Utilitarianism

Molière [Jean-Baptiste Poquelin]
Unbroken happiness is a bore: it should have ups and
downs.
   Les fourberies de Scapin

Lady Mary Wortley Montagu
One would suffer a great deal to be happy.
   Letter, 1759

Thomas Moore
Earth has no sorrow that Heaven cannot heal.
   Come, Ye Disconsolate

Alexander Pope
O happiness! our being's end and aim!
   Essay on Man

John Ray
Little children, little sorrows; big children, big sorrows.
   English Proverbs

Bertrand (Arthur William) Russell, 3rd Earl Russell
The secret of happiness is this: let your interests be as

wide as possible, and let your reactions to the things and persons that interest you be as far as possible friendly rather than hostile.

The Conquest of Happiness

Men who are unhappy, like men who sleep badly, are always proud of the fact.

In *The Faber Book of Aphorisms*

Thomas Shadwell
No man is happy but by comparison.

The Virtuoso

William Shakespeare
Sorrow breaks seasons and reposing hours,
Makes the night morning, and the noon-tide night.

Richard III 1

More in sorrow than in anger.

Hamlet 1

When sorrows come, they come not single spies,
But in battalions!

Ibid 4

All's cheerless, dark, and deadly.

King Lear 5

Sorrow concealed, like an oven stopp'd,
Doth burn the heart to cinders where it is.

Titus Adronicus 3

George Bernard Shaw
We have no more right to consume happiness without producing it than to consume wealth without producing it.

Candida

250

A lifetime of happiness! No man alive could bear it: it would be hell on earth.
Man and Superman

Richard Brinsley Sheridan
'Tis now six months since Lady Teazle made me the happiest of men—and I've been the most miserable dog ever since.
The School for Scandal

(Lloyd) Logan Pearsall Smith
There are few sorrows, however poignant, in which a good income is of no avail.
Afterthoughts

C(harles) H(addon) Spurgeon
Sorrows are visitors that come without invitation.
John Ploughman

Robert Louis Stevenson
There is no duty we so much underrate as the duty of being happy.
Virginibus Puerisque

Publilius Syrus
No man is happy unless he believes he is.
Sententiae

Horace Walpole, 4th Earl of Oxford
The world is a comedy to those that think, a tragedy to those that feel.
Letter, 1776

Oscar (Fingall O'Flahertie Wills) Wilde
Where there is sorrow, there is holy ground.
De Profundis

MONEY, WEALTH AND POVERTY

John Quincy Adams
The extremes of opulence and want are more remarkable, and more constantly obvious, in this country than in any other that I ever saw.
Diary

Abbé Leonor Jean d'Allainval
L'embarrases des richesses.
The embarrassment of riches.
Title of a play

Aristotle
Men are divided between those who are as thrifty as if they would live forever, and those who are as extravagant as if they were going to die the next day.
Lives and Opinions of Eminent Philosophers by Diogenes Laertius

Francis Bacon
And money is like muck, not good except it be spread.
Essays: Of Seditions and Troubles

Riches are for spending.
Essays: Of Expense

Walter Bagehot

Poverty is an anomaly to rich people. It is very difficult to make out why people who want dinner do not ring the bell.
  Literary Studies

Maurice Baring

If you would know what the Lord God thinks of money, you have only to look at those to whom he gives it.
  Writers at Work by Dorothy Parker

Brendan Behan

Pound notes is the best religion in the world.
  The Hostage

Aphra Behn

Money speaks sense in a language all nations understand.
  The Rover

(Joseph) Hilaire (Pierre) Belloc

I'm tired of Love: I'm still more tired of Rhyme.
But Money gives me pleasure all the time.
  Epigrams: Fatigue

The Bible

A good name is rather to be chosen than great riches, and loving favour rather than silver and gold.
  Proverbs 22

No man can serve two masters…Ye cannot serve God and mammon.
  Matthew 6

It is easier for a camel to go through the eye of a needle, than for a rich man to enter into the kingdom of God.
  Ibid 19

For the love of money is the root of all evil.
1 Timothy 6

Henry St John, Viscount Bolingbroke

All our wants, beyond those which a very moderate
income will supply, are purely imaginary.
Letter to Jonathan Swift, 1719

Samuel Butler

It has been said that the love of money is the root of all
evil. The want of money is so quite as truly.
Erewhon

George Gordon (Noel), 6th Lord Byron

Ready money is Aladdin's lamp.
Don Juan

Thomas Carlyle

Aristocracy of the money bag.
History of the French Revolution

Cash payment is not the sole nexus of man with man.
Past and Present

Miguel de Cervantes (Saavedra)

That which costs little is less valued.
Don Quixote

There are but two families in the world as my grandmother used to say, the Haves and the Have-nots.
Ibid

Philip Dormer Stanhope, 4th Earl of Chesterfield

I knew once a very covetous, sordid fellow, who used to
say, "Take care of the pence, for the pounds will take care
of themselves."
Letters to His Son

Sir Winston (Leonard Spencer) Churchill
Saving is a very fine thing. Especially when your parents have done it for you.
   Attributed

William Cobbett
To be poor and independent is very nearly an impossibility.
   Advice to Young Men

Charles Dickens
Annual income twenty pounds, annual expenditure nineteen nineteen six, result happiness. Annual income twenty pounds, annual expenditure twenty pounds ought and six, result misery.
   David Copperfield

Benjamin Disraeli, 1st Earl of Beaconsfield
"Two nations; between whom there is no intercourse and no sympathy"…"You speak of—" said Egremont, hesitatingly. "The rich and the poor."
   Sybil

Ralph Waldo Emerson
Can anybody remember when the times were not hard and money not scarce?
   Society and Solitude: Works and Days

George Farquhar
My Lady Bountiful.
   The Beaux' Stratagem

'Tis still my maxim, that there is no scandal like rags, nor any crime so shameful as poverty.
   Ibid

Henry Fielding

Money will say more in one moment than the most
eloquent lover can in years.
  The Miser

Benjamin Franklin

Nothing but money is sweeter than honey.
  Poor Richard's Almanack 1735

Many a man would have been worse if his estate had
been better.
  Ibid 1751

J(ean) Paul Getty

If you can actually count your money then you are not
really a rich man.
  The Pendulum Years by Bernard Levin

Gracchus [François Noël Babeuf]

Let the revolting distinction of rich and poor disappear
once and for all.
  Manifesto of the Equals

E(dgar) W(atson) Howe

A man is usually more careful of his money than he is of
his principles.
  Ventures in Common Sense

Dr Samuel Johnson

There are few ways in which a man can be more inno-
cently employed than in getting money.
  Boswell's *Life of Johnson*

No man but a blockhead ever wrote except for money.
  Ibid

It is better to live rich than to die rich.
   Ibid

D(avid) H(erbert) Lawrence
Money is our madness, our vast collective madness.
   Money Madness

Edward Moore
I am rich beyond the dreams of avarice.
   The Gamester

Thomas Love Peacock
Respectable means rich, and decent means poor. I should
die if I heard my family called decent.
   Crotchet Castle

Titus Maccius Plautus
You must spend money, if you wish to make money.
   Asinaria

Jean Jacques Rousseau
Money is the seed of money, and the first guinea is
sometimes more difficult to acquire than the second
million.
   Discours sur l'origine de l'inegalité

William Shakespeare
Saint-seducing gold.
   Romeo and Juliet 1

Bell, book, and candle shall not drive me back,
When gold and silver becks me to come on.
   King John 3

Neither a borrower nor a lender be.
Hamlet 1

Percy Bysshe Shelley
Wealth is a power usurped by the few, to compel the
many to labour for their benefit.
Queen Mab, Notes

Adam Smith
No society can surely be flourishing and happy, of which
the far greater part of the members are poor and miserable.
The Wealth of Nations

(Lloyd) Logan Pearsall Smith
The wretchedness of being rich is that you live with rich
people.
Afterthoughts

William Somerville
Let all the learned say what they can,
'Tis ready money makes the man.
Ready Money

Henry David Thoreau
That man is the richest whose pleasures are the cheapest.
Journal, 11 March 1856

Mark Twain [Samuel Langhorne Clemens]
Few of us can stand prosperity. Another man's, I mean.
Pudd'nhead Wilson

Artemus Ward [Charles Farrar Browne]
Let us all be happy and live within our means, even if we

have to borrow the money to do it with.
   Natural History

H(erbert) G(eorge) Wells
I don't 'old with Wealth. What is Wealth? Labour robbed
out of the poor.
   Autocracy of Mr Parham

Success, Fame and Greatness

Woody Allen [Allen Stewart Konigsberg]
I don't want to achieve immortality through my work. I want to achieve it through not dying.
  Woody Allen and His Comedy by E. Lax

John Emerich Edward Dalberg, 1st Baron Acton
Great men are almost always bad men…There is no worse heresy than that the office sanctifies the holder of it.
  Letter to Bishop Creighton, 1887

Fred Allen [John Florence Sullivan]
A celebrity is a person who works hard all his life to become known, then wears dark glasses to avoid being recognized.
  Treadmill to Oblivion

Henri Frédéric Amiel
Great men are the real men: in them nature has succeeded.
  Journal, 13 Aug. 1865

Francis Bacon
Men in great places are thrice servants: servants of the Sovereign or State; servants of Fame; and servants of Business…It is a strange desire to seek Power and to lose Liberty.
  Essays: Of Great Place

The Bible
Let us now praise famous men.
   Ecclesiasticus 44

Elizabeth Barrett Browning
   A great man,
Leaves clean work behind him, and requires
No sweeper up of the chips.
   Aurora Leigh

Edward (George Earle Lytton) Bulwer-Lytton, 1st Baron Lytton
Beneath the rule of men entirely great,
The pen is mightier than the sword.
   Richelieu

Edmund Burke
It is the nature of all greatness not to be exact.
   Speech, 1774

Passion for fame; a passion which is the instinct of all great souls.
   Ibid

George Gordon (Noel), 6th Lord Byron
I awoke one morning and found myself famous.
   [On the success of *Childe Harold*.]

Pedro Calderón de la Barca
Fame, like water, bears up the lighter things, and lets the weighty sink.
   Adventures of Five Hours

Dante Alighieri
Chè, seggendo in piuma,

In fama non si vien, nè sotto coltre.
For fame is not won by lying on a feather bed nor under a canopy.
  Divine Comedy: Inferno

John Dryden

His grandeur he derived from Heaven alone,
For he was great, ere fortune made him so.
  Heroic Stanzas after Cromwell's Funeral

Ralph Waldo Emerson

The great man is he who in the midst of the crowd keeps with perfect sweetness the independence of solitude.
  Essays, First Series: Self-Reliance

To be great is to be misunderstood.
  Ibid

Henry Fielding

Greatness consists in bringing all manner of mischief on mankind, and goodness in removing it from them.
  Jonathan Wild the Great

Benjamin Franklin

I pronounce it as certain that there was never yet a truly great man that was not at the same time truly virtuous.
  The Busy-Body

Thomas Fuller

The great and the little have need of one another.
  Gnomologia: Adagies and Proverbs

Henry IV
Great eaters and great sleepers are incapable of doing
anything that is great.
 Attributed

George Herbert
The great would have none great, and the little all little.
 Jacula Prudentum

There would be no great ones if there were no little ones.
 Ibid

John Keats
Fame, like a wayward girl, will still be coy
To those who woo her with too slavish knees.
 Sonnet: On Fame

Jean de La Bruyère
The nearer we come to great men the more clearly we see
they are only men. They rarely seem great to their valets.
 Caractères

Henry Wadsworth Longfellow
Lives of great men all remind us
 We can make our lives sublime,
And, departing, leave behind us
 Footprints on the sands of time.
 A Psalm of Life

The heights by great men reached and kept
 Were not attained by sudden flight,
But they, while their companions slept,
 Were toiling upward in the night.
 The Ladder of Saint Augustine

Alexander Pope
Nor fame I slight, nor for her favours call;
She comes unlook'd for, if she comes at all.
  The Temple of Fame

William Shakespeare
Be not afraid of greatness: some are born great, some
achieve greatness, and some have greatness thrust upon
them.
  Twelfth Night 2

George Bernard Shaw
If a great man could make us understand him we should
hang him.
  Man and Superman: Maxims for Revolutionists

Life levels all men: death reveals the eminent.
  Ibid

Percy Bysshe Shelley
Fame is love disguised.
  Epipsychidion

Horace Walpole, (4th Earl of Oxford)
They who cannot perform great things themselves may
yet have a satisfaction in doing justice to those who can.
  Attributed

John Wolcot ["Peter Pindar"]
What rage for fame attends both great and small!
Better be d——d than mentioned not at all!
  More Lyric Odes to the Royal Academicians

BEAUTY

Anacreon
Beauty is proof against spears and shields. She who is beautiful is more formidable than fire and iron.
Fragment

Francis Bacon
There is no Excellent Beauty, that hath not some strangeness in the proportion.
Essays: Of Beauty

Aphra Behn
Do you not daily see fine clothes…are more inviting than Beauty unadorn'd?
The Rover

Robert Browning
If you get simple beauty, and nought else.
You get about the best thing God invents.
Fra Lippo Lippi

Edmund Burke
I never remember that anything beautiful…was ever shown, though it were to a hundred people, that they did not all immediately agree that it was beautiful.
The Sublime and Beautiful

George Gordon (Noel), 6th Lord Byron
She walks in beauty like the night
 Of cloudless climes and starry skies;
And all that's best of dark and bright
 Meet in her aspect and her eyes:
 She Walks in Beauty

Luis Cernuda
Everything beautiful has its moment and then passes away.
 Las Ruinas

Confucius
Everything has its beauty but not everyone sees it.
 Analects

William Congreve
There is in true beauty, as in courage, somewhat which
narrow souls cannot dare to admire.
 The Old Bachelor

John Donne
No spring nor summer beauty hath such grace
As I have seen in one autumnal face.
 Elegies: The Autumnal

Henry Havelock Ellis
Beauty is the child of love.
 Impressions and Comments

Ralph Waldo Emerson
Beauty is its own excuse for being.
 The Rhodora

Anne Frank
Think of all the beauty still left around you and be happy.
 The Diary of a Young Girl

Baltasar Gracián
Beauty and folly are generally companions.
   The Art of Wordly Wisdom

John Keats
A thing of beauty is a joy forever;
Its loveliness increases; it will never
Pass into nothingness.
   Endymion

"Beauty is truth, truth beauty,"—that is all
Ye know on earth, and all ye need to know.
   Ode on a Grecian Urn

Christopher Marlowe
Was this the face that launch'd a thousand ships
And burnt the topless towers of Ilium? [Of Helen of Troy.]
   Dr Faustus

O, thou art fairer than the evening air
Clad in the beauty of a thousand stars.
   Ibid

John Milton
Beauty is nature's coin, must not be hoarded,
But must be current.
   Comus

Beauty stands
In the admiration only of weak minds
Led captive.
   Paradise Regained

Molière [Jean-Baptiste Poquelin]
Beauty of face is a frail ornament, a passing flower, a

momentary brightness belonging only to the skin.
Les Femmes savantes

Plato
The good is the beautiful.
Lysis

Alexander Pope
Beauties in vain their pretty eyes may roll...but merit
wins the soul.
The Rape of the Lock

John Ruskin
Remember that the most beautiful things in the world are
the most useless.
The Stones of Venice

William Shakespeare
Is she kind as she is fair?
For beauty lives with kindness.
The Two Gentlemen of Verona 4

He hath a daily beauty in his life
That makes me ugly.
Othello 5

Shall I compare thee to a summer's day?
Thou art more lovely and more temperate:
Rough winds do shake the darling buds of May,
And summer's lease hath all too short a date.
Sonnets 18

James Thomson
Perfecty beauty is its own sole end.
Weddah

Count Leo (Nikolaevich) Tolstoy
It is amazing how complete is the delusion that beauty is goodness.
The Kreutzer Sonata

Lew(is) Wallace
Beauty is altogether in the eye of the beholder.
The Prince of India

Oscar (Fingall O'Flahertie Wills) Wilde
Beauty is the only thing that time cannot harm. Philosophies fall away like sand, and creeds follow one another like the withered leaves of autumn; but what is beautiful is a joy for all seasons and a possession for all eternity.
The English Renaissance of Art

It is better to be beautiful than to be good. But…it is better to be good than to be ugly.
The Picture of Dorian Gray

NATURE

Alfonso the Wise [Alfonso X]
Had I been present at the Creation, I would have given some useful hints for the better ordering of the universe.
    Attributed

St Augustine of Hippo
All nature is good.
    Of Continence

Walter Bagehot
Taken as a whole, the universe is absurd.
    Literary Studies

George Gordon (Noel), 6th Lord Byron
There is a pleasure in the pathless woods,
There is a rapture on the lonely shore,
There is society, where none intrudes,
By the deep sea and music in its roar:
I love not man the less, but Nature more...
To mingle with the Universe, and feel
What I can ne'er express, yet cannot all conceal.
    Childe Harold's Pilgrimage

Marcus Tullius Cicero
Those things are better which are perfected by nature than those which are finished by art.
De Natura Deorum

Ralph Waldo Emerson
Nature is an endless combination and repetition of very few laws. She hums the old well-known air through innumerable variations.
History

Enrico Fermi
Whatever Nature has in store for mankind, unpleasant as it may be, men must accept, for ignorance is never better than knowledge.
Atoms in the Family by Laura Fermi

Robert (Lee) Frost
How many times it thundered before Franklin took the hint! How many apples feel on Newton's head before he took the hint! Nature is always hinting at us. It hints over and over again. And suddenly we take the hint.

Horace [Quintus Horatius Flaccus]
Though you drive away Nature with a pitchfork she always returns.
Epistles

Thomas Henry Huxley
For every man the world is as fresh as it was at the first day, and as full of untold novelties for him who has the eyes to see them.
A Liberal Education

William Ralph Inge
The whole of nature is a conjugation of the verb to eat, in the active and the passive.
Outspoken Essays

Juvenal [Decimus Junius Juvenalis]
Never does nature say one thing and wisdom another.
Satires

Baron Gottfried Wilhelm von Leibnitz
In nature there can never be two beings that are exactly alike.
The Monadology

Leonardo da Vinci
Nature never breaks her own laws.
Notebooks

Carolus Linnaeus [Carl von Linné]
Nature does not proceed by leaps.
Philosophia Botanica

John Muir
The clearest way into the Universe is through a forest wilderness.
John of the Mountains

Cardinal John Henry Newman
Living Nature, not dull Art
Shall plan my ways and rule my heart.
Nature and Art

Alexander Smith
Nature never quite goes along with us. She is sombre at

weddings, sunny at funerals, and she frowns on ninety-nine out of a hundred picnics.
Dreamthorp

Adlai E(wing) Stevenson
Nature is neutral. Man has wrested from nature the power to make the world a desert or to make the deserts bloom. There is no evil in the atom; only in men's souls.
Speech, 1952

Alfred, Lord Tennyson
Nature red in tooth and claw.
In Memoriam

Henry David Thoreau
We need the tonic of wildness…We can never have enough of nature.
Walden

Voltaire [François Marie Arouet]
Men argue, nature acts.
Philosophical Dictionary

Mary Wollstonecraft
It is the preservation of the species, not of individuals, which appears to be the design of Deity throughout the whole of nature.
Letters written in Sweden, Norway and Denmark

TIME AND ETERNITY

Francis Bacon
And he that will not apply New Remedies, must expect New Evils; for Time is the greatest Innovator.
   Essays: Of Innovations

The Bible
To everything there is a season, and a time to every purpose under the heaven: A time to be born, and a time to die; a time to plant, and a time to pluck up that which is planted; A time to kill, and a time to heal; a time to break down, and a time to build up; A time to weep, and a time to laugh; a time to mourn, and a time to dance; A time to cast away stones, and a time to gather stones together; a time to embrace, and a time to refrain from embracing; A time to get, and a time to lose; a time to keep, and a time to cast away; A time to rend, and a time to sew; a time to keep silence, and a time to speak; A time to love, and a time to hate; A time of war, and a time of peace.
   Ecclesiastes 3

William Blake
To see a world in a grain of sand,

And heaven in a wild flower,
Hold infinity in the palm of your hand,
And eternity in an hour.
  Auguries of Innocence

Robert Browning
Who knows but the world may end tonight?
  The Last Ride Together

Thomas Carlyle
The illimitable, silent, never-resting thing called Time,
rolling, rushing on, swift, silent, like an all embracing
ocean-tide, on which we and all the Universe swim like
exhalations.
  Heroes and Hero Worship

Julia Fletcher Carney
Little drops of water, little grains of sand,
Make the mighty ocean and the pleasant land.
So the little minutes, humble though they be,
Make the mighty ages of eternity.
  Little Things

Philip Dormer Stanhope, 4th Earl of Chesterfield
I recommend you to take care of the minutes, for hours
will take care of themselves.
  Letters to His Son

Know the true value of time; snatch, seize and enjoy
every moment of it. No idleness, no laziness, no procrastination.
  Ibid

Sir Noel (Pierce) Coward
Time is the reef upon which all our frail mystic ships are
wrecked.
  Blithe Spirit

I don't give a hoot about posterity. Why should I worry
about what people think of me when I'm dead as a
doornail anyway.
  Present Laughter

Charles Dickens
It was the best of times, it was the worst of times, it was
the age of wisdom, it was the age of foolishness, it was
the epoch of belief, it was the epoch of incredulity, it was
the season of Light, it was the season of Darkness, it was
the spring of hope, it was the winter of despair, we had
everything before us, we had nothing before us, we were
all going direct to Heaven, we were all going direct the
other way.
  A Tale of Two Cities

Benjamin Disraeli, 1st Earl of Beaconsfield
Time is the great physician.
  Endymion

Sir Francis Drake
There's plenty of time to win this game, and to thrash the
Spaniards too. [Sighting of the Armada while playing
bowls, 1588.]

John Dryden
A very merry, dancing, drinking,
Laughing, quaffing, and unthinking time.
  Secular Masque

Ralph Waldo Emerson
A day is a miniature eternity.
   Journals

Euripides
Time will reveal everything. It is a babbler, and speaks
even when not asked.
   Fragment

Edward FitzGerald
The Bird of Time has but a little way
To fly—and Lo! the Bird is on the Wing.
   The Rubaiyat of Omar Khayyam

Benjamin Franklin
Dost thou love life? Then do not squander time, for that's
the stuff life is made of.
   Poor Richard's Almanack 1746

Lost time is never found again.
   Ibid 1748

Remember that time is money.
   Advice to a Young Tradesman

Robert Herrick
Gather ye rosebuds while ye may,
   Old Time is still a-flying:
And this same flower that smiles today,
   Tomorrow will be dying.
   Hesperides: To the Virgins, to Make Much of Time

Mark Antony de Wolfe Howe
Now, thieving Time, take what you must...
Yet leave, O leave exempt from plunder
My curiosity, my wonder!
Thieving Time

Jean de La Bruyère
Those who make the worse use of their time are the first
to complain of its brevity.
Caractères

C(live) S(taples) Lewis
The Future is something which everyone reaches at the rate
of sixty minutes an hour, whatever he does, whoever he is.
The Screwtape Letters

Lucretius
Summarum summa est aeternum.
The sum of all sums is eternity.
De Natura Rerum

Andrew Marvell
But at my back I always hear
Time's wingèd chariot drawing near.
To his Coy Mistress

W(illiam) Somerset Maugham
It is bad enough to know the past; it would be intolerable
to know the future.
Foreign Devil by Richard Hughes

John Milton
Time, the subtle thief of youth.
Sonnets 7

Friedrich Wilhelm Nietzsche
All things return eternally, and ourselves with them: we
have already existed times without number, and all things
with us.
  Thus Spake Zarathustra

Ovid [Publius Ovidius Naso]
Tempus fugit.
Time flies.
  Fasti

Tempus edax rerum.
Time the devourer of all things.
  Metamorphoses

Thomas Paine
These are the times that try men's souls.
  The American Crisis

Pliny the Younger
The happier the time, the faster it goes.
  Letters

Marcel Proust
The time which we have at our disposal every day is
elastic; the passions that we feel expand it, those that we
inspire contract it; and habit fills up what remains.
  Remembrance of Things Past

Will(iam Penn Adair) Rogers
Half our life is spent trying to find something to do with
the time we have rushed through life trying to save.
  The Autobiography of Will Rogers

Sir Walter Scott

There's a gude time coming.
  Rob Roy

Seneca

Veritatem dies aperit.
Time discovers the truth.
  De Ira

William Shakespeare

O, call back yesterday, bid time return.
  King Richard II 3

Time travels in divers paces with divers persons. I'll tell
you who Time ambles withal, who Time trots withal, who
Time gallops withal and who he stands still withal.
  As You Like It 3

For who would bear the whips and and scorns of time.
  Hamlet 3

Tomorrow, and tomorrow, and tomorrow,
Creeps in this petty pace from day to day
To the last syllable of recorded time.
  Macbeth 1

Samuel Smiles

Those who have most to do, and are willing to work, will
find the most time.
  Self-Help

Herbert Spencer

Time: that which man is always trying to kill, but which
ends in killing him.
  Definitions

Henry David Thoreau
As if you could kill time without injuring eternity.
  Walden

Virgil [Publius Vergilius Maro]
Sed fugit interea, fugit inreparabile tempus.
Time meanwhile flies, flies never to return.
  Georgics

LOVE

Jane Austen
All the privilege I claim for my own sex…is that of
loving longest, when existence or when hope is gone.
  Persuasion

Sir J(ames) M(atthew) Barrie
Let no one who loves be called altogether unhappy. Even
love unreturned has its rainbow.
  The Little Minister

Aphra Behn
Love ceases to be a pleasure when it ceases to be a secret.
  The Lover's Watch: Four o'clock

The Bible
And Jacob served seven years for Rachel; and they
seemed unto him but a few days, for the love he had to
her.
  Genesis 29

[Jonathan] thy love to me was wonderful, passing the
love of women.
  2 Samuel 1

Stay me with flagons, comfort me with apples: for I am sick of love.
Song of Solomon 2

A new commandment I give unto you, That ye love one another; as I have loved you, that ye also love one another.
John 13

Ambrose (Gwinett) Bierce
Love: a temporary insanity curable by marriage or by removal of the patient from the influences under which he incurred the disorder.
The Devil's Dictionary

William Blake
Love seeketh not itself to please,
Nor for itself hath any care,
But for another gives its ease,
And builds a heaven in hell's despair.
Songs of Experience: The Clod and the Pebble

Ancius Manlius Severinus Boethius
Who can give a law to lovers? Love is a greater law unto itself.
De Consolatione Philosophiae

Elizabeth Barrett Browning
Unless you can muse in a crowd all day
  On the absent face that fixed you;
Unless you can love, as the angels may,
  With the breadth of heaven betwixt you;
Unless you can dream that his faith is fast,
  Through behoving and unbehoving;

Unless you can die when the dream is past—
  Oh, never call it loving!
    A Woman's Shortcomings

How do I love thee? Let me count the ways.
    Sonnets from the Portugese

Robert Burns
But to see her was to love her,
Love but her, and love for ever.
    Ae Fond Kiss

O, my luve is like a red red rose,
  That's newly sprung in June.
    A Red Red Rose

Samuel Butler
'Tis better to have loved and lost than never to have lost at all.
    The Way of All Flesh

George Gordon (Noel), 6th Lord Byron
Man's love is of man's life a thing apart,
  'Tis woman's whole existence.
    Don Juan

Lewis Carroll [Charles Lutwidge Dodgson]
And the moral of that is— "Oh, 'tis love, 'tis love that makes the world go round."
    Alice's Adventures in Wonderland

Geoffrey Chaucer
Love is blind.
    The Canterbury Tales: The Merchant's Tale

Samuel Taylor Coleridge

A person once said to me that he could make nothing of love, except that it was friendship accidently combined with desire. Whence I concluded that he had never been in love.

Table-Talk

William Congreve

Heav'n has no rage like love to hatred turn'd,
Nor Hell a fury like a woman scorn'd.

The Mourning Bride

If there's delight in love, 'tis when I see
That heart, which others bleed for, bleed for me.

The Way of the World

Noel (Pierce) Coward

Mother love, particularly in America, is a highly respected and much publicized emotion and when exacerbated by gin and bourbon it can become extremely formidable.

Future Indefinite

Benjamin Disraeli, 1st Earl of Beaconsfield

The magic of first love is our ignorance that it can ever end.

Henrietta Temple

We are all born for love; it is the principle of existence and its only end.

Sybil

John Donne

For God's sake hold your tongue and let me love.

The Canonization

Lord Alfred Douglas
I am the love that dare not speak its name. [Homosexual love.]
Two Loves

John Dryden
Love's the noblest frailty of the mind.
The Indian Emperor

Pains of love be sweeter far
Than all other pleasures are.
Tyrannic Love

Edward VIII
I have found it impossible to carry the heavy burden of responsibility and to discharge my duties as king as I would wish to do without the help and support of the woman I love.
Radio broadcast, 11 Dec. 1936

Ralph Waldo Emerson
All mankind love a lover.
Essays: Love

Henry Fielding
Devil take me, if I think anything but love to be the object of love.
Amelia

Christopher (Harris) Fry
Oh, the unholy mantrap of love!
The Lady's not for Burning

John Gay
She who has never lov'd, has never liv'd.
The Captives

Oliver Goldsmith
Friendship is a disinterested commerce between equals;
love, an abject intercourse between tyrants and slaves.
The Good-Natured Man

Thomas Hardy
A lover without indiscretion is no lover at all.
The Hand of Ethelberta

Nathaniel Hawthorne
Selfishness is one of the qualities apt to inspire love. This
might be thought out at great length.
American Note-Books

James Hogg
O, love, love, love; Love is like a dizziness;
It winna let a poor body gang about his business!
Love is Like a Dizziness

Victor (Marie) Hugo
The supreme happiness of life is the conviction that we
are loved.
Les Misérables

Jerome K(lapka) Jerome
Love is like the measles; we all have to go through it.
Idle Thoughts of an Idle Fellow: On Being in Love

Douglas William Jerrold
Love's like the measles—all the worse when it comes late
in life.
A Philanthropist

Dr Samuel Johnson

Love is the wisdom of the fool and the folly of the wise.

Johnsonian Miscellanies

John Keats

La belle Dame sans Merci
Hath thee in thrall!

La Belle Dame Sans Merci

François, Duc de La Rochefoucauld

True love is like ghosts, which everybody talks about but few have seen.

Maxims

The pleasure of love is in loving. We are happier in the passion we feel than in that we arouse.

Ibid

Henry Wadsworth Longfellow

There is nothing holier, in this life of ours, than the first consciousness of love—the first fluttering of its silken wings.

Hyperion

Christopher Marlowe

Where both deliberate, the love is slight;
Whoever loved that loved not at first sight?

Hero and Leander

Come live with me, and be my love.

The Passionate Shepherd to His Love

H(enry) L(ouis) Mencken

To be in love is merely to be in a state of perpetual

anaesthesis—to mistake an ordinary young man for a
Greek god or an ordinary young woman for a goddess.
   Prejudices

Molière [Jean-Baptiste Poquelin]
On est aisement dupé par ce qu'on aime.
We are easily duped by those we love.
   Le Tartuffe

Thomas Moore
 But there's nothing half so sweet in life
   As love's young dream.
   Irish Melodies: Love's Young Dream

Napoleon I [Napoleon Bonaparte]
I have never loved anyone for love's sake, except,
perhaps Josephine—a little.
   To Gaspard Gourgaud, St Helena, 1817

Friedrich Wilhelm Nietzsche
Love is the state in which man sees things most decidedly
as they are not.
   The Antichrist

Dorothy (Rothschild) Parker
Life is a glorious cycle of song
A medley of extemporania,
And love is a thing that can never go wrong
And I am Marie of Rumania.

Blaise Pascal
Le coeur a ses raisons que la raison ne connait point.
The heart has its reasons, of which reason knows nothing.
   Pensées

Alexander Pope

Love, free as air, at sight of human ties,
Spreads his light wings, and in a moment flies.
  Eloisa to Abelard

Jean Paul Richter

Love diminishes the delicacy of women and increases
that of men.
  Titan

Samuel Rogers

Oh, she was good as she was fair!
  None—none on earth above her!
As pure in thought as angels are,
  To know her was to love her.
  Jacqueline

Bertrand (Arthur William) Russell, 3rd Earl Russell

To fear love is to fear life, and those who fear life are
already three parts dead.
  Marriage and Morals

Alexander Scott

Luve is ane fervent fire,
Kendillit without desire:
Short plesour, lang displesour,
Repentance is the hire.
  Lo! What it is to Luve

Sir Walter Scott

True love's the gift which God has given
To man alone beneath the heaven.
  The Lay of the Last Minstrel

William Shakespeare
Love comforteth like sunshine after rain,
But Lust's effect is tempest after sun;
Love's gentle spring doth always fresh remain,
Lust's winter comes ere summer half be done:
   Love surfeits not, Lust like a glutton dies;
   Love is all truth, Lust full of forged lies.
   Venus and Adonis

And when Love speaks, the voice of all the gods
Make heaven drowsy with the harmony.
   Love's Labour's Lost 4

A pair of star-cross'd lovers.
   Romeo and Juliet, Prologue

O, swear not by the moon, the inconstant moon,
That monthly changes in her circled orb,
Lest that thy love prove likewise variable.
   Ibid

The course of true love never did run smooth.
   A Midsummer Night's Dream 1

Speak low, if you speak love.
   Much Ado About Nothing 2

If thou remember'st not the slightest folly
That ever love did make thee run into,
Thou hast not loved.
   As You Like It 2

   Down on your knees,
And thank heaven, fasting, for a good man's love.
   Ibid 3

No sooner met but they looked, no sooner looked but they loved, no sooner loved but they sighed, no sooner sighed but they asked one another the reason, no sooner knew the reason but they sought the remedy.
Ibid 5

Love sought is good, but given unsought is better.
Twelfth Night 3

Doubt thou the stars are fire;
  Doubt that the sun doth move;
Doubt truth to be a liar;
  But never doubt I love.
Hamlet 2

To be wise and love
Exceeds man's might.
Troilus and Cressida 3

She loved me for the dangers I had pass'd,
And I loved her that she did pity them.
This only is the witchcraft I have used.
Othello 1

Then must you tell
Of one that loved not wisely but too well.
Ibid 5

There's beggary in the love that can be reckon'd.
Antony And Cleopatra 1

George Bernard Shaw
When we want to read of the deeds that are done for love, whither do we turn? To the murder column.
Three Plays for Puritans, Preface

Percy Bysshe Shelley
The wise want love; and those who love want wisdom.
  Prometheus Unbound

Sir Philip Sidney
My true love hath my heart and I have his,
By just exchange one for the other given.
  Arcadia

Sophocles
Love, unconquered in battle.
  Antigone

Edmund Spenser
And all for love, and nothing for reward.
  The Faerie Queen

Laurence Sterne
Love, an' please your Honour, is exactly like war, in this;
that a soldier, though he has escaped three weeks complete o' Saturday night,—may, nevertheless, be shot
through his heart on Sunday morning.
  Tristram Shandy

Alfred, Lord Tennyson
In the Spring a young man's fancy lightly turns to
thoughts of love.
  Locksley Hall

He will hold thee, when his passion shall have spent its
novel force,
Something better than his dog, a little dearer than his horse.
  Ibid

'Tis better to have loved and lost
Than never to have loved at all.
 In Memoriam

William Makepeace Thackeray
Some cynical Frenchman has said that there are two
parties to a love transaction; the one who loves and the
other who condescends to be so treated.
 Vanity Fair

Anthony Trollope
There is no happiness in love, except at the end of an
English novel.
 Barchester Towers

Those who have courage to love should have courage to
suffer.
 The Bertrams

Royall Tyler
The chains of love are never so binding as when the links
are made of gold.
 The Contrast

Virgil [Publius Vergilius Maro]
Omnia vincit amor.
Love conquers all.

George John Whyte-Melville
We always believe our first love is our last, and our last
love our first.
 Katerfekto

Oscar (Fingall O'Flahertie Wills) Wilde

To love oneself is the beginning of a lifelong romance, Phipps.

An Ideal Husband

SEX AND CHASTITY

Woody Allen [Allen Stewart Konigsberg]
Don't knock it [masturbation], it's sex with someone you love.

Maxwell Anderson
Virginity is rather a state of mind.
  Elizabeth the Queen

St Augustine of Hippo
Da mihi castitatem et continentiam, sed noli modo.
Give me chastity and continence, but not yet.
  Confessions

Charles Baudelaire
Sexuality is the lyricism of the masses.
  Journaux intimes 93

Francis Beaumont and **John Fletcher**
Kiss till the cow comes home.
  The Scornful Lady

Anthony Burgess [John Burgess Wilson]
He said it was artificial respiration but now I find I'm to have his child.
  Inside Mr Enderby

George Gordon (Noel), 6th Lord Byron
What men call gallantry, and gods adultery,
Is much more common where the climate's sultry.
   Don Juan

Mrs Patrick Campbell
I don't mind where people make love, so long as they
don't do it on the street and frighten the horses.
   Attributed

Barbara Cartland
I'll wager that in 10 years it will be fashionable again to
be a virgin.
   The Observer, 'Sayings of the Week', 20 June 1976

I said 10 years ago that in 10 years time it would be smart
to be a virgin. Now everyone is back to virgins again.
   The Observer, 'Sayings of the Week', 12 July 1987

Gaius Valerius Catullus
Give me a thousand kisses, then a hundred, then another
thousand, then a second hundred, then yet another
thousand, then a hundred.
   Carmin

Philip Dormer Stanhope, 4th Earl of Chesterfield
The pleasure is momentary, the position ridiculous and
the expense damnable
   Nature 1970

Charles Dickens
I might keep up with a young 'ooman o' large property as
hadn't a title, if she made wery fierce love to me. Not else.
   Pickwick Papers

John Donne

Licence my roving hands, and let them go,
Before, behind, between, above, below.
O my America! my new-found-land,
My kingdom, safeliest when with one man mann'd.
   'To his Mistress Going to Bed'

Full nakedness! All joys are due to thee,
As souls unbodied, bodies uncloth'd must be,
To taste whole joys.
   Ibid

John Dryden

Let not his hand within your bosom stray,
And rudely with your pretty bubbies play.
   Imitations of Ovid: Amores

Germaine Greer

No sex is better than bad sex.
   Attributed

Dr Samuel Johnson

Marriage has many pains, but celibacy has no pleasures.
   Rasselas

Juvenal [Decimus Junius Juvenalis]

To set your neighbour's bed a-shaking is now an ancient
and long-established custom. It was the silver age which
saw the first adulterers.
   Satires

D(avid) H(erbert) Lawrence

You mustn't think I advocate perpetual sex. Far from it.

Nothing nauseates me more than promiscuous sex in and out of season. [Referring to *Lady Chatterley's Lover*.]
   Letter to Lady Ottoline Morrell, 22 Dec. 1928

Frédérick Leboyer
Making love is the sovereign remedy for anguish.
   Birth without Violence

Lord Longford
No sex without responsibility.
   The Observer, 3 May 1954

Maimonides [Moses ben Maimon]
He who immerses himself in sexual intercourse will be assailed by premature ageing, his strength will wane, his eyes will weaken, and a bad odour will emit from his mouth and his armpits, his teeth will fall out and many other maladies will afflict him.
   Mishreh Torah

Christopher Marlowe
Thou hast committed—
Fornication: but that was in another country;
and besides, the wench is dead.
   The Jew of Malta

John Masefield
The new lust gives the lecher the new thrill.
   Widow in the Bye Street

George Mikes
Continental people have sex lives. The English have hot water bottles.
   How To Be An Alien

Henry Miller

Sex is one of the nine reasons for reincarnation…The other eight are unimportant.
  Big Sur and the Oranges of Hieronymus Bosch

Lord Montgomery

This sort of thing [homosexuality] may be tolerated by the French but we are British—thank God.
  Daily Mail, 27 May 1965

J. Earle Moore

Two minutes with Venus, two years with mercury.
  Aphorism

Thomas Moore

Then awake!—the heavens look bright, my dear,
'Tis never too late for delight, my dear,
  And the best of all ways
  To lengthen our days,
Is to steal a few hours from the night, my dear!
  Irish Melodies: The Young May Moon

Ovid [Publius Ovidius Naso]

Arte perennat amor.
Skill makes love unending.
  Ars Amatoria

Cynthia Payne

I know it does make people happy but to me it is just like having a cup of tea.
  Said 8 Nov. 1987

Thomas Shadwell

'Tis the way of all flesh.
  The Sullen Lovers

William Shakespeare

Is it not strange that desire should so many years outlive
performance?
Henry IV, Part II 2

Your daughter and the Moor are now making the beast
with two backs.
Othello 1

I'll canvass thee between a pair of sheets.
II Henry IV 2

Graze on my lips, and if those hills be dry,
Stray lower, where the pleasant fountains lie.
Venus and Adonis

Thomas Szasz

Masturbation: the primary sexual activity of mankind. In
the nineteenth century it was a disease; in the twentieth
it's a cure.
The Second Sin.

Henry David Thoreau

I lose my respect for the man who can make the mystery
of sex the subject of a coarse joke, yet, when you speak
earnestly and seriously on the subject, is silent.
Journal, 12 April 1852

Mary Day Winn

Sex is the tabasco sauce which an adolescent national
palate sprinkles on every course in the menu.
Adam's Rib

MARRIAGE

Susan B(rownell) Anthony
Marriage, to women as to men, must be a luxury, not a necessity; an incident of life, not all of it. And the only possible way to accomplish this great change is to accord to women equal power in the making, shaping and controlling of the circumstances of life.
   Speech, 1875

Aristophanes
A man, though he be grey-haired, can always get a wife. But a woman's time is short.
   Lysistrata

Jane Austen
Happiness in marriage is entirely a matter of chance.
   Pride and Prejudice

Lord, how ashamed I should be of not being married before three and twenty!
   Ibid

Francis Bacon
Wives are young men's mistresses; companions for middle age; and old men's nurses.
   Essays: Of Marriage and Single Life

Honoré de Balzac

No man should marry until he has studied anatomy and dissected at least one woman.

The Physiology of Marriage

Being a husband is a whole-time job. That is why so many husbands fail. They cannot give their entire attention to it.

The Title

So long as there are differences between one moment of pleasure and another a man can go on being happy with the same woman.

The Physiology of Marriage

The Bible

I say therefore to the unmarried and widows, It is good for them if they abide even as I. But if they cannot contain, let them marry: for it is better to marry than to burn.

1 Corinthians 7

Ambrose (Gwinett) Bierce

Marriage: the state or condition of a community consisting of a master, a mistress and two slaves, making in all, two.

The Devil's Dictionary

Wedding: a ceremony at which two persons undertake to become one, one undertakes to become nothing, and nothing undertakes to become supportable.

Ibid

Robert Burton

One was never married, and that's his hell; another is, and that's his plague.

The Anatomy of Melancholy

Mrs Patrick Campbell
Marriage is the result of the longing for the deep, deep peace of the double bed after the hurly-burly of the chaise longue.
Attributed

Sir Winston (Leonard Spencer) Churchill
Lady Astor: If I were your wife, I should flavour your coffee with poison!
Sir Winston: And If I were your husband, madam, I should drink it.
Attributed

Marcus Tullius Cicero
The first bond of society is marriage.
De Officiis

Charles Caleb Colton
Marriage is a feast where the grace is sometimes better than the dinner.
Lacon

William Congreve
Courtship to marriage, as a very witty prologue to a very dull play.
The Old Bachelor

Married in haste, we may repent at leisure.
Ibid

Charles Dickens
Wen you're a married man, Samivel, you'll understand a good many things as you don't understand now; but vether it's worth while goin' through so much to learn so

little, as the charity boy said ven he got to the end of the
alphabet, is a matter o' taste.
   Pickwick Papers

Benjamin Disraeli, 1st Earl of Beaconsfield
I have always thought that every woman should marry,
and no man.
   Lothair

Marriage is the greatest earthly happiness when founded
on complete sympathy.
   Letter to Gladstone

John Dryden
Here lies my wife: here let her lie,
Now she's at rest, and so am I.
   Epitaph Intended for Dryden's Wife

Benjamin Franklin
Where there's marriage without love, there will be love
without marriage.
   Poor Richard's Almanack 1734

John Gay
Do you think your mother and I should have liv'd
comfortably so long together, if ever we had been married?
   The Beggar's Opera

Sir A(lan) P(atrick) Herbert
The critical period in matrimony is breakfast time.
   Uncommon Law

Hesiod
Marry in the springtime of thy life, neither much above or

below the age of thirty. Thy wife should be a virgin in her nineteenth year.
Works and Days

Rudyard Kipling

The bachelor may risk 'is 'ide
　To 'elp you when you're downed;
But the married man will wait beside
　Till the ambulance comes round.
The Married Man

Abraham Lincoln

Marriage is neither heaven nor hell. It is simply purgatory.
Attributed, 1864

Henry Wadsworth Longfellow

The men that women marry,
And why they marry them, will always be
A marvel and a mystery to the world.
Michael Angelo

Sir (Edward Morgan) Compton Mackenzie

Prostitution. Selling one's body to keep one's soul...one might say of most marriages that they were selling one's soul to keep one's body.
The Adventures of Sylvia Scarlett

Menander

Marriage, to tell the truth, is an evil, but it is a necessary evil.
Fragment

Molière [Jean-Baptiste Poquelin]

Marriage, Agnes, is not a joke.
L'Ecole des femmes

Thomas Moore
It is time you should think, boy, of taking a wife—"
"Why, so it is, father—whose wife shall I take?"
   A Joke Versified

Thomas Love Peacock
Love is to be avoided because marriage is at best a
dangerous experiment.
   Gryll Grange

Bertrand (Arthur William) Russell, 3rd Earl Russell
The more civilized people become the less capable they
seem of lifelong happiness with one partner.
   Marriage and Morals

Saki [Hector Hugh Munro]
The Western custom of one wife and hardly any mis-
tresses.
   Reginald in Russia

William Shakespeare
Many a good hanging prevents a bad marriage.
   Twelfth Night 1

A young man married is a man that's marr'd.
   All's Well That Ends Well 2

George Bernard Shaw
Marriage…combines the maximum of temptation with
the maximum of opportunity.
   Man and Superman: Maxims for Revolutionists

Percy Bysshe Shelley

When a man marries, dies or turns Hindoo,
His best friends hear no more of him.
  Letter to Maria Gisborne

A system could not well have been devised more studiously hostile to human happiness than marriage.
  Queen Mab, Notes

Richard Brinsley Sheridan

'Tis safest in matrimony to begin with a little aversion.
  The Rivals

Robert Louis Stevenson

Marriage is like life in this—that it is a field of battle, and not a bed of roses.
  Virginibus Purerisque 1881

In marriage, a man becomes slack and selfish, and undergoes a fatty degenertion of his moral being.
  Ibid

Publilius Syrus

It is mind, not body, that makes marriage last.
  Sententiae

William Makepeace Thackeray

Remember, it's as easy to marry a rich woman as a poor woman.
  Pendennis

Oscar (Fingall O'Flahertie Wills) Wilde

Twenty years of romance make a woman look like a ruin;

but twenty years of marriage make her something like a
public building.
   A Woman of No Importance

Thornton (Niven) Wilder
The best part of married life is the fights. The rest is
merely so-so.
   The Matchmaker

Home and Hearth

(Amos) Bronson Alcott
As the homes, so the state.
Tablets

Jane Austen
A family of ten children will always be called a fine family, where there are heads, and arms, and legs enough for that number.
Northanger Abbey

Francis Bacon
He that hath wife and children, hath given hostages to fortune; for they are impediments to great enterprises, either of virtue or mishief.
Essays: Of Marriage and Single Life

Nicholas Breton
He that lives at home, sees nothing but home.
Works

Robert Burns
To make a happy fireside clime
       To weans and wife,

That's the true pathos and sublime
    Of human life.
  Epistle to Dr Blacklock

Miguel de Cervantes (Saavedra)
You are a king by your own fireside, as much as any
monarch in his throne.
  Don Quixote

Whom God loves, his house is sweet to him.
  Ibid

Marcus Tullius Cicero
Nullus est locus domestica sede jucundior.
No place is more delightful than one's own fireside.
  Epistolæ ad Familiares

Samuel Taylor Coleridge
The largest part of mankind are nowhere greater strangers
than at home.
  Table Talk

William Cowper
Domestic happiness, Thou only bliss
Of Paradise that has surviv'd the fall!
  The Task: The Garden

Sir John Davies
Every groom is a king at home.
  The Scourge of Folly

Charles Dickens
Home is home, be it ever so homely.
  Dombey and Son

Phineas Fletcher
A saint abroad, at home a fiend.
The Purple Island

Robert (Lee) Frost
Home is the place where, when you have to go there,
They have to take you in.
The Death of the Hired Man

Mrs Elizabeth Cleghorn Gaskell
A man is so in the way in the house.
Cranford

Oliver Goldsmith
I am now no more than a mere lodger in my own house.
The Good-Natured Man 1

Thomas Jefferson
The happiest moments of my life have been the few
which I have passed at home in the bosom of my family.
Letter, 1790

The happiness of the domestic fireside is the first boon of
Heaven; and it is well it is so, since it is that which is the
lot of the mass of mankind.
Ibid, 1813

F. M. Knowles
There's no place like home, and many a man is glad of
it.
A Cheerful Year Book

Christopher Morley
Joy dwells beneath a humble roof;
Heaven is not built of country seats

312

But little queer suburban streets.
>   *To the Little House*

John Howard Payne
'Mid pleasures and palaces though we may roam,
Be it ever so humble, there's no place like home.
>   *Clari, the Maid of Milan*

Samuel Pepys
Home, and, being washing day, dined upon cold meat.
>   *Diary,* 4 April 1666

Pliny the Elder
Home is where the heart is.
>   Attributed

Alexander Pope
I find that by all you have been telling,
That 'tis a house, but not a dwelling.
>   *On the Duke of Marlborough's House*

Samuel Rogers
To fireside happiness, to hours of ease,
Blest with that charm, the certainty to please.
>   *Human Life*

William Shakespeare
>   As 'tis ever common
That men are merriest when they are from home.
>   *King Henry V* 1

George Bernard Shaw
Home is the girl's prison and the woman's workhouse.
>   *Man and Superman: Maxims for Revolutionists*

Home life as we understand it is no more natural to us than a cage is natural to a cockatoo.
Getting Married

Dodie Smith
That dear octopus from whose tentacles we never quite escape, nor in our innermost hearts never quite wish to.
Dear Octopus

Sydney Smith
A comfortable house is a great source of happiness. It ranks immediately after health and a good conscience.
Letter to Lord Murray, 29 Sept. 1843

WOMEN

Anacreon

Nature gave horns to bulls, hooves to horses, speed to hares, the power of swimming to fishes, that of flying to birds, and understanding to men. She had nothing left to give to women save beauty.

Fragment

Simone de Beauvoir

One is not born a woman, one becomes one.

The Second Sex

It is in great part the anxiety of being a woman that devastates the feminine body.

Womansize by Kim Chernin

Sir Max Beerbohm

"After all," as a pretty girl once said to me, "women are a sex by themselves, so to speak."

The Pervasion of Rouge

The Bible

Favour is deceitful, and beauty is vain: but a woman that feareth the Lord, she shall be praised.

Proverbs 31

Philip Dormer Stanhope, 4th Earl of Chesterfield
Women are much more like each other than men: they
have, in truth, but two passions, vanity and love.
Letters to His Son

Hannah Cowley
What is woman?—only one of Nature's agreeable
blunders.
Who's the Dupe!

Edwina Currie
The strongest possible piece of advice I would give to
any young woman is: Don't screw around and don't
smoke.
The Observer, 'Sayings of the Week', 3 April 1988

Christian Dior
Women are most fascinating between the ages of thirty-
five and forty, after they have won a few races and know
how to pace themselves. Since few women ever pass
forty, maximum fascination can continue indefinitely.
Colliers Magazine, 10 June 1955

George Eliot [Mary Ann Evans]
I'm not denyin' the women are foolish: God Almighty
made 'em to match the men.
Adam Bede

I should like to know what is the proper function of
women, if it is not to make reasons for husbands to stay
at home, and still stronger reasons for bachelors to go
out.
The Mill on the Floss

The happiest women, like the happiest nations, have no history.
   Ibid

Elizabeth I
I know I have the body of a weak and feeble woman, but I have the heart and stomach of a king, and of a king of England too.
   Speech, 1588

George Farquhar
How a little love and good company improves a woman.
   The Beaux' Stratagem

Sigmund Freud
   What does a woman want?

Betty (Naomi) Friedan
It is easier to live through someone else than to become complete yourself.
   The Feminine Mystique

Erich Fromm
Women are equal because they are not different any more.
   The Art of Loving

Thomas Hardy
Time and circumstance, which enlarge the views of most men, narrow the views of women almost invariably.
   Jude the Obscure

Juvenal [Decimus Junius Juvenalis]
Nothing is more intolerable than a wealthy woman.
   Satires

John Keats
I have met with women whom I really think would like to
be married to a poem, and to be given away by a novel.
   Letter, 1819

François, Duc de La Rochefoucauld
One can find women who have never had a love affair,
but it is rare to find a woman who has had only one.
   Maxims

Groucho (Julius Henry) Marx
You're the most beautiful woman I've ever seen, which
doesn't say much for you.
   Animal Crackers

Friedrich Wilhelm Nietzsche
God created woman. And boredom did indeed cease from
that moment—but many other things ceased as well!
Woman was God's second mistake.
   The Antichrist

In revenge, as in love, woman is always more barbarous
than man.
   Beyond Good and Evil

Woman likes to believe that love can achieve anything. It
is her peculiar superstition.
   Ibid

When a woman becomes a scholar there is usually
something wrong with her sexual organs.
   In *Bartlett's Unfamiliar Quotations*

Thomas Otway
O woman! lovely woman! Nature made thee
To temper man: we had been brutes without you.
   Venice Preserv'd

Arthur Schopenhauer
Women exist in the main solely for the propagation of the
species.

Sir Walter Scott
O Woman! in our hours of ease,
Uncertain, coy, and hard to please…
When pain and anguish wring the brow
A ministering angel thou!
   Marmion: Lochinvar

William Makepeace Thackeray
'Tis strange what a man may do, and a woman yet think
him an angel.
   The History of Henry Esmond

This I set down as a positive truth. A woman with fair
opportunities and without an absolute hump, may marry
whom she likes.
   Vanity Fair

Margaret (Hilda) Thatcher
No woman in my time will be Prime Minister or Chancellor or Foreign Secretary—not the top jobs.
The Sunday Telegraph, 1969

Oscar (Fingall O'Flahertie Wills) Wilde
Women have become so highly educated that nothing should surprise them except happy marriages.
A Woman of No Importance

All women become like their mothers. That is their tragedy. No man does. That is his.
Ibid

PARENTS AND OFFSPRING

Anonymous
The law of heredity is that all undesirable traits come from the other parent.

Francis Bacon
The joys of parents are secret, and so are their griefs and fears.
Essays: Of Parents and Children

Children sweeten labours, but they make misfortunes more bitter.
Ibid

The Bible
He that spareth his rod hateth his son: but he that loveth him chasteneth.
Proverbs 13

The fathers have eaten sour grapes, and the children's teeth are set on edge.
Ezekiel 18

Lewis Carroll [Charles Lutwidge Dodgson]
Speak roughly to your little boy.
  And beat him when he sneezes:

He only does it to annoy,
  Because he knows it teases.
   Alice's Adventures in Wonderland

Marcus Tullius Cicero

Quid dulcius hominum generi ab natura datum est quam
sui cuique liberi?
Of all nature's gifts to the human race, what is sweeter to
a man than his children?
   Post Reditum ad Quirites

Mrs Dinah Maria Craik

Oh, my son's my son till he gets him a wife,
But my daughter's my daughter all her life.
   Young and Old

Bernard le Bovier de Fontenelle,

The follies of the fathers are no warning to the children.
   Dialogues des morts

Benjamin Franklin

"Late children," says the Spanish proverb, "are early
orphans."
   Letter to John Alleyn

Jean de La Fontaine

It is impossible to please all the world and also one's
father.
   Fables

William Langland

Who so spareth the spring spoileth his children.
   Piers Plowman

Stephen Butler Leacock
The parent who could see his boy as he really is, would
shake his head and say: "Willie is no good: I'll sell him."
The Lot of the Schoolmaster

Menander
A daughter is an embarrassing and ticklish possession.
Perinthis

Napoleon I [Napoleon Bonaparte]
It is horrible to see oneself die without children.
To Gaspard Gourgaud, St Helena, 1817

John Ray
Children suck the mother when they are young, and the
father when they are grown.
English Proverbs

Samuel Richardson
Children when they are little make parents fools, when
great, mad.
Clarissa Harlowe

Sir Walter Scott
A mother's pride, a father's joy.
Rokeby

William Shakespeare
It is a wise father that knows his own child.
The Merchant of Venice 2

How sharper than a serpent's tooth it is
To have a thankless child!
King Lear 1

Laurence Sterne

I wish either my father or my mother, or indeed both of them, as they were in duty both equally bound to it, had minded what they were about when they begot me.

Tristram Shandy

Sir Henry Taylor

A spoilt child never loves its mother.

Notes from Life

Oscar (Fingall O'Flahertie Wills) Wilde

Children begin by loving their parents, After a time they judge them. Rarely, if ever, do they forgive them.

A Woman of No Importance

TRAVEL

Francis Bacon
Travel, in the younger sort, is a part of education; in the elder, a part of experience.
   Essays: Of Travel

Giuseppe Baretti
Travellers…seem to have no other purpose by taking long journeys but to procure themselves the pleasure of railing at everything they have seen or heard.
   An Account of the Manners and Customs of Italy

Sir Thomas Beecham
I have recently been all round the world and have formed a very poor opinion of it.

Fanny Burney [Frances, Madame d'Arblay]
Travelling is the ruin of all happiness. There's no looking at a building here after seeing Italy.
   Cecilia

Albert Camus
There is no pleasure in travelling, and I look upon it more as an occasion for spiritual testing.
   Notebooks

Philip Dormer Stanhope, 4th Earl of Chesterfield
Those who travel heedlessly from place to place, observing only their distance from each other, and attending only to their accommodation at the inn at night, set out fools, and will certainly return so.
Letters to His Son

René Descartes
Travelling is almost like talking with men of other centuries.
Le Discours de la Méthode

Benjamin Disraeli, 1st Earl of Beaconsfield
Travel teaches toleration.
Contarini Fleming

Ralph Waldo Emerson
All educated Americans, first or last, go to Europe.
The Conduct of Life: Culture

Carlo Goldoni
A wise traveller never despises his own country.
Pamela Nubile

William Hazlitt
I should like to spend the whole of my life travelling, if I could anywhere borrow another life to spend at home.
Table Talk

Ernest Hemingway
If you are lucky enough to have lived in Paris as a young man, then wherever you go for the rest of your life, it stays with you, for Paris is a moveable feast.
A Moveable Feast

Homer
There is nothing worse for mortals than a wandering life.
  Odyssey

James Henry Leigh Hunt
Travelling in the company of those we love is home in
motion.
  The Indicator

Juvenal [Decimus Junius Juvenalis]
Travel light and you can sing in the robber's face.
  Satires

Rudyard Kipling
He travels the fastest who travels alone.
  The Winners

Herman Melville
I love to sail forbidden seas, and land on barbarous coasts.
  Moby Dick

Edna St Vincent Millay
My heart is warm with the friends I make,
And better friends I'll not be knowing;
Yet there isn't a train I wouldn't take,
No matter where it's going.
  Travel

Jonathan Raban
In an underdeveloped country don't drink the water, in a
developed country, don't breathe the air.
  Reader's Digest, 1976

John Ruskin

All travelling becomes dull in exact proportion to its rapidity.

Modern Painters

Seneca

Every change of scene is a delight.

Epistolæ ad Lucilium

William Shakespeare

Farewell, Monsieur Traveller: look you lisp and wear strange suits, disable all the benefits of your own country, be out of love with your nativity, and almost chide God for making you the countenance you are, or I will scarce think you have swum in a gondola.

As You Like It 4

Philip Henry Sheridan

If I owned Texas and Hell, I would rent out Texas and live in Hell.

Said 1855

Laurence Sterne

A man should know something of his own country, too, before he goes abroad.

Tristram Shandy

They order, said I, this matter better in France.

A Sentimental Journey

Robert Louis Stevenson

For my part, I travel not to go anywhere, but to go. I travel for travel's sake. The great affair is to move.

Travels with a Donkey; Cheylard and Luc

To travel hopefully is a better thing than to arrive.
   Virginibus Puerisque: El Dorado

Wealth I ask not, hope nor love,
Nor a friend to know me;
All I ask, the heaven above
And the road below me.
   Songs of Travel: The Vagabond

Mark Twain [Samuel Langhorne Clemens]
To forget pain is to be painless; to forget care is to rid of
it; to go abroad is to accomplish both.
   Autobiography

Sir Laurens Van der Post
I have travelled so much because travel has enabled me to
arrive at unknown places within my clouded self.

William Carlos Williams
Most of the beauties of travel are due to the strange hours
we keep to see them.
   Selected Poems, 'January Morning'

William Wordsworth
I have travelled among unknown men
   In lands beyond the sea;
Nor, England! did I know till then
   What love I bore to thee.
   I Travelled among Unknown Men

FRIENDSHIP AND ENMITY

Henry (Brooks) Adams
A friend in power is a friend lost.
  The Education of Henry Adams

Friends are born not made.
  Ibid

Aristotle
The perfect friendship is that between good men, alike in their virtue.
  The Nicomachean Ethics

Without friends no one would choose to live, though he had all other goods.
  Ibid

Francis Bacon
The worst solitude is to be destitute of sincere friendship.
  De Augmentis Scientiarum

The Bible
A friend loveth at all times, and a brother is born for adversity.
  Proverbs 17

Greater love hath no man than this, that a man lay down his life for his friends.
  John 15

A faithful friend is a strong defence: and he that hath found such a one hath found a treasure.
  Ecclesiasticus 6

A faithful friend is the medicine of life.
  Ibid

Forsake not an old friend; for the new is not comparable to him; a new friend is as new wine; when it is old, thou shalt drink it with pleasure.
  Ibid 9

Ambrose (Gwinett) Bierce
Acquaintance: a person whom we know well enough to borrow from, but not well enough to lend to.
  The Devil's Dictionary

Friendless: having no favours to bestow. Destitute of fortune. Addicted to utterance of truth and common sense.
  Ibid

Nicholas Breton
I wish my deadly foe no worse
Than want of friends, and empty purse.
  A Farewell to Town

"Beau" (George Bryan) Brummell
Who's your fat friend? [Of the Prince of Wales.]

Robert Burns

I want someone to laugh with me, someone to be grave
with me, someone to please me and help my discrimina-
tion with his or her own remark, and at times, no doubt,
to admire my acuteness and penetration.

Commonplace Book

Should auld acquaintance be forgot,
  And days o' auld lang syne.
  Auld Lang Syne

George Gordon (Noel) Byron, 6th Lord Byron

Friendship is Love without his wings.
  Hours of Idleness

George Canning

But of all plagues, good Heaven, thy wrath can send,
Save, save, oh save me from the candid friend!
  New Morality

George Chapman

Trust not a reconciled friend, for good turns cannot blot
out old grudges.
  Alphonsus

Marcus Tullius Cicero

A friend is, as it were, a second self.
  De Amicitia

Charles Caleb Colton

Friendship often ends in love; but love, in friendship—
never.
  Lacon

If you want enemies, excel others; if you want friends, let
others excel you.
   Ibid

William Cowper
How sweet, how passing sweet, is solitude!
But grant me still a friend in my retreat,
Whom I may whisper—solitude is sweet.
   Retirement

Abbé Jacques Delille
Fate chooses our relatives, we choose our friends.
   Malheur et Pitié

Charles Dickens
Fan the sinking flame of hilarity with the wing of friend-
ship; and pass the rosy wine.
   The Old Curiosity Shop

Wery glad to see you, indeed, and hope our acquaintance
may be a long 'un, as the gen'l'm'n said to the fi' pun'
note.
   Pickwick Papers

George Louis Palmella Busson Du Maurier
I have no talent for making new friends, but oh, such a
genius for fidelity to old ones.
   Peter Ibbetson

George Eliot [Mary Ann Evans]
Friendships begin with liking or gratitude—roots that can
be pulled up.
   Daniel Deronda

Benjamin Franklin
There are three faithful friends—an old wife, an old dog, and ready money.
  Poor Richard's Almanac 1738

William Hazlitt
I like a friend the better for having faults that one can talk about.
  Plain Speaker

Thomas Jefferson
An injured friend is the bitterest of foes.
  French Treaties Opinion

I find friendship to be like wine, raw when new, ripened with age, the true old man's milk and restorative cordial.
  Letter, 1811

Dr Samuel Johnson
If a man does not make new acquaintance as he advances through life, he will soon find himself left alone. A man, sir, should keep his friendship in constant repair.
  Boswell's *Life of Johnson*

Ben Jonson
  True happiness
Consists not in the multitude of friends,
But in the worth and choice.
  Cynthia's Revels

Paul de Kock
The best way to keep your friends is to never borrow
from them and never lend them anything.
  Homme aux trois culottes

Leonardo da Vinci
Reprove a friend in secret, but praise him before others.
  Notebooks

Ovid [Publius Ovidius Naso]
The vulgar estimate friends by the advantage to be
derived from them.
  Epistulæ ex Ponto

Blaise Pascal
I lay it down as a fact that if all men knew what others
say of them, there would not be four friends in the
world.
  Pensées

William Penn
A true friend unbosoms freely, advises justly, assists
readily, adventures boldly, takes all patiently, defends
courageously, and continues a friend unchangeably.
  Some Fruits of Solitude

Alexander Pope
Histories are more full of examples of the fidelity of dogs
than of friends.
  Letter, 1709

John Selden
Old friends are best. King James used to call for his old
shoes; they were easiest for his feet.
  Table Talk: Friends

William Shakespeare
I count myself in nothing else so happy
As in a soul remembering my good friends.
King Richard II 2

Our plot is as good a plot as ever was laid; our friends
true and constant; a good plot, good friends, and full of
expectation; an excellent plot, very good friends.
King Henry IV, Par: I 2

Sophocles
An enemy should be hated only so far as one may be
hated who may one day be a friend.
Ajax

Alfred, Lord Tennyson
He makes no friend who never made a foe.
Idylls of the King: Lancelot and Elaine

Mark Twain [Samuel Langhorne Clemens]
The holy passion of Friendship is of so sweet and steady
and loyal and enduring a nature that it will last through a
whole lifetime, if not asked to lend money.
Pudd'nhead Wilson

Voltaire [François Marie Arouet]
I have never made but one prayer to God, a very short
one: "O Lord, make my enemies ridiculous." And God
granted it.
Letter, 1767

Walt Whitman
I no doubt deserved my enemies, but I don't believe I
deserved my friends.
Bradford's *Biography and the Human Heart*

Oscar (Fingall O'Flahertie Wills) Wilde

I choose my friends for their good looks, my acquaintances for their characters, and my enemies for their brains.

The Picture of Dorian Gray

Edward Young

Friendship's the wine of life.

Night Thoughts

WAR AND PEACE

Lewis Addison Armistead
Give them the cold steel, boys!
   Battle of Gettysburg, 1863

Bernard M(annes) Baruch
We are today in the midst of a cold war.
   To Senate Committee, 1948

Sir John Betjeman
Gracious Lord, oh bomb the Germans.
   In Westminster Abbey

The Bible
How are the mighty fallen, and the weapons of war
perished!
   2 Samuel 1

Blessed are the peacemakers: for they shall be called the
children of God.
   Matthew 5

Put up again thy sword into his place: for all they that
take the sword shall perish with the sword.
   Ibid 26

Ambrose (Gwinett) Bierce
Peace: in international affairs, a period of cheating
between two periods of fighting.
  The Devil's Dictionary

Gaius Julius Caesar
In war trivial causes produce momentous events.
  The Gallic War

Sir Winston (Leonard Spencer) Churchill
I cannot forecast to you the action of Russia. It is a riddle
wrapped in a mystery inside an enigma.
  Radio broadcast, 1939

"I have nothing to offer but blood, toil, tears and sweat."
  House of Commons speech, 13 May 1940

We shall not flag or fail. We shall go on to the end, we
shall fight in France, we shall fight on the seas and
oceans…we shall fight on the beaches, we shall fight on
the landing grounds, we shall fight in the fields and in the
streets, we shall fight in the hills; we shall never surren-
der.
  Ibid 4 June 1940

Never in the field of human conflict was so much owed
by so many to so few [Battle of Britain pilots].
  Ibid 20 Aug. 1940

Karl von Clausewitz
War is the continuation of politics by other means.
  On War

Ferdinand Foch

Mon centre cède, ma droite recule, situation excellente, j'attaque.

My centre is giving way, my right is pushed back, situation excellent, I am attacking.

Battle of the Marne, 1914

Benjamin Franklin

There never was a good war or a bad peace.

Letter, 1773

Oliver Goldsmith

He who fights and runs away
May live to fight another day.

The Art of Poetry on a New Plan

The first blow is half the battle.

She Stoops to Conquer

Ulysses S(impson) Grant

The art of war is simple enough. Find out where your enemy is. Get at him as soon as you can. Strike him as hard as you can and as often as you can, and keep moving on.

On the Art of War

Thomas Hobbes

The first and fundamental law of nature…is to seek peace and follow it.

Leviathan

Oliver Wendell Holmes

The peaceful are the strong.

A Voice of the Loyal North

Herbert (Clark) Hoover
Older men declare war. But it is youth that must fight and die.
   Speech, 1944

John Paul II [Karol Wojtyla]
War should belong to the tragic past, in history. It should find no place on humanity's agenda for the future.
   Coventry, 1982

John Fitzgerald Kennedy
Mankind must put an end to war or war will put an end to mankind.
   United Nations, 1961

Rudyard Kipling
For it's Tommy this, an' Tommy that, an' "Chuck him out, the brute!"
But it's "Saviour of 'is country" when the guns begin to shoot.
   Barrack Room Ballads

Henry Wadsworth Longfellow
Buried was the bloody hatchet;
Buried was the dreadful war-club;
Buried were all war-like weapons,
And the war-cry was forgotten,
Then was peace among the nations.
   The Song of Hiawatha

Martin Luther
War is the greatest plague that can afflict humanity; it destroys religion, it destroys states, it destroys families. Any scourge is preferable to it.
   Table Talk

Dr John McCrae

In Flanders fields the poppies blow
Between the crosses, row on row.
  In Flanders Fields

Mao Tse-Tung

Politics is war without bloodshed, while war is politics
with bloodshed.
  Quotations from Chairman Mao

Helmuth Karl Bernard, Count von Moltke

Everlasting peace is a dream, and not even a beautiful one.
  Letter, 1880

Napoleon I [Napoleon Bonaparte]

What a beautiful fix we are in now: peace has been
declared!
  Following Treaty of Amiens, 1802

Frederick, Lord North, 2nd Earl of Guildford

I do not know whether our generals will frighten the
enemy, but I know they frighten me whenever I think of
them.
  Attributed

William Shakespeare

Once more into the breach, dear friends, once more:
Or close the wall up with our English dead!
In peace ther's nothing so becomes a man
As modest stillness and humility:
But when the blast of war blows in our ears,
Then imitate the action of the tiger;
Stiffen the sinews, summon up the blood,

Disguise fair nature with hard-favour'ed rage;
Then lend the eye a terrible aspect.
   King Henry V 3

Follow your spirit; and, upon this charge
Cry "God for Harry! England and Saint George!"
   Ibid

O war! thou son of hell!
   II Henry VI 5

Cry, "Havoc," and let slip the dogs of war.
   Julius Caesar 3

Let me have war, say I; it exceeds peace as far as day
does night; it's spritely, waking, audible, and full of vent.
Peace is a very apoplexy, lethargy: mulled, deaf, sleep,
insensible; a getter of more bastard children than war's a
destroyer of men.
   Coriolanus 5

William (Tecumseh) Sherman

War is at best barbarism…Its glory is all moonshine. It
is only those who have neither fired a shot nor heard
the shrieks and groans of the wounded who cry aloud
for blood, more vengeance, more desolation. War is
hell.
   Attributed, 1879

Peter (Alexander) Ustinov

Generals are fascinating cases of arrested development—
after all, at five we all of us wanted to be generals.
   The Illustrated London News, 1968

George Washington

There is nothing so likely to produce peace as to be well prepared to meet an enemy.

Letter, 1780

Oscar (Fingall O'Flahertie Wills) Wilde

As long as war is regarded as wicked, it will always have its fascination. When it is looked upon as vulgar, it will cease to be popular.

The Critic as Artist

HEALTH AND SICKNESS

Joseph Addison
Health and cheerfulness mutually beget each other.
  The Spectator, 1712

Anonymous
Get up at five, have lunch at nine,
Super at five, retire at nine.
And you will live to ninety-nine.
  Rabelais's *Works*

Francis Bacon
The remedy is worse than the disease.
  Essays: Of Seditions and Troubles

The Bible
Be not slow to visit the sick.
  Ecclesiasticus 7

Health and good estate of body are above all gold.
  Ibid 30

Sir Thomas Browne
We all labour against our own cure, for death is the cure
of all diseases.
  Religio Medici

Samuel Butler

I reckon being ill as one of the greatest pleasures of life, provided one is not too ill and is not obliged to work till one is better.

The Way of All Flesh

Chauncey Depew

I get my exercise acting as a pallbearer to my friends who exercise.

Attributed

Mary Baker Glover Eddy

Health is not a condition of matter, but of mind.

Science and Health

Ralph Waldo Emerson

A person seldom falls sick, but the bystanders are animated with a faint hope that he will die.

The Conduct of Life: Considerations By the Way

Henry Ford

Exercise is bunk. If you are healthy, you don't need it: if you are sick, you shouldn't take it.

Attributed

Hippocrates

Natural forces within us are the true healers of disease.

Aphorisms

James Gibbons Huneker

My corns ache, I get gouty, and my prejudices swell like varicose veins.

Old Fogy

Dr Samuel Johnson
Disease generally begins that equality which death completes.
   The Rambler

How few of his friends' houses would a man choose to be at when sick.
   Boswell's *Life of Johnson*

Charles Lamb
What have I gained by health? Intolerable dullness. What by early hours and moderate meals? A total blank.
   Letter to Wordsworth, 1830

To be sick is to enjoy monarchal prerogatives.
   Last Essays of Elia, 'The Convalescent'.

How sickness enlarges the dimensions of a man's self to himself.
   Ibid

François, Duc de La Rochefoucauld
It is a boresome disease to try to keep health by following too strict a regimen.
   Maxims

Plato
Attention to health is the greatest hinderance to life.

Alexander Pope
Here am I dying of a hundred good symptoms.
   Said to George Lyttleton, 15 May 1744

John Ray
Diseases are the tax on pleasures.
   English Proverbs

Jules Romains

Every man who feels well is a sick man neglecting himself.

Knock, ou le triomphe de la médecine

Seneca

It is part of the cure to wish to be cured.

Phaedra

James Thomson

Health is the vital principle of bliss.

The Castle of Indolence

Henry David Thoreau

'Tis healthy to be sick sometimes.

Virgil [Publius Vergilius Maro]

He destroys his health by labouring to preserve it.

Aeneid

Oscar (Fingall O'Flahertie Wills) Wilde

One knows so well the popular idea of health. The English country gentleman galloping after a fox—the unspeakable in full pursuit of the uneatable.

A Woman of No Importance

DOCTORS AND MEDICINE

The Bible
Honour a physician with the honour due unto him for the
uses which ye may have of him: for the Lord hath created
him.
  Ecclesiasticus 38

He that sinneth before his Maker, let him fall into the
hand of the physician.
  Ibid

Physician, heal thyself.
  Luke 4

Ambrose (Gwinett) Bierce
Homeopathy: A school of medicine midway between
Allopathy and Christian Science. To the last both the
others are distinctly inferior, for Christian Science will
cure imaginary diseases, and they can not.
  The Devil's Dictionary

Physician: One upon whom we set our hopes when ill and
our dogs when well.
  Ibid

James Bryce, Viscount Bruce
Medicine is the only profession that labours incessantly
to destroy the reason for its own existence.
   New York, 1914

Anton Pavlovich Chekhov
Doctors are just the same as lawyers; the only difference
is that lawyers merely rob you, whereas doctors rob you
and kill you, too.
   Ivanov

Marcus Tullius Cicero
Because all the sick do not recover, therefore medicine is
no art.
   De Natura Deorum

J. Chalmers Da Costa
A fashionable surgeon like a pelican can be recognized
by the size of his bill.
   The Trials and Triumphs of the Surgeon

Samuel Goldwyn
Anbody who goes to see a psychiatrist ought to have his
head examined.
   Attributed

Hippocrates
Wherever the art of medicine is loved, there also is love
of humanity.
   Aphorisms

Oliver Wendell Holmes

I firmly believe that if the whole *materia medica*, as now used, could be sunk to the bottom of the sea, it would be all the better for mankind—and all the worse for the fishes.

Massachusetts Medical Society, 1860

Baron Gottfried Wilhelm von Leibnitz

I often say a great doctor kills more people than a great general.

Attributed

Leonardo da Vinci

Strive to preserve your health; and in this you will the better succeed in proportion as you keep clear of the physicians.

Notebooks

John Coakley Lettsom

When people's ill, they come to I,
I physics, bleeds, and sweats 'em;
Sometimes they live, sometimes they die.
What's that to I? I let's 'em.

On Dr Lettsom, by Himself

Molière [Jean-Baptiste Poquelin]

Nearly all men die of their medicines, not of their diseases.

Le malade imaginaire

Michel Eyquem de Montaigne

No doctor takes pleasure in the health even of his friends.

Essays

351

Napoleon I [Napoleon Bonaparte]
You medical people will have more lives to answer for in
the other world than even we generals.
    To Barry E. O'Meara, St Helena, 1817

Sir William Osler
The desire to take medicine is perhaps the greatest feature
which distinguishes men from animals.
    Science and Immortality

A physician who treats himself has a fool for a patient.
    Sir William Osler: Aphorisms by William B. Bean

Ovid [Publius Ovidius Naso]
The art of medicine is generally a question of time.
    Remedia Amoris

Medicine sometimes snatches away health, sometimes
gives it.
    Tristia

John Owen
God and the doctor we alike adore
But only when in danger, not before;
The danger o'er, both are alike requited,
God is forgotten, and the doctor slighted.
    Epigrammata

Matthew Prior
Cured yesterday of my disease,
I died last night of my physician.
    The Remedy Worse than the Disease

You tell your doctor that y' are ill,
And what does he do but write a bill?
Alma

Jean-Paul Sartre
Doctors, priests, magistrates, and officers know men as
thoroughly as if they had made them.
Nausea

William Shakespeare
With the help of a surgeon, he might yet recover, and
prove an ass.
A Midsummer Night's Dream 5

George Bernard Shaw
The most tragic thing in the world is a sick doctor.
The Doctor's Dilemma

Jonathan Swift
The best doctors in the world are Doctor Diet,
Doctor Quiet and Doctor Merryman.

Publilius Syrus
That sick man does badly who makes his physician his
heir.
Sententiae

FOOD AND GLUTTONY

Kingsley Amis
Outside every fat man is an even fatter man trying to close in.
One Fat Englishman

R(ichard) H(arris) Barham ["Thomas Ingoldsby"]
'Tis not her coldness, father,
That chills my labouring breast;
It's that confounded cucumber
I've eat and can't digest.
The Ingoldsby Legends, 'The Confession'

Sir John Betjeman
Phone for the fish-knives, Norman,
    As Cook is a little unnerved.
    How to Get On in Society

The Bible
Let us eat and drink for tomorrow we shall die.
    Psalms 22

And when he had taken the five loaves and the two fishes, he looked up to heaven, and blessed, and brake the loaves, and gave them to his disciples to set before them; and the two fishes divided he among them all. And they

did all eat, and were filled. And they took up twelve
baskets full of the fragments, and of the fishes. And they
that did eat of the loaves were about five thousand men.
   Mark 6

Arnold Bennett
A man of sixty has spent twenty years in bed and over
three years eating.
   In *Bartlett's Unfamiliar Quotations*

Ambrose (Gwinett) Bierce
Eat: To perform successively (and successfully) the
functions of mastication, humectation, and deglutition.
   The Devil's Dictionary

Edible: good to eat, and wholesome to digest, as a worm
to a toad, a toad to a snake, a snake to a pig, a pig to a
man, and a man to a worm.
   Ibid

Glutton: A person who escapes the evils of moderation by
committing dyspepsia.
   Ibid

Hospitality: the virtue which induces us to feed and lodge
certain persons who are not in need of food and lodging.
   Ibid

Sauce: the one infallible sign of civilization and enlight-
enment. A people with no sauces has one thousand vices;
a people with one sauce has only nine hundred and
ninety-nine.
   Ibid

Rupert Chawner Brooke

Stands the Church clock at ten to three?
And is there honey still for tea.
   'The Old Vicarage, Grantchester'

Robert Browning

So munch on, crunch on, take your muncheon
Breakfast, supper, dinner, luncheon!
   The Pied Piper of Hamelin

Edmund Burke

And having looked to government for bread, on the very
first scarcity they will turn and bite the hand that fed
them.
   Thoughts and Details on Scarcity

Robert Burns

The halesome parritch, chief of Scotia's food.
   The Cottar's Saturday Night

Great chieftain o' the pudding-race.
   Address to a Haggis

Some hae meat and canna eat,
   And some wad eat that want it;
But we hae meat, and we can eat,
   And sae the Lord be thankit.
   The Selkirk Grace

George Gordon (Noel), 6th Lord Byron

  All human history attests
That happiness for man—the hungry sinner!—
Since Eve ate apples, much depends on dinner.
   Don Juan

Lewis Carroll [Charles Lutwidge Dodgson]
Jam tomorrow and jam yesterday—but never jam today.
Through the Looking-Glass and What Alice Found There

Cicero
One should eat to live, not live to eat.
Rhetoricum

Cyril Connolly
Imprisoned in every fat man a thin one is wildly signalling to be let out.
The Unquiet Grave

The one way to get thin is to re-establish a purpose in life.
Ibid

Obesity is a mental state, a disease brought on by boredom and disappointment
Ibid

Charles T. Copeland
To eat is human, to digest divine.

T(homas) S(tearns) Eliot
Should I, after tea and cakes and ices,
Have the strength to force the moment to its crisis?
The Love Song of J. Alfred Prufrock

Epicurus
We should look for someone to eat and drink with before looking for something to eat and drink, for dining alone is leading the life of a lion or wolf.
Aphorisms

Ludwig Andreas Feuerbach

Der Mensch is was er isst.

Man is what he eats.

　　Moleschott's *Lehre der Nahrungsmittel, Preface*

Benjamin Franklin

To lengthen thy life, lessen thy meals.

　　Poor Richard's Almanac 1733

Mahatma Gandhi (Mohandas Karamchand Gandhi)

I eat to live, to serve, and also, if it so happens, to enjoy, but I do not eat for the sake of enjoyment.

　　Attributed

Hebrew Proverb

He that eats till he is sick must fast till he is well.

Dr Samuel Johnson

For a man seldom thinks with more earnestness of anything than he does of his dinner.

　　Mrs Piozzi's *Anecdotes of Samuel Johnson*

Fran Lebowitz

Food is an important part of a balanced diet.

　　Metropolitan Life, "Food for Thought and Vice Versa"

Henry Sambrooke Leigh

If you wish to grow thinner, diminish your dinner,
　And take to light claret instead of pale ale;
Look down with an utter contempt upon butter,
　And never touch bread till it's toasted—or stale.

　　Carols of Cockayne

Food and Gluttony

Marie Antoinette
Qu'ils mangent de la brioche.
Let them eat cake.
  Attributed

W(illiam) Somerset Maugham
At a dinner party one should eat wisely but not too well,
and talk well but not too wisely.
  A Writer's Notebook

George Meredith
Kissing don't last: cookery do!
  The Ordeal of Richard Feverel

A(lan) A(lexander) Milne
I do like a little bit of butter to my bread.
  When We Were Very Young

Molière [Jean-Baptiste Poquelin]
He makes his cook his merit, and the world visits his
dinners and not him.
  Le Misanthrope

Il faut manger pour vivre et non pas vivre pour manger.
One should eat to live, not live to eat.
  L'Avare

Ogden Nash
You two can be what you like, but since I am the big
fromage in this family, I prefer to think of myself as the
Gorgon Zola.
  Medusa and the Mot Juste

Alexander Pope

Fame is at best an unperforming cheat;
But 'tis substantial happiness, to eat.
  Prologue for Mr D'Urfey's Last Play

François Rabelais

L'appetit vient en mangeant.
The appetite comes with eating.
  Gargantua

Harry Secombe

My advice if you insist on slimming: Eat as much a you
like—just don't swallow it.
  The Daily Herald, 5 Oct. 1962

William Shakespeare

He hath eaten me out of house and home.
  King Henry IV, Part II 2

I am a great eater of beef and I believe that does harm to
my wit.
  Twelfth Night 1

  He was a man
Of an unbounded stomach.
  King Henry VIII 4

George Bernard Shaw

There is no love sincerer than the love of food.
  Man and Superman

Sydney Smith
Madam, I have been looking for a person who disliked
gravy all my life; let us swear eternal friendship.
Lady Holland's *Memoir of the Rev. Sydney Smith*

I am convinced digestion is the great secret of life.
Letter to Arthur Kinglake

Socrates
Bad men live that they may eat and drink, whereas good
men eat and drink that they may live.
Plutarch's *How Young Men Ought to hear Poems*

Jonathan Swift
Fingers were made before forks, and hands before knives.
Polite Conversation

DRINK AND ABSTINENCE

Alvan L. Bach
An alcoholic has been lightly defined as a man who
drinks more than his own doctor.
  Journal of the American Medical Association, 1962

Pierre-Augustin Caron de Beaumarchais
Drinking when we are not thirsty and making love all
year round, madam; that is all there is to distinguish us
from other animals.
  The Marriage of Figaro

Thomas Becon
For when the wine is in, the wit is out.
  Catechism

The Bible
Wine is a mocker, strong drink is raging: and whosoever
is deceived thereby is not wise.
  Proverbs 20

They reel to and fro, and stagger like a drunken man, and
are at their wit's end.
  Psalms 107

Drink no longer water, but use a little wine for thy stomach's sake.
  I Timothy 5

Wine is as good as life to a man, if it be drunk moderately: what life is then to a man that is without wine? for it was made to make men glad.
  Ecclesiasticus 31

Ambrose (Gwinett) Bierce
Wine, madame, is God's next best gift to man.
  The Devil's Dictionary

Anthelme Brillat-Savarin
A meal without wine is like a day without sunshine.
  The Physiology of Taste

Robert Burns
Freedom and whisky gang the gither!
  The Author's Earnest Cry and Prayer

George Gordon (Noel), 6th Lord Byron
There's nought, no doubt, so much the spirit calms
  As rum and true religion.
  Don Juan

Let us have wine and women, mirth and laughter,
Sermons and soda water the day after.
  Ibid

Miguel de Cervantes (Saavedra)
I drink when I have occasion for it, and sometimes when I have not.
  Don Quixote

Samuel Taylor Coleridge
Water, water, everywhere.
Nor any drop to drink.
The Ancient Mariner

T(homas) S(tearns) Eliot
I have measured out my life with coffee spoons.
The Love Song of J. Alfred Prufrock

Epictetus
He is a drunkard who takes more than three glasses.
Encheiridion

François de Salignac de la Mothe Fénélon
Some of the most dreadful mischiefs that afflict mankind
proceed from wine; it is the cause of disease, quarrels,
sedition, idleness, aversion to labour, and every species of
domestic disorder.
Télémaque

Henry Fielding
I am as sober as a judge.
Don Quixote in England

F(rancis) Scott (Key) Fitzgerald
First you take a drink, then the drink takes a drink, then
the drink takes you.
Ackroyd by Jules Feiffer

George Herbert
He that goes to bed thirsty rises healthy.
Jacula Rudentum

Drink not the third glasse,— which thou can'st not tame.
The Temple: The Church Porch

A(lfred) E(dward) Housman
And malt does more than Milton can
To justify God's ways to man.
Ale, man, ale's the stuff to drink
For fellows whom it hurts to think.
   A Shropshire Lad

Washington Irving
They who drink beer will think beer.
   The Sketch-book: Stratford

Thomas Jefferson
I wish to see this beverage [beer] become common
instead of the whiskey which kills one third of our
citizens, and ruins their families.
   Letter, 1815

Jerome K(lapka) Jerome
We drink one another's health and spoil our own.
   Idle Thoughts of an Idle Fellow

H(enry) L(ouis) Mencken
I've made it a rule never to drink by daylight and never to
refuse a drink after dark.
   New York Post, 1945

John Motley Morehead
It's a long time between drinks.
   Said when Governor of North Carolina

Ogden Nash
Candy
Is dandy

But liquor
Is quicker
  Hard Lines, 'Reflection on Ice-Breaking'

John Selden
'Tis not the drinking that is to be blamed, but the excess.
  Table Talk: Humility

William Shakespeare
I have very poor and unhappy brains for drinking: I could
wish courtesy would invent some other custom of
entertainment.
  Othello 2

Good wine is a good familiar creature, if it be well used.
  Ibid

It provokes the desire, but it takes away the performance.
Therefore much drink may be said to be an equivocator
with lechery.
  Macbeth 2

George Bernard Shaw
I'm only a beer teetotaller, not a champagne teetotaller.
  Candida

Sir J(ohn) C(ollings) Squire
But I am not so think as you drunk I am.
  Ballade of Soporific Absorption

Horace Walpole, (4th Earl of Oxford)
I have a partiality for drunkenness, though I never
practised it: it is a reality; but what is sobriety, only the
absence of drunkenness?
  Letter, 1789

WORK AND ENTERPRISE

Dean Acheson
A memorandum is written not to inform the reader but to protect the writer.

(Joseph) Hilaire (Pierre) Belloc
Lord Finchley tried to mend the Electric Light
Himself. It struck him dead: and serve him right!
It is the business of the wealthy man
To give employment to the artisan.
Epigrams

Ambrose (Gwinett) Bierce
Corporation: an ingenious device for obtaining individual profit without individual responsibility.
The Devil's Dictionary

Merchant: one engaged in a commercial pursuit. A commercial pursuit is one in which the thing pursued is a dollar.
Ibid

Otto von Bismarck
To youth I have but three words of counsel—work, work, work.
Sayings of Bismarck

367

George Gordon (Noel), 6th Lord Byron

Such hath it been—shall be—beneath the sun
The many still must labour for the one.
  The Corsair

Thomas Carlyle

A man willing to work, and unable to find work, is
perhaps the saddest sight that fortune's inequality exhibits
under the sun.
  Chartism

Blessed is he who has found his work; let him ask no
other blessedness.
  Past and Present

Captains of industry.
  Ibid

Work is the grand cure of all the maladies and miseries
that ever beset mankind.
  Rectorial address, Edinburgh, 1866

Philip Dormer Stanhope, 4th Earl of Chesterfield

Without some dissimulation no business can be carried on
at all.
  Letters to His Son

Henry Clay

The call for free trade is as unavailing as the cry of a
spoiled child for the moon. It never has existed; it never
will exist.
  Senate speech, 1832

R(obin) G(eorge) Collingwood

Perfect freedom is reserved for the man who lives by his own work and in that work does what he wants to do.
  Speculum Mentis

Charles Caleb Colton

Of the professions it may be said that soldiers are becoming too popular, parsons too lazy, physicians too mercenary, and lawyers too powerful.
  Lacon

Calvin Coolidge

The business of America is business.
  Speech, 1925

Sir Noel (Pierce) Coward

Work is much more fun than fun.
  The Observer, 1963

Clarence Seward Darrow

With all their faults, trade unions have done more for humanity than any other organization of men that ever existed.
  The Railroad Trainman

Charles Dickens

Here's the rule, for bargains: "Do other men, for they would do you." That's the true business precept.
  Martin Chuzzlewit

W(illiam) E(dward) B(urghardt) Du Bois

The return from your work must be the satisfaction which that work brings you and the world's need of that work. With this, life is heaven, or as near heaven as you can get.

Without this—with work which you despise, which
bores you, and which the world doest not need—this
life is hell.
  To His Newborn Great-Grandson

John Kenneth Galbraith

The salary of the chief executive of the large corporation
is not a market award for achievement. It is frequently in
the nature of a warm personal gesture by the individual to
himself.
  Annals of an Abiding Liberal

Oliver Goldsmith

And honour sinks where commerce long prevails.
  The Traveller

Samuel Goldwyn

I don't want any yes-men around me. I want everybody to
tell me the truth even if it costs them their jobs.
  Attributed

Richard Long Harkness

What is a committee? A group of the unwilling, picked
from the unfit, to do the unnecessary.
  New York Herald Tribune, 1960

Sir A(lan) P(atrick) Herbert

This high official, all allow,
Is grossly overpaid.
There wasn't any Board; and now
There isn't any trade.
  On the President of the Board of Trade

David Hume

Avarice, the spur of industry.
  Essays: Of Civil Liberty

Jerome K(lapka) Jerome

I like work; it fascinates me. I can sit and look at it for
hours. I love to keep it by me: the idea of getting rid of it
nearly breaks my heart.
  Three Men in a Boat

Dr Samuel Johnson

Trade could not be managed by those who manage it if it
had much difficulty.
    Letter to Mrs Hester Thrale

Abraham Lincoln

My father taught me to work; he did not teach me to love it.

Ogden Nash

I sit in an office at 244 Madison Avenue,
And say to myself You have a responsible job,
havenue?
  Spring comes to Murray Hill

Sir William Osler

The effective, moving, vitalizing work of the world is
done between the ages of twenty-five and forty.
  Life of Sir William Osler by Harvey Cushing

My second fixed idea is the uselessness of men above
sixty years of age, and the incalculable benefit it would
be…men stopped work at this age.
  Ibid

Cyril Northcote Parkinson

Work expands so as to fill the time available for its completion.

Parkinson's Law, The Pursuit of Progress

Laurence Johnston Peter

Most hierarchies were established by men, who now monopolize the upper levels, thus depriving women of their rightful share of opportunities to achieve incompetence.

The Peter Principle

An economist is an expert who will know tomorrow why the things he predicted yesterday didn't happen today.

Peter's Quotations

Franklin Delano Roosevelt

No business which depends for existing on paying less than living wages to its workers has any right to continue in this country.

Address, 1933

Theodore Roosevelt

No man needs sympathy because he has to work…Far and away the best prize that life offers is the chance to work hard at work worth doing.

Address, 1903

William Shakespeare

To business that we love we rise betime,
And go to 't with delight.

Antony and Cleopatra 4

Let me have no lying: it becomes none but tradesmen.

The Winter's Tale 4

Adam Smith

The real price of every thing, what every thing really costs to the man who wants to acquire it, is the toil and trouble of acquiring it.

The Wealth of Nations

People of the same trade seldom meet together, even for merriment and diversion, but the conversation ends in a conspiracy against the public, or in some contrivance to raise prices.

Ibid

Robert Louis Stevenson

Everyone lives by selling something.

Across the Plains

Studs (Louis) Terkel

Perhaps it is this spectre that most haunts working men and women: the planned obsolescence of people that is of a piece with the planned obsolescence of the things they make. Or sell.

Working

William Makepeace Thackeray

"No business before breakfast, Glum!" says the King. "Breakfast first, business next."

The Rose and the Ring

Virgil [Publius Vergilius Maro]

Labor omnia vincit.
Work conquers all.

Georgics

Voltaire [François Marie Arouet]
Work keeps us from three great evils, boredom, vice, and need.
Candide

Arthur Wellesley, 1st Duke of Wellington
My rule always was to do the business of the day in the day.
Stanhope's Notes of Conversations with the Duke of Wellington

Katherine Whitehorn
I yield to no one in my admiration for the office as a social centre, but it's no place to get any work done.
Sunday Best

Oscar (Fingall O'Flahertie Wills) Wilde
Work is the refuge of people who have nothing better to do.
The Soul of Man under Socialism

IDLENESS

James Albery
He slept beneath the moon,
He basked beneath the sun;
He lived a life of going-to-do,
And died with nothing done.
  Epitaph Written for Himself

Thomas Becon
Idleness, which is the well-spring and root of all vice.
  Early Works

The Bible
Woe to the idle shepherd that leaveth the flock.
  Habakkuk 11

Go to the ant, thou sluggard; consider her ways, and be wise.
  Proverbs 6

John Bodenham
Idleness is the canker of the mind.
  Belvedere

Robert Burton
Idleness is an appendix to nobility.
  Anatomy of Melancholy

Thomas Carlyle
The foul sluggard's comfort: "It will last my time."
Count Cagliostro: Flight Last

Philip Dormer Stanhope, 4th Earl of Chesterfield
Idleness is only the refuge of weak minds.
Letters to His Son

Christina of Sweden
We grow older more through indolence, than through age.
Maxims (1660–1680)

John Clarke
Ever sick of the slothful guise,
Loath to bed and loath to rise.
Paræmiologia

Samuel Taylor Coleridge
As idle as a painted ship
Upon a painted sea.
The Ancient Mariner

William Cowper
Absence of occupation is not rest,
A mind quite vacant is a mind distress'd.
Retirement

William Henry Davies
What is this life if, full of care,
We have no time to stand and stare?
Leisure

Ralph Waldo Emerson
That man is idle who can do something better.

George Farquhar
Says little, thinks less, and does nothing at all, faith!
The Beaux' Stratagem

Thomas Fuller
Idlenss makes the wit rust.
Gnomologia

John Kenneth Galbraith
Meetings are indispensable when you don't want to do anything.
Ambassador's Journal

Horace [Quintus Horatius Flaccus]
Strenua inertia.
Masterly inactivity.
Epistles

Nathiel Howe
To do nothing is the way to be nothing.
A Chapter of Proverbs

Victor (Marie) Hugo
Nothing is more dangerous than discontinued labour; it is habit lost. A habit easy to abandon, difficult to resume.
Les Misérables

Jerome K(lapka) Jerome
It is impossible to enjoy idling thoroughly unless one has plenty of work to do.
The Idle Thoughts of an Idle Fellow

Dr Samuel Johnson

Perhaps man is the only being that can properly be called idle.

The Idler

To do nothing is in every man's power.

The Rambler

Franz Kafka

There are two cardinal sins from which others spring: impatience and laziness.

Franz Kafka by Max Brod

Rudyard Kipling

Kiddies and grown ups too-oo-oo,
If we haven't enough to do-oo-oo,
    We get the hump,
    Cameelious hump,
The lump that is black and blue!

Just-So Stories: The Camel's Hump

Charles Lamb

I am sure that indolence—indefeasible indolence—is the true state of man, and business the invention of the old Teazer.

Letter to Wordsworth, 28 Sept. 1805

Michel Eyquem de Montaigne

I have ever loved to repose myself, whether sitting or lying, with my heels as high or higher than my head.

Essays

Friedrich Wilhelm Nietzsche

Idleness is the parent of all psychology.

Twilight of the Idols

Alexander Pope
She went from opera, park, assembly, play,
To morning walks, and prayers three times a day;
To part her time 'twixt reading and bohea,
To muse, and spill her solitary tea,
Or o'er cold coffee trifle with the spoon,
Count the slow clock, and dine exact at noon.
   Epistle to Mrs. Teresa Blount

John Ray
An idle brain is the devil's workshop.
   English Proverbs

Seneca
Nihilque tam certum est quam otii vitia negotio discuti.
Nothing is so certain as that the evils of idleness can be
shaken off by hard work.
   Epistulæ as Lucilium

William Shakespeare
If all the year were playing holidays,
To sport would be as tedious as to work.
   King Henry IV, Part 1

George Bernard Shaw
The ghostliest of all unrealities, the non-working man.
   The Irrational Knot

A man who has has no office to go to—I don't care who
he is—is a trial of which you can have no conception.
   Ibid

Richard Steele
The insupportable labour of doing nothing.
Spectator

James Thomson
Their only labour was to kill time;
And labour dire it is, and weary woe.
Castle of Indolence

Martin Farquhar Tupper
It is well to lie fallow for a while.
Of Good in Things Evil: Of Recreation

George Turberville
Eschew the idle life,
Flee, flee from doing nought:
For never was there idle brain
But bred an idle thought.
The Lover to Cupid for Mercy

Artemus Ward [Charles Farrar Browne]
I am happiest when I am idle. I could live for months
without performing any kind of labour, and at the expira-
tion of that time I should feel fresh and vigorous enough
to go right on in the same way for numerous more
months.
Natural History

R. T. Wombat
The lazy man gets round the sun
As quickly as the busy one
Quatrains

THE ARTS

Aristotle
Art is a higher type of knowledge than experience.
Metaphysics

In part, art completes what nature cannot elaborate; and
in part, it imitates nature.
Physics

Charlie Chaplin [Sir Charles Spencer Chaplin]
There are more valid facts and details in works of art than
there are in history books.
My Autobiography

Victor Cousin
L'art pour l'art.
Art for art's sake.
Sorbonne Lectures

T(homas) S(tearns) Eliot
No artist produces great art by a deliberate attempt to
express his own personality.
Essay: Four Elizabethan Dramatists

Henry Havelock Ellis
Every artist writes his own autobiography.
The New Spirit

Ralph Waldo Emerson

Every genuine work of art has as much reason for being as the earth and the sun.
Society and Solitude: Civilization

Art is a jealous mistress, and if a man have a genius for painting, poetry, music, architecture, or philosophy, he makes a bad husband and an ill provider.
Conduct of Life: Wealth

Artists must be sacrificed to their art. Like bees, they must put their lives into the sting they give.
Letters and Social Aims: Inspiration

E(dward) M(organ) Forster

Works of art, in my opinion, are the only objects in the material universe to possess internal order, and that is why, though I don't believe that only art matters, I do believe in Art for Art's sake.
Art for Art's Sake

Paul Gauguin

Many excellent cooks are spoiled by going into the arts.
Cournos' *Modern Plutarch*

Art is either a plagiarist or a revolutionist.
Pathos of Distance by James Huneker

Elbert Hubbard

Art is not a thing: it is a way.
Epigrams

James Gibbon Huneker

Great Art is an instant arrested in eternity.
Pathos of Distance

Henry James

Art is nothing more than the shadow of humanity.
   Lectures: University in Arts

John Keats

The excellence of every art is its intensity, capable of making all disagreeables evaporate, from their being in close relationship with beauty and truth.
   Letter to his brothers, 1817

So I do believe...that works of genius are the first things in this world.
   Ibid 1818

Rudyard Kipling

But the Devil whoops, as he whooped of old:
   "It's clever, but is it Art?"
   The Conundrum of the Workshops

H(enry) L(ouis) Mencken

The great artists of the world are never Puritans, and seldom even ordinarily respectable.
   Prejudices

George Augustus Moore

Art must be parochial in the beginning to be cosmopolitan in the end.
   Hail and Farewell

George Jean Nathan

Great art is as irrational as great music. It is mad with its own loveliness.
   House of Satan

Art is a reaching out into the uglinesss of the world for vagrant beauty and the imprisonment of it in a tangible dream.
  Critic and the Drama

Dorothy (Rothschild) Parker

Authors and actors and artists and such
Never know nothing and never know much...
Playwrights and poets and such horses' necks
Start off from anywhere, end up at sex.
  Bohemia

Edgar Allan Poe

Were I called upon to define, very briefly, the term "art," I should call it "the reproduction of what the senses perceive in nature through the veil of the soul."
  Marginalia

Quintillian [Marcus Fabius Quintilianus]

The height of art is to conceal art.
  De institutione oratoria

John Ruskin

All great art is the work of the whole living creature, body and soul, and—chiefly of the soul.
  The Stones of Venice

No one can explain how the notes of a Mozart melody, or the folds of a piece of Titian's drapery, produce their essential effects. If you do not feel it, no one can by reasoning make you feel it.
  Ibid

Life without industry is guilt, industry without art is brutality.
  Lectures on Art

George Bernard Shaw
The true artist will let his wife starve, his children go
barefoot, his mother drudge for his living at seventy,
sooner than work at anything but his art.
  Man and Superman

Count Leo (Nikolaevich) Tolstoy
Art is not a handicraft, it is a transmission of feeling the
artist has experienced.
  What is Art?

James (Abbott) McNeill Whistler
Art happens—no hovel is safe from it, no Prince may
depend on it, the vastest intelligence cannot bring it
about.
  "Ten O'Clock."

Oscar (Fingall O'Flahertie Wills) Wilde
The final revelation is that Lying, the telling of beautiful
untrue things, is the proper aim of Art.
  Intentions: The Decay of Lying

The secret of life is in art.
  The English Renaissance

Art should never try to be popular.
  The Soul of Man under Socialism

MUSIC

Joseph Addison

Music, the greatest good that mortals know,
And all of heaven we have below.
Song for St Cecilia's Day

Jane Austen

I consider music as a very innocent diversion, and
perfectly compatible with the profession of a clergy-
man.
Pride and Prejudice

Sir Thomas Beecham

Music first and last should sound well, should allure and
enchant the ear. Never mind the inner significance.
Atkins' and Newman's *Beecham Stories*

The function of music is to release us from the tyranny of
conscious thought.
Ibid

A distinguished British historian...declares that solo
singing is favour-ed in an aristocratic society and com-
munal or choral in a democratic.
A Mingled Chime

Jazz! Bah—nothing but the debasement of noble brass
instruments by blowing them into mutes, hats, caps,
nooks, crannies, holes and corners!
   Brymer's *From Where I Sit*

Sir Max Beerbohm

"I don't," she added, "know anything about music, really.
But I know what I like."
   Zuleika Dobson

The Bible

O sing unto the Lord a new song: sing unto the Lord, all
the earth.
   Psalms 96

Ambrose (Gwinett) Bierce

Opera: a play representing life in another world, whose
inhabitants have no speech but song, no motions but
gestures and no postures but attitudes.
   The Devil's Dictionary

Piano: a parlor utensil for subduing the impenitent visitor.
It is operated by depressing the keys of the machine and
the spirits of the audience.
   Ibid

William Cobbett

Dancing is at once rational and healthful.
   Advice to Young Men

Samuel Taylor Coleridge

Swans sing before they die—'twere no bad thing
Should certain persons die before they sing.
   Epigram on a Volunteer Singer

William Congreve
Music alone with sudden charms can bind
The wandering sense, and calm the troubled mind.
  Hymn to Harmony

Music has charms to soothe a savage breast.
  The Mourning Bride

Sir Noel (Pierce) Coward
Extraordinary how potent cheap music is.
  Private Lives

Aldous (Leonard) Huxley
After silence, that which comes nearest to expressing the
inexpressible is music.
  In Time

Gioacchino Antonio Rossini
Beethoven is the greatest composer—but Mozart is the
only one.
  Attributed

William Shakespeare
I am never merry when I hear sweet music.
  The Merchant of Venice 1

The man that hath no music in himself,
Nor is not moved with concord of sweet sounds,
Is fit for treasons, stratagems and spoils...
Let no such man be trusted.
  Ibid 5

If music be the food of love, play on.
   Twelfth Night 1

George Bernard Shaw
At every one of those concerts in England you will find
rows of weary people who are there, not because they
really like classical music, but because they think they
ought to like it.
   Man and Superman

Percy Bysshe Shelley
Music, when soft voices die,
Vibrates in the memory.
   To —: Music When Soft Voices

Artemus Ward [Charles Farrar Browne]
I can't sing. As a singist I am not a success. I am saddest
when I sing. So are those who hear me. They are sadder
even than I am.
   Artemus Ward, His Travels

Edith Wharton
An unalterable and unquestioned law of the musical
world required that the German text of French operas
sung by Swedish artists should be translated into Italian
for the clearer understanding of English-speaking audi-
ences.
   The Age of Innocence

PAINTING AND SCULPTURE

Sir Thomas Browne
I can look for a whole day with delight upon a handsome
picture, though it be but of an horse.
  Religio Medici

Robert Browning
Your business is to paint the souls of men.
  Fra Lippo Lippi

Works done least rapidly, Art most cherishes.
  Old Pictures in Florence

That's my last Duchess painted on the wall
Looking as if she were alive.
  My Last Duchess

Sir Edward Coley Burne-Jones
I mean by a picture a beautiful, romantic dream of
something that never was, never will be.
  Letter

Miguel de Cervantes (Saavedra)
Good painters imitate nature, bad ones regurgitate it.
  El Licenciado Vidriera

Oliver Cromwell
Mr Lely, I desire you would use all your skill to paint my
picture freely like me, and not flatter me at all; but
remark all these roughnesses, pimples, and everything
as you see me, otherwise I will never pay a farthing for
it.
   Attributed

Charles Dickens
There are only two styles of portrait painting; the serious
and the smirk.
   Nicholas Nickleby

Oliver Goldsmith
When they talk'd of their Raphaels, Correggios, and stuff,
He shifted his trumpet, and only took snuff.
   Retaliation

William Hazlitt
Landscape painting is the obvious resource of misan-
thropy.
   Criticisms on Art

Indifferent pictures, like dull people, must absolutely be
moral.
   Ibid

Dr Samuel Johnson
I had rather see the portrait of a dog that I know than all
the allegorical paintings…in the world.
   Boswell's *Life of Johnson*

Henry Wadsworth Longfellow

Sculpture is more divine, and more like Nature,
That fashions all her works in high relief,
And that is sculpture. This vast ball, the Earth,
Was moulded out of clay, and baked in fire;
Men, women, and all animals that breathe
Are statues and not paintings.

Michael Angelo

H(enry) H(art) Milman

And the cold marble leapt into life a god.

The Belvedere Apollo

"Grandma" (Anna Mary) Moses

A primitive artist is an amateur whose work sells.

Alexander Pope

Then marble, soften'd into life, grew warm.

Imitations of Horace: Epistles

John Ruskin

No picture can be good which deceives by its imitation,
for the very reason that nothing can be beautiful which is
not true.

Modern Painters

They are good furniture pictures, unworthy of praise, and
undeserving of blame.

Ibid

James Thomson

So stands the statue [the Venus de Medici] that enchants
the world.

The Seasons: Summer

Ivan Sergeyevich Turgenev
A picture shows me at a glance what it takes dozen of pages of a book to expound.
Fathers and Sons

C(harles) D(udley) Warner
A great artist can paint a great picture on a small canvas.
Washington Irving

James Abbott McNeill Whistler
A life passed among pictures makes not a painter—else the policeman in the National Gallery might assert himself. As well assert that he who lives in a library must needs be a poet.
The Gentle Art of Making Enemies

POETRY

Matthew Arnold
Poetry is simply the most beautiful, impressive and widely effective mode of saying things, and hence its importance.
Essays in Criticism: Heinrich Heine

Not deep the Poet sees, but wide.
Resignation

Thomas Beer
I agree with one of your reputable critics that a taste for drawing-rooms has spoiled more poets than ever did a taste for gutters.
The Mauve Decade

Robert Browning
Would you have your songs endure?
Build on the human heart!
Sordello

Robert Burns
Hail, Poesie! thou nymph reserv'd!

In chase o' thee, what crowds hae swerv'd
Frae Common Sense, or sunk ennerv'd
  'Mang heaps o' clavers.
  Sketch

Robert Burton

All poets are mad.
  Anatomy of Melancholy.

Samuel Butler

For rhyme the rudder is of verses,
With which, like ships, they steer their courses.
  Hudibras

Marcus Tullius Cicero

Adhuc neminem cognovi poetam, qui sibi non optimus
videretur.
I have never yet known a poet who did not think himself
the best.
  Tusculanarum Disputationum

Samuel Taylor Coleridge

No man was ever yet a great poet, without being at the
same time a profound philosopher.
  Biographia Literaria

That willing suspension of disbelief for the moment,
which constitutes poetic faith.
  Ibid

Not the poem which we have read, but that to which we
return, with the greatest pleasure, possesses the genuine
power, and claims the name of essential poetry.
  Lectures on Shakespeare and Milton

I wish our clever young poets would remember my homely definitions of prose and poetry; that is, prose = words in their best order; poetry = the best words in the best order.
Table Talk

Charles Caleb Colton
Subtract from many modern poets all that may be found in Shakespeare, and trash will remain.
Lacon

William Cowper
There is a pleasure in poetic pains
Which only poets know.
The Task II: The Timepiece

Isaac D'Israeli
A poet is the painter of the soul.
Literary Characters of Men of Genius

John Donne
I am two fooles, I know,
For loving, and for saying so
In whining Poetry.
The Triple Foole

Ralph Waldo Emerson
Homer's words are as costly and admirable to Homer as Agamemnon's victories are to Agamemnon.
Essays: Second Series

Poets often have nothing poetical about them except their verses.
Conduct of Life: Behaviour

James Elroy Flecker
The poet's business is not to save the soul of man but to
make it worth saving.
    Untermeyer's *Modern British Poetry*

Johann Wolfgang von Goethe
Neuere Poeten thun viel Wasser in die Tinte.
Modern poets mix too much water with their ink.
    Sprüche in Prosa

(Sir) Anthony Hope (Hawkins)
I wish you would read a little poetry sometimes. Your
ignorance cramps my conversation.
    The Dolly Dialogues

Horace [Quintus Horatius Flaccus]
Genus irritabile vatum.
The touchy race of poets.
    Epistles

Incomposito pede currere versus.
His verses run with a halting foot.
    Satires

The man is mad, or else he's writing verses.
    Ibid

Poets, the first instructors of mankind.
    Ars Poetica

Ben(jamin) Jonson
A good poet's made as well as born.
    To the Memory of Shakespeare

(Alfred) Joyce Kilmer
I think that I shall never see
A poem lovely as a tree.
   Trees

Poems are made by fools like me,
But only God can make a tree.
   Ibid

The Koran
Those who err follow the poets.
   Ch. 26

Thomas Babington Macaulay, 1st Baron Macaulay
Perhaps no person can be a poet, or even can enjoy
poetry, without a certain unsoundness of mind.
   Essays: On Milton

H(enry) L(ouis) Mencken
Nine-tenths of the best poetry of the world has been
written by poets less than thirty years old; a great deal
more than half of it has been written by poets under
twenty-five.
   Prejudices

Plato
Poets utter great and wise things which they do not
themselves understand.
   The Republic

Alexander Pope
It stands on record, that in Richard's times

A man was hang'd for very honest rhymes.
  Imitations of Horace: Satires

William Shakespeare
The lunatic, the lover and the poet
Are of imagination all compact.
  A Midsummer Night's Dream 5

Tear him for his bad verses, tear him for his bad verses.
  Julius Caesar 3

This is the very false gallop of verses.
  As you Like It 3

Percy Bysshe Shelley
Poetry is the record of the best and happiest moments of
the happiest and best minds.
  A Defence of Poetry

Alfred, Lord Tennyson
The passionate heart of the poet is whirl'd
    into folly and vice.
  Maud

Dylan Thomas
These poems, with all their crudities, doubts, and confu-
sions, are written for the love of Man and in praise of
God, and I'd be a damn' fool if they weren't.
  Collected Poems, Note

Franz Woepcke
I have seized life by the the poetic side.
  Journals of Ralph Waldo Emerson, 1868

William Wordsworth
We poets in our youth begin in gladness;
But thereof comes in the end despondency and madness.
  The Leech-Gatherer; or Resolution and Independence

Poetry is the spontaneous overflow of powerful feelings:
it takes its origin from emotion recollected in tranquility.
  Lyrical Ballads, Preface

BOOKS AND READING

(Amos) Bronson Alcott
One must be a wise reader to quote wisely and well.
  Table Talk: Quotation

Jane Austen
I think I may boast myself to be, with all possible vanity,
the most unlearned and uninformed female who ever
dared to be an authoress.
  Letter, 1815

"And what are you reading, Miss ——?" "Oh! it is only a
novel!" replies the young lady; while she lays down her
book with affected indifference, or momentary shame.
  Northanger Abbey

Francis Bacon
Some books are to be tasted, others to be swallowed, and
some few to be chewed and digested.
  Essays: Of Studies

(Joseph) Hilaire (Pierre) Belloc
When I am dead, I hope it may be said
"His sins were scarlet, but his books were read."
  On His Books

The Bible

Of making many books there is no end; and much study is a weariness of the flesh.

Ecclesiastes 12

Ambrose (Gwinett) Bierce

Novel: a short story padded.

The Devil's Dictionary

The first three essentials of the literary art are imagination, imagination and imagination.

Ibid

Charlotte Brontë

Novelists should never allow themselves to weary of the study of real life.

The Professor

Robert Burton

Hence it is clear how much more cruel the pen is than the sword.

Anatomy of Melancholy

George Gordon (Noel) Byron, 6th Lord Byron

'Tis pleasant, sure, to see one's name in print;
A book's a book, although there's nothing in 't.

English Bards and Scotch Reviewers

If I could always read, I should never feel the want of society.

Journal

Thomas Carlyle

My books are friends that never fail me.

Letter, 1817

A well-written Life is amost as rare as a well-spent one.
   Critical and Miscellaneous Essays

Lewis Carroll [Charles Lutwidge Dodgson]
"What is the use of a book," thought Alice, "without
pictures or conversations?"
   Alice's Adventures in Wonderland

G(ilbert K(eith) Chesterton
There is a great deal of difference between the eager man
who wants to read a book, and the tired man who wants a
book to read.
   Charles Dickens

William Cowper
 Thousands...
Kiss the book's outside who ne'er look within.
   Expostulation

Benjamin Disraeli, 1st Earl of Beaconsfield
An author who speaks about his own books is almost as
bad as a mother who talks about her own children.
   Banquet, 1873

When I want to read a novel I write one.
   Moneypenny and Buckle's *Life of Disraeli*

Isaac D'Israeli
There is an art of reading, as well as an art of thinking,
and an art of writing.
   The Literary Character

T(homas) S(tearns) Eliot
Many are engaged in writing books and printing them
Many desire to see their names in print,

Many read nothing but the race reports.
The Rock

Ralph Waldo Emerson
Never read any book that is not a year old.
Society and Solitude: Books

Edward Gibbon
My early and invincible love of reading...I would not
exchange for the treasures of India.
Memoirs

William Henry, Duke of Gloucester
Another damned, thick, square book! Always scribble,
scribble, scribble. Eh! Mr Gibbon?
Attributed

Heinrich Heine
Wherever they burn books they will also, in the end, burn
human beings.
Almansor: A Tragedy

Ernest Hemingway
All modern American literature comes from one book by
Mark Twain called Huckleberry Finn.
Green Hills of Africa

Aldous (Leonard) Huxley
The proper study of mankind is books.
Chrome Yellow

William Ralph Inge
Literature flourishes best when it is half a trade and half
an art.
The Victorian Age

Henry James
It takes a great deal of history to produce a little litera-
ture.
   Life of Nathaniel Hawthorne

Dr Samuel Johnson
What is written without effort is in general read without
pleasure.
   Johnsonian Miscellanies

A man ought to read just as inclination leads him; for
what he reads as a task will do him little good.
   Boswell's *Life of Johnson*

[When asked if he had read a new book through] No, Sir,
do you read books through?
   Ibid

A man will turn over half a library to make one book.
   Ibid

Helen (Adams) Keller
Literature is my Utopia. Here I am not disfranchised. No
barrier of the senses shuts me out from the sweet, gracious discourse of my book friends. They talk to me
without embarrassment or awkwardness.
   The Story of My Life

Georg Christoph Lichtenberg
There can hardly be a stranger commodity in the world
than books. Printed by people who don't understand

them; sold by people who don't understand them; bound, criticized and read by people who don't understand them, and now even written by people who don't understand them.

A Doctrine of Scattered Occasions

Samuel Lover

When once the itch of literature comes over a man, nothing can cure it but the scratching of a pen.

Handy Andy

Martin Luther

The multitude of books is a great evil.

Table-Talk

Michel Eyquem de Montaigne

All the world knows me in my book, and my book in me.

Essays

John Morley, 1st Viscount Morley of Blackburn

Literature, the most seductive, the most deceiving, the most dangerous of professions.

Burke

Dorothy (Rothschild) Parker

This is not a novel to be tossed aside lightly. It should be thrown with great force.

Will(iam Penn Adair) Rogers

When you put down the good things you ought to have done, and leave out the bad ones you did do—that's memoirs.

The Autobiography of Will Rogers

John Ruskin

All books are divisible into two classes: the books of the hour, and the books of all time.
Seasame and Lilies

If a book is worth reading, it is worth buying.
Ibid

William Shakespeare

He hath never fed of the dainties that are bred in a book; he hath not eat paper, as it were; he hath not drunk ink.
Love's Labour's Lost 1

Knowing I loved my books, he furnish'd me
From mine own library with volumes that
I prize above my dukedom.
The Tempest 1

(Lloyd) Logan Pearsall Smith

A bestseller is the gilded tomb of a mediocre talent.
Afterthoughts: Art and Letters

People say that life is the thing, but I prefer reading.
Ibid: Myself

Sydney Smith

No furniture so charming as books.
Lady Holland's *Memoirs of the Rev. Sydney Smith*

Sir Richard Steele

Reading is to the mind what exercise is to the body.
The Tatler

Robert Louis Stevenson

Books are good enough in their own way, but they are a mighty bloodless substitute for life.
Virginibus Puerisque: An Apology for Idlers

Jonathan Swift
Satire is a sort of glass, wherein beholders do generally
discover everybody's face but their own.
The Battle of the Books

William Makepeace Thackeray
There are a thousand thoughts lying within a man that he
does not know till he takes up the pen to write.
The History of Henry Esmond

Thomas à Kempis
Verily, when the day of judgment comes, we shall not be
asked what we have read, but what we have done.
De Imitatione Christi

Henry David Thoreau
How many a man has dated a new era in his life from the
reading of a book.
Walden

Martin Farquhar Tupper
A good book is the best of friends, the same today and for
ever.
Proverbial Philosophy: Of Reading

Mark Twain [Samuel Langhorne Clemens]
A classic is something that everybody wants to have read
and nobody wants to read.
Speeches: The Disappearance of Literature

John Wesley
Beware you be not swallowed up in books! An ounce of
love is worth a pound of knowledge.
Southey's *Life of Wesley*

Oscar (Fingall O'Flahertie Wills) Wilde

There is no such thing as a moral or an immoral book.
Books are well written or badly written. That is all.
   The Picture of Dorian Gray

You should study the Peerage, Gerald. It is the one book a
young man about town should know thoroughly, and it is
the best thing in fiction the English have done.
   A Woman of No Importance

I never travel without my diary. One should always have
something sensational to read in the train.
   The Importance of Being Earnest

William Wordsworth

Every great and original writer, in proportion as he is
great and original, must himself create the taste by which
he is to be relished.
   Letter

FILM AND THEATRE

Robert Benchley
There's less in this than meets the eye.
[After viewing an art film.]
   Halliwells' *Filmgoer's and Video Viewer's Companion*

Marlon Brando
An actor's a guy who if you ain't talkin' about him, ain't listening.
   The Observer, 1956

Fanny Burney [Frances, Madame d'Arblay]
"Do you come to the play without knowing what it is?"
"Oh, yes, sir, yes, very frequently. I have not time to read playbills. One merely comes to meet one's friends, and show that one's alive."
   Evelina

Oliver Goldsmith
On the stage he was natural, simple, affecting;
'Twas only that when he was off he was acting.
   Retaliation

Moss Hart
One begins with two people on a stage and one of them
had better say something pretty damn quick!
  Contemporary Dramatists, 1977

Katharine Hepburn
Acting's just waiting for a custard pie. That's all.

Sir Alfred (Joseph) Hitchcock
The length of a film should be directly related to the
endurance of the human bladder.
  The Observer, 1960

If I made Cinderella, the audience would be looking out
for a body in the coach.

Auguste (Marie Louis Nicolas) Lumière
Young man, you may be grateful that my invention is
not for sale, for it would undoubtedly ruin you. It can
be exploited for a certain time as a scientific curiosity,
but apart from that it has no commercial value whatso-
ever.
  Said 1895

George Augustus Moore
Acting is therefore the lowest of the arts, if it is an art at
all.
  Mummer-Worship

Francis Quarles
Judge not the play before the play is done:
  Epigram: Respice Finem

William Shakespeare
The play, I remember, pleased not the million; 'twas
caviare to the general.
Hamlet 2

The play's the thing
Wherein I'll catch the conscience of the king.
Ibid

Speak the speech, I pray you, as I pronounced it to you,
trippingly on the tongue: but if you mouth it, as many of
your players do, I had as lief the town-crier spoke my
lines. Nor do not saw the air too much with your hand,
thus, but use all gently.
Ibid

Suit the action to the word, the word to the action; with
this special observance, that you o'erstep not the modesty
of nature.
Ibid

The purpose of playing, whose end, both at the first and
now, was and is, to hold, as 'twere, the mirror up to
nature.
Ibid

Exit, pursued by a bear.
The Winter's Tale 3, stage direction

Spencer Tracy
Acting in not an important job in the scheme of things.
Plumbing is.

I'm too tired and old and rich for all this. so let's do the scene.
[To a director with "artistic" pretensions.]
  Halliwells' *Filmgoer's and Video Viewer's Companion*

Billy Wilder
Johnny, keep it out of focus. I want to win the foreign picture award.
[To his cinematographer]
  Halliwells' *Filmgoer's and Video Viewer's Companion*

MASS MEDIA

Jean Anouilh
Have you noticed that life, real honest to goodness life,
with murders, and catastrophes and fabulous inheritances,
happens almost exclusively in newspapers?
The Rehearsal

W(ystan) H(ugh) Auden
What the mass media offer is not popular art, but entertainment which is intended to be consumed like food,
forgotten, and replaced by a new dish.
The Dyer's Hand: The Poet and the City

(Enoch) Arnold Bennett
Journalists say a thing that they know isn't true in the
hope that if they keep on saying it long enough it will be
true.
The Title

(Mark) James (Walter) Cameron
The press can only be a mirror—albeit a distorting mirror,
according to its politics or the smallness of its purpose—
but it rarely lies because it dare not.
The Listener, 1979

Quentin Crisp

If any reader of this book is in the grip of some habit of which he is deeply ashamed, I advise him not to give way to it in secret but to do it on television...People will cross the road at the risk of losing their own lives in order to say "We saw you on the telly."

How to Become a Virgin

Charles Anderson Dana

When a dog bites a man that is not news, but when a man bites a dog that is news.

'What is News?', *New York Sun*, 1882

T(homas) S(tearns) Eliot

[TV] is a medium of entertainment which permits millions of people to listen to the same joke at the same time, and yet remain lonesome.

New York Post, 1963

David (Parradine) Frost

Television is an invention that permits you to be entertained in your living room by people you wouldn't have in your home.

David Frost Revue, CBS TV, 1971

Samuel Goldwyn

Why should people go out and pay money to see bad films when they can stay at home and see bad television for nothing?

The Observer, 1956

Richard Ingrams

Children watch too much television not only because
indolent parents allow them to, but because the standard
of most programmes is pitched at their level.
The Observer

Thomas Jefferson

Where the press is free and every man able to read, all is
safe.
Writings, Vol. XIV

"Junius" [?Sir Philip Francis]

The liberty of the press is the Palladium of all the civil,
political, and religious rights of an Englishman.
Letters, Dedication

Louis Kronenberger

It is the gossip columnist's business to write about what is
none of his business.
The Cart and the Horse

(Herbert) Marshall McLuhan

The medium is the message.
Understanding Media

Advertising is the greatest art form of the twentieth
century.
Advertising Age

Norman Mailer

Once a newspaper touches a story, the facts are lost
forever, even to the protagonists.
The Presidential Papers

Groucho (Julius Henry) Marx
I find television very educational. Every time someone
switches it on I go into another room and read a good book.
   The Groucho Papers

George Mason
The freedom of the press is one of the great bulwarks of
liberty, and can never be restrained but by despotic
governments.
   Virginia Bill of Rights, 1776

Sir Yehudi Menuhin
Whenever I see a newspaper, I think of the poor trees. As
trees they provide beauty, shade and shelter, but as paper
all they provide is rubbish.
   Said 1970

Arthur Miller
A good newspaper is a nation talking to itself.
   The Observer, 1961

**Alfred Charles William Harmsworth, Viscount
Northcliffe**
A profession [journalism] whose business it is to explain
to others what it personally does not understand.

Adolph Simon Ochs
All the news that's fit to print.
   [Motto of the New York Times.]

John (Henry) O'Hara
Hot lead can be almost as effective coming from a
linotype as from a firearm.
   The Portable F. Scott Fitzgerald, Introduction

Theodore Roosevelt
The men with the muck-rake are often indispensable to the well-being of society, but only if they know when to stop raking the muck.
   Address, 1906

C(harles) P(restwich) Scott
Television? The word is half Latin and half Greek. No good can come of it.
   Attributed

Richard Brinsley Sheridan
The newspapers! Sir, they are the most villainous— licentious—abominable—infernal—Not that I ever read them—no—I make it a rule never to look into a newspaper.
   The Critic

Susan Sontag
Reality has come to seem more and more like what we are shown by cameras.
   'Photography Unlimited', *New York Review of Books,* 1977

Voltaire [François Marie Arouet]
In the case of news, we should always wait for the sacrament of confirmation.

Barbara Ward
The modern world is not given to uncritical admiration. It expects its idols to have feet of clay, and can be reasonably sure that press and camera will report their exact dimensions.
   Saturday Review, 1961

Oscar (Fingall O'Flahertie Wills) Wilde

As for modern journalism, it is not my business to defend it. It justifies its own existence by the great Darwinian principle of the survival of the vulgarist.

Intentions: The Critic as Artist

There is much to be said in favour of modern journalism. By giving us the opinions of the uneducated, it keeps us in touch with the ignorance of the community.

Ibid

Billy Wilder

Television is…a twenty-one inch person. I'm delighted with it, because it used to be that films were the lowest form of art. Now we've got something to look down on.

Halliwell's *Filmgoer's Book of Quotations*

FOOLISHNESS AND WISDOM

Phineas Taylor Barnum
You can fool some of the people all the time, and all of
the people some of the time, but you can't fool all of the
people all the time.
   Attributed

The Bible
Wisdom is the principal thing; therefore get wisdom: and
with all thy getting get understanding.
   Proverbs 4

Even a fool, when he holdeth his peace, is counted wise:
and he that shutteth his lips is esteemed a man of understanding.
   Ibid 17

It is an honour for a man to cease from strife: but every
fool will be meddling.
   Ibid 20

Answer not a fool according to his folly, lest thou also be
like unto him. Answer a fool according to his folly, lest he
be wise in his own conceit.
   Ibid 26

For in much wisdom is much grief: and he that increaseth knowledge increaseth sorrow.
   Ecclesiastes 1

The heart of the wise is in the house of mourning: but the heart of fools is in the house of mirth. It is better to hear the rebuke of the wise, than for a man to hear the song of fools.
   Ibid 7

For ye suffer fools gladly, seeing ye yourselves are wise.
   2 Corinthians 11

William Blake
A fool sees not the same tree that a wise man sees.
   Marriage of Heaven and Hell: Proverbs of Hell

Nicolas Boileau-Despréaux
A fool always finds a greater fool to admire him.
   L'Art poétique

Miguel de Cervantes (Saavedra)
He's a muddled fool, full of lucid intervals.
   Don Quixote

Charles Caleb Colton
The follies of the fool are known to the world, but are hidden from himself; the follies of the wise are known to himself, but hidden from the world.
   Lacon

Confucius
For one word a man is often deemed to be wise, and for one word he is often deemed to be foolish. We should be careful indeed what we say.
   Analects

William Cowper

How much a dunce that has been sent to roam
Excels a dunce that has been kept at home.
  The Progress of Error

Knowledge is proud that he has learn'd so much;
Wisdom is humble that he knows no more.
  The Task: The Winter Walk at Noon

Albert Einstein

Before God we are all equally wise—equally foolish.
  Adress at the Sobonne

Epicharmus

The wise man must be wise before, not after, the event.
  Fabulæ Incertæ

Benjamin Franklin

Experience keeps a dear school, but fools will learn in no
other.
  Poor Richard's Almanack 1743

It is ill manners to silence a fool, and cruelty to let him go
on.
  Ibid 1754

The first degree of folly is to conceit one's self wise; the
second to profess it; the third to despise counsel.
  Ibid

Baltasar Gracián

Self-reflection is the school of wisdom.
  The Art of Worldly Wisdom

Thomas Gray
Where ignorance is bliss,
  'Tis folly to be wise.
  Ode on a Distant Prospect of Eton College

Henry IV
The wisest fool in Christendom. [James VI of Scotland
and I of England.]
  Attributed

Thomas Hobbes
For words are wise men's counters, they do but reckon by
them; but they are the money of fools.
  Leviathan

Thomas Henry Huxley
The only medicine for suffering, crime, and all the other
woes of mankind, is wisdom.
  Science and Education

Ben(jamin) Jonson
To be a fool born is a disease incurable.
  Volpone

Rudyard Kipling
Take my word for it, the silliest woman can manage a clever
man; but it needs a very clever woman to manage a fool.
  Three and—an Extra

Abraham Lincoln
You can fool some of the people all of the time, and all of
the people some of the time, but you cannot fool all of the
people all the time.
  Attributed, 1856

Better to remain silent and be thought a fool than to speak
out and remove all doubt.
    Attributed

Lady Mary Wortley Montagu
I enjoy vast delight in the folly of mankind; and, God be
praised, that is an inexhaustible source of entertainment.
    Letter, 1725

Edgar Allan Poe
I have great faith in fools:—self-confidence my friends
will call it.
    Marginalia

Alexander Pope
Pride, the never-failing vice of fools.
    Essay on Criticism

For fools rush in where angels fear to tread.
    Ibid

No creature smarts so little as a fool.
    Epistle to Dr Arbuthnot

Sir Walter Raleigh
Tell wisdom she entangles
Herself in overwiseness.
    The Lie

Allan Ramsay
For when I dinna clearly see,
I always own I dinna ken,
And that's the way with wisest men.
    Eclogue

Theodore Roosevelt
Nine-tenths of wisdom is being wise in time.
  Speech, 14 June 1917

William Shakespeare
Lord, what fools these mortals be!
  A Midsummer Night's Dream 3

I had rather have a fool to make me merry than experience to make me sad.
  As You Like It 4

The fool doth think he is wise, but the wise man knows himself to be a fool.
  Ibid 5

He uses his folly like a stalking-horse and under the presentation of that he shoots his wit.
  Ibid

William Shenstone
A fool and his words are soon parted; a man of genius and his money.
  Essays on Men and Manners: On Reserve

Charles Hadden Spurgeon
The doorstep to the temple of wisdom is a knowledge of our own ignorance.
  Gleanings among the Sheaves: The First Lesson

Laurence Sterne
Sciences may be learned by rote, but Wisdom not.
  Tristram Shandy

Alfred, Lord Tennyson
Knowledge comes, but wisdom lingers.
Locksley Hall

Thomas Tusser
A fool and his money be soon at debate.
Five Hundred Points of Good Husbandry

Samuel Warren
There is probably no man living, though ever so great a
fool, that cannot do something or other well.
Ten Thousand a Year

Oscar (Fingall O'Flahertie Wills) Wilde
There is no sin except stupidity.
Intentions: The Critic as Artist

TEACHERS, SCHOLARS AND CRITICS

Henry (Brooks) Adams
A teacher affects eternity; he can never tell where his influence stops.
The Education of Henry Adams

Anonymous Critic
Mr Dickens writes too often and too fast…If he persists much longer in this course, it requires not gift of prophecy to foretell his fate—he has risen like a rocket, and he will come down like a stick.
Review of *Pickwick Papers,* 1838

Antiphanes of Macedonia
Idly inquisitive tribe of grammarians, who dig up the poetry of others by the roots…Get away, bugs, that bite secretly at the eloquent.
Greek Anthology

Walter Bagehot
A schoolmaster should have an atmosphere of awe, and walk wonderingly, as if he was amazed at being himself.
Literary Studies

Henry Peter Brougham, 1st Baron Brougham and Vaux

The schoolmaster is abroad, and I trust to him, armed
with his primer, against the soldier in full military array.

House of Commons speech, 1828

Robert Burns

Thou eunuch of language: thou butcher, imbruing thy
hands in the bowels of orthography: thou arch-heretic in
pronunciation: thou pitch-pipe of affected emphasis: thou
carpenter, mortising the awkward joints of jarring sen-
tences: thou squeaking dissonance of cadence: thou pimp
of gender: thou scape-gallows from the land of syntax:
thou scavenger of mood and tense: thou murderous
accoucheur of infant learning: thou ignis fatuus, misleading the steps of benighted ignorance: thou pickle-herring
in the puppet-show of nonsense.

[On an unidentified critic]

Critics!—appall'd I venture on the name,
Those cut-throat bandits in the paths of fame.

Second Epistle to Robert Graham of Fintry

His locked, letter'd, braw brass collar,
Show'd him the gentleman and scholar.

The Twa Dogs

Robert Burton

And to this day is every scholar poor;
Gross gold from them runs headlong to the door.

Anatomy of Melancholy

George Gordon (Noel) Byron, 6th Lord Byron
With just enough of learning to misquote.
English Bards and Scotch Reviewers

Thomas Carlyle
Respectable Professors of the Dismal Science.
Latter-Day Pamphlets

George Chapman
And let a scholar all Earth's volumes carry,
He will be but a walking dictionary.
Tears of Peace

Charles Churchill
Dull, superstitious readers they deceive,
Who pin their easy faith on critic's sleeve,
And knowing nothing, every thing believe.
The Apology

Though by whim, envy, or resentment led,
They damn those authors whom they never read.
The Candidate

Confucius
The scholar who cherishes the love of comfort, is not fit
to be deemed a scholar.
Analects

Destouches [Philippe Néricault]
Criticism is easy, art is difficult.
Le Glorieux

Ralph Waldo Emerson
The man who can make hard things easy is the educator.
Journals, 1861

The scholar must be a solitary, modest, and charitable
soul. He must embrace solitude as a bride…that he may
become acquainted with his thoughts.
Nature, Addresses, and Lectures: Literary Ethics

I offer perpetual congratulation to the scholar; he has
drawn the white lot in life.
Lectures and Biographical Sketches: The Man of Letters

George Savile, 1st Marquis of Halifax
The vanity of teaching often tempteth a man to forget he
is a blockhead.
Works

Oliver Wendell Holmes
The world's great men have not commonly been great
scholars, nor its great scholars great men.
The Autocrat of the Breakfast Table

Elbert Hubbard
Now owls are not really wise—they only look that way.
The owl is a sort of college professor.
Epigrams

Aldous (Leonard) Huxley
The solemn foolery of scholarship for scholarship's sake.
The Perennial Philosophy

Dr Samuel Johnson
You may abuse a tragedy, though you cannot write one.
You may scold a carpenter who has made you a bad table,
though you cannot make a table. It is not your trade to make
tables.
Boswell's *Life of Johnson*

Mark what ills the scholar's life assail,
Toil, envy, want, the patron, and the jail.
   The Vanity of Human Wishes

Ben(jamin) Jonson

Very few men are wise by their own counsel; or learned
by their own teaching. For he that was only taught by
himself, had a fool to his master.
   Explorata: Consilia

H(enry) L(ouis) Mencken

The average schoolmaster is and always must be essen-
tially an ass, for how can one imagine an intelligent man
engaging in so puerile an avocation.
   Prejudices

Mohammed

The ink of the scholar is more sacred than the blood of
the martyr.
   Tribute to Reason

Alexander Pope

Let such teach others who themselves excel,
And censure freely who have written well.
   Essay on Criticism

Some have at first for Wits then Poets past,
Turn'd Critics next, and prov'd plain fools at last.
   Ibid

The generous Critic fann'd the Poet's fire,
And taught the world with reason to admire.
   Ibid

Hugh Rhodes
Men learn when they teach.
  Boke of Nurture

George Bernard Shaw
A drama critic is a man who leaves no turn unstoned.
  New York Times, 1950

He who can, does. He who cannot, teaches.
  Maxims for Revolutionists

Sydney Smith
I never read a book before reviewing it; it prejudices a
man so.
  The Smith of Smiths by H. Pearson

Oscar (Fingall O'Flahertie Wills) Wilde
Everybody who is incapable of learning has taken to
teaching.
  The Decay of Lying

John Wolcot
Proud to find faults and raptured with defect! [Of critics.]
  Benevolent Epistle to Sylvanus Urban

IGNORANCE AND LEARNING

Joseph Addison
Education is a companion which no misfortune can depress, no crime can destroy, no enemy can alienate, no despotism can enslave. At home a friend, abroad an introduction, in solitude a solace, and in society an ornament. It chastens vice, it guides virtue, it gives, at once, grace and government to genius. Without it, what is man? A splendid slave, a reasoning savage.
The Spectator

(Amos) Bronson Alcott
To be ignorant of one's ignorance is the malady of the ignorant.
Table Talk: Discourse

Francis Bacon
I have taken all knowledge to be my province.
Letter, 1592

Sir J(ames) M(atthew) Barrie
Facts were never pleasing to him. He acquired them with reluctance and got rid of them with relief. He was never on terms with them until he had stood them on their heads.
Love Me Never or For Ever

The Bible
He that hath knowledge spareth his words.
Proverbs 17

Paul, thou art beside thyself; much learning doth make thee mad.
Acts 26

Ambrose (Gwinett) Bierce
Education: that which discloses to the wise and disguises from the foolish their lack of understanding.
The Devil's Dictionary

Erudition: dust shaken out of a book into an empty skull.
Ibid

Learning: the kind of ignorance distinguishing the studious.
Ibid

Charlotte Brontë
Prejudices, it is well known, are most difficult to eradicate from the heart whose soil has never been loosened or fertilized by education; they grow there, firm as weeds among stones.
Jane Eyre

Henry Peter Brougham, 1st Baron Brougham and Vaux
Education makes a people easy to lead, but difficult to drive; easy to govern, but impossible to enslave.
Attributed

Charles V [Charles the Wise]
I speak Spanish to God, Italian to women, French to men, and German to my horse.
Attributed

Sir Winston (Leonard Spencer) Churchill

It is a good thing for an uneducated man to read books of
quotations...The quotations when engraved upon the
memory give you good thoughts. They also make you
anxious to read the authors and look for more.
Roving Commission: My Early Life

Confucius

Learning without thought is labour lost; thought without
learning is perilous.
Analects

Charles Dickens

A smattering of everything and a knowledge of nothing.
Sketches by Boz

"Now what I want is, Facts. Teach these boys and girls
nothing but Facts. Facts alone are wanted in life. Plant
nothing else, and root out everything else...Stick to Facts, sir!"
Hard Times

Diogenes

The foundation of every state is the education of its
youth.
Stobaeus' *Florilegium*

Diogenes Laertius

On one occasion Aristotle was asked how much educated
men were superior to those uneducated; "As much," said
he, "as the living are to the dead."
Lives of Eminent Philosophers

Henry Fielding

Public schools are the nurseries of all vice and immorality.
Joseph Andrews

Martin H. Fischer

All the world's a laboratory to the inquiring mind.
Fischerisms by Howard Fabing and Ray Marr

Thomas Fuller

Learning hath gained most by those books by which the printers have lost.
The Holy State and the Profane State: Of Books

James Abram Garfield

Next in importance to freedom and justice is popular education, without which neither freedom nor justice can be permanently maintained.
Letter of Acceptance, 1880

Oliver Goldsmith

In arguing too, the parson own'd his skill,
For e'en though vanquish'd, he could argue still;
While words of learned length and thund'ring sound
Amazed the gazing rustics rang'd around,
And still they gaz'd, and still the wonder grew,
That one small head could carry all he knew.
The Deserted Village

William Hazlitt

It is better to be able neither to read nor write than to be able to do nothing else.
Table Talk: On the Ignorance of the Learned

Georg Wilhelm Friedrich Hegel

But what experience and history teach is this, that peoples and government have never learned anything from history.
The Philosophy of History

William Harvey
All we know is still infinitely less than all that still
remains unknown.
De Motu Cordis et Sanguinis

Thomas Hughes
Life isn't all beer and skittles; but beer and skittles, or
something better of the same sort, must form a good part
of every Englishman's education.
Tom Brown's Schooldays

Thomas Henry Huxley
The great tragedy of Science: the slaying of a beautiful
hypothesis by an ugly fact.
'Biogenesis and Abigenesis'

Dr Samuel Johnson
Integrity without knowledge is weak and useless, and
knowledge without integrity is dangerous and dreadful.
Rasselas

A man is in general better pleased when he has a good
dinner upon his table than when his wife talks Greek.
Johnsonian Miscellanies

Maimonides [Moses ben Maimon]
Teach thy tongue to say "I do not know".

Christopher Marlowe
I count religion but a childish toy,
And hold there is no sin but ignorance.
The Jew of Malta

William Lamb, 2nd Viscount Melbourne
I don't know, Ma'am, why they make all this fuss about
education; none of the Pagets can read or write, and they
get on well enough.
Remark to Queen Victoria

Alexander Pope
A little learning is a dangerous thing;
Drink deep, or taste not the Pierian spring:
Essay on Criticism

The proper study of mankind is man.
Moral Essays

Sir Walter Alexander Raleigh
In an examination those who do not wish to know ask
questions of those who cannot tell.
Laughter from a Cloud: Some Thoughts on Examinations

Bertrand Russell
Science is what you know, philosophy is what you don't
know.

Sir Walter Scott
All men who have turned out worth anything have had
the chief hand in their own education.
Letter, 1830

William Shakespeare
Away with him, away with him! he speaks Latin.
King Henry VI, Part II 4

John Sheffield, 1st Duke of Buckingham and Normanby

Learn to write well, or not to write at all.
   Essay on Satire

Socrates

There is only one good, knowledge, and one evil, ignorance.
   Lives of Eminent Philosophers by Diogenes Laertius

Herbert Spencer

Science is organized knowledge.
   Essays on Education

Charles Maurice de Talleyrand-Perigord

Ils n'ont rien appris, ni rien oublié.
They have learned nothing and forgotten nothing.
   Attributed

Alfred, Lord Tennyson

To follow knowledge like a sinking star,
Beyond the utmost bound of human thought.
   Ulysses

George Macaulay Trevelyan

Education...has produced a vast population able to read but unable to distinguish what is worth reading.
   English Social History

Oscar (Fingall O'Flahertie Wills) Wilde

Education is an admirable thing, but it is well to remember from time to time that nothing that is worth knowing can be taught.
   Intentions: The Critic as Artist

Edward Young

Some for renown, on scraps of learning dote,
And think they grow immortal as they quote.
Love of Fame

POLITICS AND POLITICIANS

John Emerich Edward Dalberg, 1st Baron Acton
Power tends to corrupt, and absolute power corrupts
absolutely.
   Letter to Bishop Creighton, 1887

Aristophanes
You have all the characteristics of a popular politician: a
horrible voice, bad breeding, and a vulgar manner.
   Knights

Francis Bacon
It is as hard and severe a thing to be a true politician as to
be truly moral.
   The Advancement of Learning

Aneurin Bevan
We know what happens to people who stay in the middle
of the road. They get run over.
   The Observer, 1953

Ambrose (Gwinett) Bierce
Elector: one who enjoys the sacred privilege of voting for
the man of another man's choice.
   The Devil's Dictionary

Politics: a strife of interests masquerading as a contest of principles. The conduct of public affairs for private advantage.

Ibid

Otto von Bismarck

Politics is the doctrine of the possible, the attainable.

Speech, 1863

Winston (Leonard Spencer) Churchill

Politics are almost as exciting as war, and quite as dangerous. In war you can only be killed once, but in politics many times.

Said 1920

Ralph Waldo Emerson

Politics is a deleterious profession, like some poisonous handicrafts.

The Conduct of Life

John Kenneth Galbraith

Politics is not the art of the possible. It consists in choosing between the disastrous and the unpalatable.

Ambassador's Journal

John Gay

That politician tops his part,
Who readily can lie with art.

Fables

Sir William Schwenck Gilbert

I always voted at my party's call,
And I never thought of thinking for myself at all.

HMS Pinafore

Isaac Goldberg
Diplomacy is to do and say
The nastiest thing in the nicest way.
   The Reflex

Thomas Hardy
When shall the softer, saner politics,
Whereof we dream, have play in each proud land?
   Departure

Richard Hooker
He that goeth about to persuade a multitude, that they are
not so well governed as they ought to be, shall never want
attentive and favourable hearers.
   Laws of Ecclesiastical Polity

Thomas Jefferson
I have no ambition to govern men. It is a painful and
thankless office.
   Letter, 1796

Politics is such a torment that I would advise every one I
love not to mix with it.
   Ibid, 1800

Dr Samuel Johnson
Why, Sir, most schemes of political improvement are
very laughable things.
   Boswell's *Life of Johnson*

John Maynard Keynes, 1st Baron Keynes of Tilton
This long run is a misleading guide to current affairs. In
the long run we are all dead.
   A Tract on Monetary Reform

Thomas Babington Macaulay, 1st Baron Macaulay
Timid and interested politicians think much more about
the security of their seats than about the security of their
country.
House of Commons speech, 1842

Thomas Moore
The minds of some of our own statesmen, like the pupil
of the human eye, contract themselves the more, the
strong light there is shed upon them.
Corruption and Intolerance, Preface

Wendell Phillips
Politicians are like the bones of a horse's foreshoulder—
not a straight one in it.
Speech, 1864

Sir John Robert Seeley
History is past politics and politics present history.
The Growth of British Policy

William Shakespeare
  Get thee glass eyes;
And, like a scurvy politician, seem
To see the things thou dost not.
King Lear 4

Robert Louis Stevenson
Politics is perhaps the only profession for which no
preparation is thought necessary.
Familiar Studies of Men and Books: Yoshida-Torajiro

Jonathan Swift
Politics, as the word is understood, are nothing but
corruptions.
Thoughts on Various Subjects

Margaret (Hilda) Thatcher

Anyway, I wouldn't want to be Prime Minister, you have
to give yourself 100 per cent.

The Sunday Telegraph, 1969

James Grover Thurber

If you can't stand the heat, get out of the kitchen.

Mr Citizen

Voltaire [François Marie Arouet]

The pleasure of governing must certainly be exquisite if
we may judge from the vast numbers who are eager to be
concerned with it.

Philisophical Dictionary

John Webster

A politician imitates the Devil, as the Devil imitates a
cannon: wheresoever he comes to do mischief, he comes
with his backside towards you.

The White Devil

GOVERNMENT AND STATE

Fisher Ames
A monarchy is a merchantman which sails well, but will
sometimes strike on a rock, and go to the bottom; a
republic is a raft which will never sink, but then your feet
are always in the water.
  House of Representatives speech, 1795

Susan B(rownell) Anthony
The true Republic: men, their rights and nothing more;
women, their rights and nothing less.
  Said 1872

Aristotle
A democracy is a government in the hands of men of low
birth, no property, and vulgar employments.
  Politics

Clement Richard Attlee, 1st Earl Attlee
Democracy means government by discussion, but it is
only effective if you can stop people talking.
  Anatomy of Britain

Sir William Blackstone

That the king can do no wrong, is a necessary and fundamental principle of the English constitution.
Commentaries

(John) Anthony Burgess (Wilson)

The U.S. Presidency is a Tudor monarchy plus telephones.
Writers at Work

Sir Charles Pratt, 1st Earl Camden

The British parliament has no right to tax the Americans...Taxation and representation are inseparably united. God hath joined them: no British parliament can put them asunder.
House of Lords speech, 1765

G(ilbert) K(eith) Chesterton

Democracy means government by the uneducated, while aristocracy means government by the badly educated.
New York Times, 1931

You can never have a revolution in order to establish a democracy. You must have a democracy in order to have a revolution.
Tremendous Trifles

Winston (Leonard Spencer) Churchill

It has been said that democracy is the worst form of government, except for all those other forms that have been tried from time to time.
House of Commons speech, 1947

Confucius

In a country well governed, poverty is something to be ashamed of. In a country badly governed, wealth is something to be ashamed of.
Analects

James Fenimore Cooper

Contact with the affairs of state is one of the most corrupting of the influences to which men are exposed.
The American Democrat

Benjamin Disraeli, 1st Earl of Beaconsfield

No Government can be long secure without a formidable Opposition.
Coningsby

Conservatism discards Prescription, shrinks from Principle, disavows Progress; having rejected all respect for antiquity, it offers no redress for the present, and makes no preparation for the future.
Ibid

A Conservative government is an organized hypocrisy.
House of Commons speech, 1845

Albert Einstein

The State is made for man, not man for the State.
The World As I See It

Benjamin Franklin

In rivers and bad governments the lightest things swim at the top.
Poor Richard's Almanack 1754

Milton Friedman

Governments never learn. Only people learn.
The Observer, 1980

The government solution to a problem is usually as bad
as the problem.
Attributed

David Hume

Nothing appears more surprising to those who consider
human affairs with a philosophical eye, than the easiness
with which the many are governed by the few.
Essays Moral and Political

Thomas Jefferson

The care of human life and happiness, and not their
destruction, is the first and only legitimate object of good
government.
Speech in Maryland, 1809

Abraham Lincoln

No man is good enough to govern another man without
that other's consent.
Speech, 1854

The ballot is stronger than the bullet.
Ibid, 1856

As I would not be a slave, so I would not be a master.
This expresses my idea of democracy.
Said when Vice-President, 1858

Louis XIV

L'Etat, c'est moi.
I am the State.
Attributed

Niccolo Machiavelli

All well-governed states and wise princes have taken care
not to reduce the nobility to despair, nor the people to
discontent.
  The Prince

Joseph Marie, Comte de Maistre

Toute nation a le gouvernement qu'elle merite.
Every nation has the government it deserves.
  Letter from Russia, 1811

Karl Marx and Friedrich Engels

In this sense, the theory of the Communists may be summed
up in the single sentence: Abolition of private property.
  The Communist Manifesto

John Stuart Mill

The worth of a state, in the long run, is the worth of the
individuals composing it.
  On Liberty

Charles Louis de Secondat, Baron de Montesquieu

When a government lasts a long while, it deteriorates by
insensible degrees.
  The Spirit of the Laws

The deterioration of every government begins with the
decay of the principles on which it was founded.
  Ibid

Jawaharlal Nehru

The forces of a capitalist society, if left unchecked, tend
to make the rich richer and the poor poorer.
  Credo

James Otis

Taxation without representation is tyranny.
   Attributed, 1763

Thomas Paine

Society in every state is a blessing, but government, even
in its best state, is but a necessary evil; in its worst state,
an intolerable one.
   Common Sense

William Penn

No system of government was ever so ill devised that,
under proper men, it wouldn't work well enough.
   Some Fruits of Solitude

Let the people think they govern and they will be governed.
   Ibid

Plato

Democracy...is a charming form of government, full of
variety and disorder, and dispensing a kind of quality to
equals and unequals alike.
   The Republic

The rulers of the State are the only ones who should have
the privilege of lying, either at home or abroad; they may
be allowed to lie for the good of the State.
   Ibid

Our object in the construction of the state is the
greatest happiness of the whole, and not that of any
one class.
   Ibid

Alexander Pope
The right divine of kings to govern wrong.
The Dunciad

Jean Jacques Rousseau
If there were a nation of gods they would be governed
democratically, but so perfect a government is not
suitable to men.
The Social Contract

William Shakespeare
Not all the water in the rude rough sea
Can wash the balm from an anointed king.
King Richard II 3

Uneasy lies the head that wears a crown.
King Henry IV, Part II 3

Something is rotten in the state of Denmark.
Hamlet 1

George Bernard Shaw
Democracy substitutes election by the incompetent many
for appointment by the corrupt few.
Man and Superman: Maxims for Revolutionists

Herbert Spencer
The Republican form of government is the highest form
of government; but because of this it requires the highest
type of human nature—a type nowhere at present existing.
Essays: The Americans

Voltaire [François Marie Arouet]
Democracy seems suitable only to a very little country.
  Philosohical Dictionary

In general, the art of government consists in taking as
much money as possible from one class of citizens to
give to the other.
  Ibid

FREEDOM AND OPPRESSION

Joseph Addison
A day, an hour of virtuous liberty
Is worth a whole eternity in bondage.
   Cato

St Augustine of Hippo
He that is good is free, though he be a slave; he that is
evil is a slave, though he be a king.
   The City of God

Bertrand Barère de Vieuzac
*L'arbre de la liberté ne croît qu'arrosé par le sang des
tyrans.*
The tree of liberty grows only when watered by the blood
of tyrants.
   Speech, 1792

The Bible
The truth shall make you free.
   John 8

With a great sum obtained I this freedom. And Paul said,
But I was free born.
   Acts 22

Edmund Burke
Abstract liberty, like other mere abstractions, is not to be found.
  On Conciliation with America: The Thirteen Resolutions

Robert Burns
Freedom and whisky gang thegither,
Tak aff your dram!
  The Author's Earnest Cry and Prayer

Liberty's in every blow!—
Let us do or die!
  Bruce before Bannockburn

A fig for those by law protected!
Liberty's a glorious feast!
  Love and Liberty or The Jolly Beggars

We labour soon, we labour late,
To feed the titled knave, man,
And a' the comfort we're to get,
Is that ayont the grave, man.
  The Tree of Liberty

George Gordon (Noel), 6th Lord Byron
Yet, Freedom! yet thy banner, torn, but flying,
Streams like the thunderstorm against the wind.
  Childe Harold's Pilgrimage

Hereditary Bondsmen! know ye not
Who would be free themselves must strike the blow?
  Ibid

Albert Camus

Fascism…represents the exaltation of the executioner by the executioner.…Russian Communism…represents the exaltation of the executioner by the victim. The former never dreamed of liberating all men, but only of liberating the few by subjugating the rest. The latter, in its most profound principle, aims at liberating all men by provisionally enslaving them all.

The Rebel

Lydia Maria Child

They [slaves] have stabbed themselves for freedom—jumped into the waves for freedom—fought like very tigers for freedom! But they have been hung, and burned, and shot—and their tyrants have been their historians.

An Appeal on Behalf of That Class of Americans called Africans

William Cowper

Freedom has a thousand charms to show,
That slaves, howe'er contented, never know.
Table-Talk

Slaves cannot breathe in England; if their lungs
Receive our air, that moment they are free;
They touch our country, and their shackles fall.
The Task: The Timepiece

John Philpot Curran

The condition upon which God hath given liberty to men is eternal vigilance; which condition if he break, servitude is at once the consequence of his crime, and the punishment of his guilt.

   Speech, 1790

Charles Dickens

Oh, let us love our occupations,
Bless the squire and his relations,
Live upon our daily rations,
And always know our proper stations.

   The Chimes

John Dryden

I am as free as Nature first made man,
Ere the base laws of servitude began,
When wild in woods the noble savage ran.

   The Conquest of Granada

Paul Laurence Dunbar

It is not a carol of joy or glee,
But a prayer that he sends from his heart's deep core...
I know why the caged bird sings!

   Sympathy

Benjamin Franklin

They that can give up essential liberty to obtain a little temporary safety deserve neither liberty nor safely.

   Historical Review of Pennsylvania

Oliver Goldsmith

This is Liberty-hall, gentlemen.
She Stoops to Conquer

Samuel Gompers

Show me the country that has no strikes and I'll show the country in which there is no liberty.
Speech

W(illiam) E(rnest) Henley

I am the master of my fate:
I am the captain of my soul.
Echoes: In Memoriam

Patrick Henry

Is life so dear, or peace so sweet, as to be purchased at the price of chains and slavery?...as for me, give me liberty or give me death!
Speech, 1775

Oliver Wendell Holmes

The freeman casting with unpurchased hand
The vote that shakes the turrets of the land.
Poetry: a Metrical Essay

Henrik Ibsen

The most dangerous enemy to truth and freedom in our midst is the compact majority. Yes, the damned, compact, liberal majority.
An Enemy of the People

You should never put on your best trousers when you go out to fight for freedom and truth.
Ibid

James I

The bird, the beast, the fish eke in the sea,
They live in freedom everich in his kind;
And I a man, and lackith liberty.
   The Kingis Quair

Thomas Jefferson

The God who gave us life gave us liberty at the same time.
   Summary View of the Rights of British America

We hold these truths to be self-evident,—that all men are
created equal; that they are endowed by their Creator with
certain inalienable rights; that among these are life,
liberty, and the pursuit of happiness.
   The Declaration of Independence

The tree of liberty must be refreshed from time to time with
the blood of patriots and tyrants. It is its natural manure.
   Letter, 1787

Martin Luther King

I have a dream that one day on the red hills of Georgia
the sons of former slaves and the sons of former slave-
owners will be able to sit down together at the table of
brotherhood.
   Speech, 1963

Emma Lazarus

Give me your tired, your poor,
Your huddled masses yearning to breathe free,
The wretched refuse of your teeming shore.
   The New Colossus (inscribed on the pedestal of the Statue of
   Liberty)

Nikolai Lenin [Vladimir Ilyich Ulyanov]
It is true that liberty is precious—so precious that it must
be rationed.
  Attributed

Abraham Lincoln
That this nation, under God, shall have a new birth of
freedom, and that government of the people, by the
people, and for the people, shall not perish from the earth.
  The Gettysburg Address, 1863

Whenever I hear anyone arguing for slavery, I feel a
strong impulse to see it tried on him personally.
  Address to an Indiana regiment, 1865

Karl Marx and **Friedrich Engels**
The workers have nothing to lose but their chains. They
have a world to gain. Workers of the world, unite!
  The Communist Manifesto

John Stuart Mill
The liberty of the individual must be thus far limited; he
must not make himself a nuisance to other people.
  On Liberty

John Milton
Give me the liberty to know, to utter, and to argue freely
according to conscience, above all liberties.
  Areopagitica

No man who knows aught, can be so stupid to deny that
all men naturally were born free.
  Tenure of Kings and Magistrates

Molière [Jean-Baptiste Poquelin]

Il se faut réserver une arrière boutique...en laquelle nous établissions notre vraie liberté.

We must keep a little back shop...where we may establish our own true liberty.

   Essais

George Orwell [Eric Arthur Blair]

All animals are equal, but some animals are more equal than others.

   Animal Farm

William Pitt the Younger

Necessity is the plea for every infringement of human freedom. It is the argument of tyrants; it is the creed of slaves.

   House of Commons speech, 1783

Marie Jeanne Philipon Roland de la Platière

O Liberté! que de crimes on commet en ton nom!

O Liberty! what crimes are committed in your name!

   From the scaffold, seeing a statue of Liberty

Jean Jacques Rousseau

L'homme est né libre, et partout il est dans les fers.

Man is born free, and everywhere he is in chains.

   The Social Contract

George Bernard Shaw

Liberty means responsibility. That is why most men dread it.

   Man and Superman: Maxims for Revolutionists

Herbert Spencer
No one can be perfectly free till all are free.
Social Statics

James Thomson and **David Malloch** or **Mallet**
"Rule, Britannia, rule the waves;
Britons never will be slaves."
Alfred: A Masque

Voltaire [François Marie Arouet]
La Liberté est née en Angleterre des querelles des tyrans.
Liberty was born in England from the quarrels of tyrans.
Lettres Philosophiques

George Washington
Liberty, when it begins to take root, is a plant of rapid growth.
Letter, 1788

Thomas Woodrow Wilson
The history of liberty is a history of resistance.
Speech, 1812

William Wordsworth
We must be free or die, who speak the tongue
That Shakespeare spake; the faith and morals hold
Which Milton held.
Sonnet: It is not to be thought of

LAWYERS AND THE LAW

Francis Bacon
One of the Seven was wont to say: "That laws were like cobwebs; where the small flies were caught, and the great brake through."
  Apothegms

Henry Ward Beecher
Riches without law are more dangerous than is poverty without law.
  Proverbs from Plymouth Pulpit

Jeremy Bentham
Every law is an evil, for every law is an infraction of liberty.
  Principles of Morals and Legislation

The Bible
For as many as have sinned without law shall also perish without law: and as many as have sinned in the law shall be judged by the law.
  Romans 2

These, not having the law, are a law unto themselves.
  Ibid 2

Ambrose (Gwinett) Bierce
Lawyer: one skilled in circumvention of the law.
The Devil's Dictionary

Litigation: a machine which you go into as a pig and
come out of as a sausage.
Ibid

Henry Peter Brougham, Baron Brougham and Vaux
All we see about us, Kings, Lords, and Commons, the
whole machinery of the State, all the apparatus of the
system, and its varied workings, end in simply bringing
twelve good men into a box.
The Present State of the Law

William Camden
Agree, for the law is costly.
Remains Concerning Britain

Charles Dickens
"If the law supposes that," said Mr Bumble..."the law is
a ass—a idiot."
Oliver Twist

George Eliot [Mary Ann Evans]
The law's made to take care o' raskills.
The Mill on the Floss

Anatole France [Jacques Anatole Thibault]
The law, in its majestic equality, forbids the rich as well
as the poor to sleep under bridges, to beg in the streets,
and to steal bread.
Cournos' *Modern Plutarch*

Christopher (Harris) Fry

I know I am not
A practical person; legal matters and so forth
Are Greek to me, except, of course,
That I understand Greek.
  The Lady's not for Burning

Sir William Schwenck Gilbert

And many a burglar I've restored
  To his friends and his relations.
  Trial by Jury

When constabulary duty's to be done,
A policeman's lot is not a happy one.
  The Pirates of Penzance

Oliver Goldsmith

Laws grind the poor, and rich men rule the law.
  The Traveller

Ulysses S(impson) Grant

I know of no method to secure the repeal of bad or
obnoxious laws so effective as their stringent execution.
  Inaugural address, 1869

Charles Macklin

The law is a sort of hocus-pocus science, that smiles in
yer face while it picks yer pocket: and the glorious
uncertainty of it is of mair use to the professors than the
justice of it.
  Love à la Mode

Charles Louis de Secondat, Baron de Montesquieu

Useless laws weaken the necessary laws.
  The Spirit of the Laws

Christopher North [John Wilson]
Laws were made to be broken.
 Noctes Ambrosianae

William Pitt the Elder
Where law ends, tyranny begins.
 House of Lords speech, 1770

Jean Jacques Rousseau
Good laws lead to the making of better ones; bad ones
bring about worse.
 The Social Contract

John Selden
Ignorance of the law excuses no man; not that all men
know the law, but because 'tis an excuse every man will
plead, and no man can tell how to refute him.
 Table Talk: Judgments

William Shakespeare
The first thing to do is kill all the lawyers.
 King Henry VI, Part II 4

Old father antic the law
 King Henry IV, Part I 1

JUSTICE AND MERCY

Martin Luther King
Injustice anywhere is a threat to justice everywhere.
  Letter, 1963

Francis Bacon
Revenge is a kind of wild justice.
  Essays: Of Revenge

Guillaume de Salluste, Seigneur du Bartas
Mercy and Justice, marching cheek by jowl.
  Divine Weeks and Works: Week 1, Day 1

Ambrose (Gwinett) Bierce
Justice: a commodity which in a more or less adulterated
condition the State sells to the citizen as a reward for his
allegiance, taxes and personal service.
  The Devil's Dictionary

Mercy: an attribute beloved of detected offenders.
  Ibid

Albert Camus
Absolute freedom mocks at justice. Absolute justice
denies freedom.
  The Rebel

Marcus Tullius Cicero
The fundamentals of justice are that no one shall suffer wrong, and that the public good be served.
De Officiis

John Dryden
Our mercy is become our crime.
Absalom and Achitophel

George Eliot [Mary Ann Evans]
There is a mercy which is weakness, and even treason against the common good.
Romola

Henry Fielding
Thwackum was for doing justice, and leaving mercy to heaven.
Tom Jones

Lord Gordon Hewart
It is not merely of some importance but is of fundamental importance that justice should not only be done, but should manifestly and undoubtedly be seen to be done.
Jackson's *The Chief*

Richard Hovey
Ah, to be just, as well as kind,—
It costs so little and so much!
Contemporaries

Walter Savage Landor
Delay of justice is injustice.
Imaginary Conversations: Peter Leopold and President Du Paty

James Russell Lowell

Exact justice is commonly more merciful in the long run than pity, for it tends to foster in men those stronger qualities which make them good citizens.
  Among My Books: Dante

Magna Carta

To no one will we sell, to no one will we refuse or delay right or justice.
  Article 40

Lord Mansfield

Consider what you think justice requires, and decide accordingly. But never give your reasons; for your judgement will probably be right, but your reasons will certainly be wrong.
  Campbell's *Lives of the Chief Justices*

H(enry) L(ouis) Mencken

Injustice is relatively easy to bear; what stings is justice.
  Prejudices

John Milton

Yet I shall temper so
Justice with mercy, as may illustrate most
Them fully satisfied, and thee appease.
  Paradise Lost

Blaise Pascal

Justice without strength is helpless, strength without justice is tyrannical...Unable to make what is just strong, we have made what is strong just.
  Pensées

William Shakespeare

The quality of mercy is not strain'd,
It droppeth as the gentle rain from heaven.
  The Merchant of Venice 3

But mercy is above this sceptred sway;
It is enthroned in the hearts of kings,
It is an attribute to God himself;
And earthly power doth then show likest God's
When mercy seasons justice.
  Ibid 4

Sparing justice feeds iniquity.
  The Rape of Lucrece

William Watson

Fiat justitia et ruant coeli.
Let justice be done though the heavens fall.
  Questions Concerning Religion and State

Oscar (Fingall O'Flahertie Wills) Wilde

For Man's grim Justice goes its way,
  And will not swerve aside:
It slays the weak, it slays the strong,
  It has a deadly stride.
  The Ballad of Reading Goal

Mary Wollstonecraft

It is justice, not charity, that is wanting in the world.
  A Vindication of the Rights of Women

CRIME AND PUNISHMENT

Woody Allen [Allen Stewart Konigsberg]
I think crime pays. The hours are good, you travel a lot.
  Take the Money and Run

Francis Bacon
Opportunity makes a thief.
  Letter, 1598

Jeremy Bentham
All punishment is mischief; all punishment in itself is evil.
  Principles of Morals and Legislation

The Bible
My father hath chastised you with whips, but I will
chastise you with scorpions.
  I Kings 12

Stolen waters are sweet.
  Proverbs 9

**Charles Synge Christopher Bowen, Baron Bowen of
Colwood**
The rain it raineth on the just
  And also on the unjust fella:
But chiefly on the just, because
  The unjust steals the just's umbrella.
  Sichel's *Sands of Time*

Marcus Tullius Cicero

The greatest incitement to crime is the hope of escaping punishment.

Pro Milone

Let the punishment be equal with the offence.

De Legibus

William Congreve

See how love and murder will out.

The Double Dealer

Thomas De Quincey

If once a man indulge himself in murder, very soon he comes to think little of robbing; and from robbing he next comes to drinking and Sabbath-breaking, and from that to incivility and procrastination.

Murder Considered as One of the Fine Arts

Sir Arthur Conan Doyle

Singularity is almost invariably a clue. The more featureless and commonplace a crime is, the more difficult it is to bring it home.

The Adventures of Sherlock Holmes

George Eliot [Mary Ann Evans]

That is the bitterest of all,—to wear the yoke of our wrong-doing.

Daniel Deronda

Ralph Waldo Emerson

Wherever a man commits a crime, God finds a witness...Every secret crime has its reporter.

Uncollected Lectures: Natural Religion

There is no den in the wide world to hide a rogue.
Commit a crime and the earth is made of glass.
  Essays, First Series: Compensation

Joseph Fouché
C'est plus qu'un crime; c'est une faute.
It is worse than a crime; it is a blunder.
  Memoirs

Sir William Schwenck Gilbert
  My object all sublime
  I shall achieve in time—
To let the punishment fit the crime.
  The Mikado 2

George Herbert
Punishment is lame, but it comes.
  Jacula Prudentum

E(dgar) W(atson) Howe
The greatest punishment is to be despised by your
neighbors, the world, and members of your family.
  Howe's Monthly

Dr Samuel Johnson
Depend upon it, sir, when a man knows he is to be hanged
in a fortnight, it concentrates his mind wonderfully.
  Boswell's *Life of Johnson*

Juvenal [Decimus Junius Juvenalis]
Quisnam hominum est quem tu contentum videris uno
Flagitio?
What man have you ever seen who was contented with
one crime only?
  Satires

Abraham Lincoln
He reminds me of the man who murdered both his parents, and then, when sentence was about to be pronounced, pleaded for mercy on the grounds that he was an orphan.
   Gross's *Lincoln's Own Stories*

Napoleon I [Napoleon Bonaparte]
The contagion of crime is like that of the plague.
   Sayings of Napoleon

Alexander Pope
The hungry judges soon the sentence sign,
And wretches hang that jurymen may dine.
   The Rape of the Lock

Robert Rice
Crime is a logical extension of the sort of behaviour that is often considered perfectly respectable in legitimate business.
   The Business of Crime

Seneca
There is no crime without a precedent.
   Hippolytus

Cui podest scelus Is fecit.
Who profits by a crime commits the crime.
   Medea

William Shakespeare
The most peaceable way for you, if you do take a thief, is to let him show himself what he is and steal out of your company.
   Much Ado About Nothing 3

Murder most foul, as in the best it is.
  Hamlet 1

It hath the primal eldest curse upon't,
A brother's murder.
  Ibid 3

Every true man's apparel fits your thief.
  Measure for Measure 4

Thou shalt be whipp'd with wire, and stew'd in brine,
Smarting in lingering pickle.
  Antony and Cleopatra 2

Bid that welcome
Which comes to punish us, and we punish it
Seeming to bear it lightly.
  Ibid 2

Herbert Spencer
Every unpunished delinquency has a family of delinquencies.
  The Study of Sociology, Postscript

Publilius Syrus
Injuriam ipse facias ubi non vindices.
You yourself are guilty of a crime when you do not
punish crime.
  Sententiæ

Qui culpæ ignoscit uni, suadet pluribus.
Pardon one offense and you encourage the commission of
many.
  Ibid

Voltaire [François Marie Arouet]
Fear follows crime, and is its punishment.
Semiramis

It is better to risk saving a guilty person than to condemn an innocent one.
Zadig

Mary Wollstonecraft
Executions, far from being useful examples to the survivors, have, I am persuaded, a quite contrary effect, by hardening the heart thay ought to terrify.
Letters written in Sweden, Norway and Denmark

GOD, FAITH AND RELIGION

Lancelot Andrewes
The nearer the Church the further from God.
  Sermon

St Augustine of Hippo
We can know what God is not, but we cannot know what
he is.
  De Trinitate

There is no salvation outside the church.
  De Bapt.

Walter Bagehot
So long as there are earnest believers in the world, they
will always wish to punish opinions, even if their judgment tells them it is unwise, and their conscience that it is
wrong.
  Literary Studies

Honoré de Balzac
I believe in the incomprehensibility of God.
  Letter, 1837

The Bible

I know that my redeemer liveth, and that he shall stand at the latter day upon the earth.

Job 9

The Lord is my shepherd; I shall not want. He maketh me to lie down in green pastures: he leadeth me beside the still waters. He restoreth my soul: he leadeth me in the paths of righteousness for his name's sake. Yea, though I walk through the valley of the shadow of death, I will fear no evil: for thou art with me; thy rod and thy staff they comfort me.

Psalms 23

God is our refuge and strength, a very present help in trouble.

Ibid 46

I will lift up mine eyes unto the hills, from whence cometh my help. My help cometh from the Lord, which made heaven and earth.

Ibid 121

The Lord shall preserve thy going out and thy coming in from this time forth, and even for evermore.

Ibid

Fear God, and keep his commandments: for this is the whole duty of man.

Ecclesiastes 12

Blessed are the poor in spirit: for theirs is the kingdom of heaven. Blessed are they that mourn: for they shall be comforted. Blessed are the meek: for they shall inherit the

earth. Blessed are they which do hunger and thirst after righteousness: for they shall be filled. Blessed are the merciful: for they shall obtain mercy. Blessed are the pure in heart: for they shall see God. Blessed are the peacemakers: for they shall be called the children of God.
   Matthew 5

Our Father which art in heaven, Hallowed be thy name. Thy kingdom come. Thy will be done in earth, as it is in heaven. Give us this day our daily bread. And forgive us our debts, as we forgive our debtors. And lead us not into temptation, but deliver us from evil. For thine is the kingdom, and the power, and the glory, for ever. Amen.
   Ibid 6

Thou art Peter, and upon this rock I will build my church; and the gates of hell shall not prevail against it. And I will give unto thee the keys of the kingdom of heaven.
   Ibid 16

Verily I say unto you, Except ye be converted, and become as little children, ye shall not enter into the kingdom of heaven.
   Ibid 18

For many are called, but few are chosen.
   Ibid 22

The sabbath was made for man, and not man for the sabbath.
   Mark 2

Glory to God in the highest, and on earth peace, good will toward men.
   Luke 2

Likewise joy shall be in heaven over one sinner that repenteth, more than over ninety and nine just persons, which need no repentance.
Ibid 15

In the beginning was the Word, and the Word was with God, and the Word was God.
John 1

If God be for us, who can be against us?
Romans 8

I have fought a good fight, I have finished my course, I have kept the faith.
2 Timothy 4

Now faith is the substance of things hoped for, the evidence of things not seen.
Hebrews 11

I am Alpha and Omega, the beginning and the ending, saith the Lord.
Revelation 1

William Blake
I will not cease from mental fight,
  Nor shall my sword sleep in my hand,
Till we have built Jerusalem
  In England's green and pleasant land.
Milton, Preface

Emily Jane Brontë
He was...the wearisomest, self-righteous pharisee that ever ransacked a Bible to rake the promises to himself and fling the curses on his neighbours.
Wuthering Heights

Sir Thomas Browne

Persecution is a bad and indirect way to plant religion.
  Religio Medici

Robert Browning

I show you doubt, to prove that faith exists.
  Bishop Blougram's Apology

The lark's on the wing;
The snail's on the thorn:
God's in his heaven—
All's right with the world!
  Pippa Passes

Ah, but a man's reach should exceed his grasp,
Or what's a heaven for?
  Andrea del Sarto

Edmund Burke

Politics and the pulpit are terms that have little agreement.
  Reflections on the Revolution in France

Robert Burton

One religion is as true as another.
  The Anatomy of Melancholy

Roger, Comte de Bussy-Rabutin

As you know, God is usually on the side of the big squadrons and against the small ones.
  Letter, 1677

Samuel Butler

An apology for the Devil: it must be remembered that we have heard only one side of the case. God has written all the books.

Note Books

An honest God's the noblest work of man.

Further Extracts from the Note-Books

George Gordon (Noel), 6th Lord Byron

"Whom the gods love die young" was said of yore.

Don Juan

Thomas Carlyle

The three great elements of modern civilization, Gunpowder, Printing, and the Protestant Religion.

Critical and Miscellaneous Essays: State of German Literature

Philip Dormer Stanhope, 4th Earl of Chesterfield

Religion is by no means a proper subject of conversation in a mixed company.

Letter to his godson

Marcus Tullius Cicero

Nature herself has imprinted on the minds of all the idea of a God.

De Natura Deorum

Charles Caleb Colton

Men will wrangle for religion; write for it; fight for it; die for it; anything but—live for it.

Lacon

Sir Noel (Pierce) Coward
Life without faith is an arid business.
Blithe Spirit

Daniel Defoe
And of all plagues with which mankind are curst,
Ecclesiastic tyranny's the worst.
The True-Born Englishman

Charles Dickens
"God bless us every one!" said Tiny Tim.
A Christmas Carol

Diogenes
I do not know whether there are gods, but there ought to be.
Tertullian's *Ad Nationes*

John Dryden
Gods they had tried of every shape and size
That godsmiths could produce or priests devise.
Absalom and Achitophel

Albert Einstein
Science without religion is lame, religion without science
is blind.
Out of My Later Years

Henry Havelock Ellis
The whole religious complexion of the modern world is
due to the absence from Jerusalem of a lunatic asylum.
Impressions and Comments

Ralph Waldo Emerson
Shove Jesus and Judas equally aside.
Essays, First Series: Self-Reliance

I like the silent church before the sevice begins, better than any preaching.
  Ibid

Demonology is the shadow of theology.
  Demonology

Empedocles
The nature of God is a circle of which the centre is everywhere and the circumference is nowhere.
  Attributed

Epicurus
It is folly for a man to pray to the gods for that which he has the power to obtain for himself.
  Vatican Sayings

Heinrich Heine
Christianity is an idea, and as such is indestructible and immortal, like every idea.
  History of Religion and Philosophy in Germany

Henry II
Will no one free me of this turbulent priest [Thomas à Becket]?
  Attributed

Thomas Hood
But now 'tis little joy
To know I'm farther off from heav'n
Than when I was a boy.
  I remember, I remember

Gerard Manley Hopkins
The world is charged with the grandeur of God.
  Poems: God's Grandeur

William Ralph Inge
The modern town-dweller has no God and no Devil; he lives without awe, without admiration, without fear.
  Outspoken Essays: Our Present Discontents

Douglas William Jerrold
Religion's in the heart, not in the knees.
  The Devil's Ducat

Martin Luther
I cannot and I will not recant anything, for to go against conscience is neither right nor safe. Here I stand. I cannot do otherwise. God help me. Amen.
  Diet of Worms speech, 1521

Thomas Babington Macaulay, 1st Baron Macaulay
She [the Roman Catholic church] may still exist in undiminished vigour when some traveller from New Zealand shall, in the midst of a vast solitude, take his stand on a broken arch of London Bridge to sketch the ruins of St Paul's.
  On Leopold von Ranke's *History of the Popes*

Karl Marx
Religion is the sigh of the oppressed creature, the feeling of a heartless world and the soul of soulless circumstances. It is the opium of the people.
  Critique of the Hegelian Philosophy of Right

The first requisite for the happiness of the people is the abolition of religion.
  Ibid

William Lamb, 2nd Viscount Melbourne

Things have come to a pretty pass when religion is allowed to invade the sphere of private life.

Attributed

John Milton

New Presbyter is but old Priest writ large.

Sonnet: On the New forcers of Conscience under the Long Parliament

What in me is dark
Illumine, what is low raise and support;
That to the highth of this great argument
I may assert eternal Providence,
And justify the ways of God to men.

Paradise Lost

Better to reign in hell, than serve in heav'n.

Ibid

Michel Eyquem de Montaigne

Man cannot make a worm, yet he will make gods by the dozen.

Essays

Charles Louis de Secondat, Baron de Montesquieu

If triangles had a god, he would have three sides.

Lettres Persanes

Novalis [Friedrich Leopold von Hardenberg]

Gott-trunkener Mensch.
A God-intoxicated man [Spinoza].

Sir William Osler

Nothing in life is more wonderful than faith—the one great moving force which we can neither weigh in the balance nor test in the crucible.
  British Medical Journal, 1910

Ovid [Publius Ovidius Naso]

There is a god within us, and we glow when he stirs us.
  Fasti

Thomas Paine

Every religion is good that teaches man to be good.
  The Rights of Man

Blaise Pascal

Men never do evil so completely and cheerfully as when they do it from religious conviction.
  Pensées

William Pitt the Elder

We have a Calvinistic creed, a Popish liturgy, and an Arminian clergy.
  House of Lords speech, 1770

Alexander Pope

  Some to church repair
Not for the doctrine, but the music there.
  Essay on Criticism

Laugh where we must, be candid where we can;
But vindicate the ways of God to man.
  An Essay on Man

An honest Man's the noblest work of God.
  Ibid

Ernest Renan
O Lord, if there is a Lord, save my soul, if I have a soul.
  Prière d'un Sceptique

Arthur Schopenhauer
Faith is like love: it cannot be forced.
  Parerga und Paralipomena

William Shakespeare
He wears his faith but as the fashion of his hat.
  Much Ado About Nothing 1

There are no tricks in plain and simple faith.
  Julius Caesar 4

There are more things in heaven and earth, Horatio,
Than are dreamt of in your philosophy.
  Hamlet 1

Our remedies oft in ourselves do lie,
Which we ascribe to heaven.
  All's Well That Ends Well 1

As flies to wanton boys, are we to gods;
They kill us for their sport.
  King Lear 4

Heaven is above all yet; there sits a judge
That no king can corrupt.
  King Henry VIII 3

George Bernard Shaw
There is only one religion, though there are a hundred
versions of it.
  Plays Unpleasant, Preface

In heaven an angel is nobody in particular.
   Man and Superman: Maxims for Revolutionists

Must then a Christ perish in torment in every age to save
those that have no imagination?
   St Joan

Percy Bysshe Shelley
Earth groans beneath religion's iron age
And priests dare babble of a God of peace
Even whilst their hands are red with guiltless blood.
   Queen Mab

Hell is a city much like London—
   A populous and a smoky city.
   Peter Bell the Third

Sydney Smith
As the French say, there are three sexes—men, women,
and clergymen.
   Lady Holland's *Memoir of the Rev. Sydney Smith*

Jonathan Swift
We have just enough religion to make us hate, but not
enough to make us love one another.
   Thoughts on Various Subjects; from Miscellanies

Thomas Szasz
If you talk to God, you are praying, if God talks to you,
you have schizophrenia. If the dead talk to you, you are a
spiritualist, if God talks to you, you are a schizophrenic.
   The Second Sin

Alfred, Lord Tennyson

Kind hearts are more than coronets,
  And simple faith than Norman blood.
  Lady Clara Vere de Vere

There lives more faith in honest doubt,
Believe me, than in half the creeds.
  In Memoriam

One God, one law, one element,
  And one far-off divine event,
To which the whole creation moves.
  Ibid

More things are wrought by prayer
Than this world dreams of.
  Idylls of the King: The Passing of Arthur

William Makepeace Thackeray

'Tis not the dying for a faith that's so hard, Master
Harry—every man of every nation has done that—'tis the
living up to it that is difficult.
  The History of Henry Esmond

Virgil [Publius Vergilius Maro]

The will of the gods was otherwise.
  Aeneid

Rudolf Virchow

There can be no scientific dispute with respect to faith,
for science and faith exclude one another.
  Disease, Life, and Man

Voltaire [François Marie Arouet]

Si Dieu n'existait pas, il faudrait l'inventer.

If God did not exist, it would be necessary to invent him.
Epitre à l'auteur du nouveau livre des trois imposteurs.
God is always on the side of the heaviest battalions.
    Letter, 1770

Oscar (Fingall O'Flahertie Wills) Wilde
Religions die when they are proved to be true. Science is
the record of dead religions.
    Phrases and Philosophies: for the Use of the Young:
    Chameleon

(Adeline) Virginia Woolf
I read the book of Job last night—I don't think God
comes well out of it.
    Letter to Lytton Strachey

William Wordsworth
But trailing clouds of glory do we come
    From God, who is our home:
Heaven lies about us in our infancy!
    Ode on Intimations of Immortality

Thomas Russell Ybarra
A Christian is a man who feels
Repentance on a Sunday
For what he did on Saturday
And is going to do on Monday.
    The Christian

Edward Young
A God all mercy, is a God unjust
    Night Thoughts

491

MANKIND

Aristotle
The high-minded man does not bear grudges, for it is not the mark of a great soul to remember injuries, but to forget them.
The Nicomachean Ethics

At his best man is the noblest of all animals; separated from law and justice, he is the worst.
Politics

Man is by nature a political animal.
Ibid

Neil (Alden) Armstrong
That's one small step for a man, one giant leap for mankind.
Stepping on to the moon's surface, 21 July 1969

Phineas Taylor Barnum
There's a sucker born every minute.
Attributed

Simone de Beauvoir
It is not in giving but in risking life that man is raised above the animal; that is why superiority has been

accorded in humanity not to the sex that brings forth but
to that which kills.
  The Second Sex

Carl Lotus Becker

[Man] alone can stand apart imaginatively and, regarding
himself and the universe in their eternal aspects, pronounce a judgment: the significance of man is that he is
insignificant and is aware of it.
  Progress and Power

Ambrose (Gwinett) Bierce

Man: An animal so lost in rapturous contemplation of
what he thinks he is as to overlook what he indubitably
ought to be.
  The Devil's Dictionary

Karen Blixen [Isak Dinesen]

What is man, when you come to think upon him, but a
minutely set, ingenious machine for turning, with infinite
artfulness, the red wine of Shiraz into urine?
  Seven Gothic Tales, 'The Dreamers'

Robert Browning

Love, hope, fear, faith—these make humanity;
These are its sign and note and character.
  Paracelsus

Robert Burns

Man's inhumanity to man.
  Man Was Made to Mourn

Confucius
The nature of men is always the same; it is their habits
that separate them.
  Analects

Ralph Waldo Emerson
No law can be sacred to me but that of my nature. Good
and bad are but names very readily transferable to that or
this; the only right is what is after my own constitution;
the only wrong what is against it.
  Essays: Self-Reliance

Clifton Fadiman
Experience teaches you that this man who looks you
straight in the eye, particularly if he adds a firm hand-
shake, is hiding something.
  Enter, Conversing

Anne Frank
In spite of eveything I still believe that people are really
good at heart.
  The Diary of a Young Girl

Sir W(illiam) S(chwenck) Gilbert
Man is Nature's sole mistake.
  Princess Ida

(Henry) Graham Greene
In human relations kindness and lies are worth a thousand
truths.
  The Heart of the Matter

Ernest Hemingway
I know only that what is moral is what you feel good after
and what is immoral is what you feel bad after.
  Death in the Afternoon

Homer
Of all the creatures that creep and breathe on the earth
there is none more wretched than man.
  Iliad

Aldous (Leonard) Huxley
That all men are equal is a proposition to which, at
ordinary times, no sane individual has ever given his assent.
  Proper Studies

Rudyard Kipling
Horrible, hairy, human.
  The Truce of the Bear

Charles Lamb
The human species, according to the best theory I can
form of it, is composed of two distinct races, the men
who borrow, and the men who lend.
  Essays of Elia: The Two Races of Men

François, Duc de La Rochefoucauld
Nothing is rarer than true good nature; they who are
reputed to have it are generally only pliant and weak.
  Maxims

Marcus Aurelius
Let us put an end, once for all, to this discussion of what
a good man should be—and be one.
  Meditations

W(illiam) Somerset Maugham

I'll give you my opinion of the human race...Their heart's in the right place, but their head is a thoroughly inefficient organ.

The Summing Up

Charles Louis de Secondat, Baron de Montesquieu

The lower animals have not the high advantages that we have, but they have something that we lack. They know nothing of our hopes, but they also know nothing of our fears; they are subject to death as we are, but they are not aware of it.

The Spirit of the Laws

George Augustus Moore

Humanity is a pigsty where liars, hypocrites and the obscene in spirit congregate.

Confessions of a Young Man

Octavio Paz

Solitude lies at the lowest depth of the human condition. Man is the only being who feels himself to be alone and the only one who is searching for the Other.

The Labyrinth of Solitude

Plato

Man is a tame, a domesticated animal.

Laws

Pliny the Elder

Man is the only animal that knows nothing, and can learn nothing without being taught. He can neither speak nor

walk nor eat, nor do anything at the prompting of nature,
but only weep.
　Natural History

Alexander Pope

Hope springs eternal in the human breast:
Man never is, but always to be blest.
　An Essay on Man

Francis Quarles

Man is Heaven's masterpiece.
　Emblems, Bk 2

Sir Walter Alexander Raleigh

I wish I loved the Human Race;
I wish I loved its silly face;
I wish I liked the way it walks;
I wish I liked the way it talks;
And when I'm introduced to one
I wish I thought What Jolly Fun!
　Laughter from a Cloud

Antoine de Saint-Exupéry

It is only with the heart that one can see rightly; what is
essential is invisible to the eye.
　The Little Prince

George Santayana

The mass of mankind is divided into two classes, the
Sancho Panzas who have a sense for reality, but no
ideals, and the Don Quixotes with a sense for ideals,
but mad.
　Interpretations of Poetry and Religion, Preface

Franz (Peter) Schubert

Let us take men as they are, not as they ought to be.
  Diary, 16 June 1816

Charles Monroe Schulz

I love mankind, it's people I can't stand.
  Go Fly a Kite, Charlie Brown

Seneca

Man is a social animal.
  De Beneficiis

Man is a reasoning animal.
  Epistolæ ad Lucilium

William Shakespeare

  Love all, trust a few,
Do wrong to none: be able for thine enemy
Rather in power than use, and keep thy friend
Under thy own life's key: be check'd for silence,
But never tax'd for speech.
  All's Well That Ends Well 1

Richard Brinsley Sheridan

Certainly nothing is unnatural that is not physically
impossible.
  The Critic

Robert Southey

Man is a dupable animal. Quacks in medicine, quacks in
religion, and quacks in politics know this, and act upon
that knowledge.
  The Doctor

Terence [Publius Terentius Afer]
Homo sum; humani nihil a me alienum puto.
I am a man; and nothing human is foreign to me.
  Heauton Timoroumenos

Henry David Thoreau
The mass of men lead lives of quiet desperation. What is
called resignation is confirmed desperation.
  Walden

Mark Twain [Samuel Langhorne Clemens]
The noblest work of God? Man. Who found it out? Man.
  Autobiography

Man is the only animal that blushes. Or needs to.
  Following the Equator

The fact that man knows right from wrong proves his
intellectual superiority to the other creatures; but the fact
that he can do wrong proves his moral inferiority to any
creature that cannot.
  What is Man?

Sir Jan Laurens Van der Post
Human beings are perhaps never more frightening than
when they are convinced beyond doubt that they are
right.
  The Lost World of the Kalahari

Marquis de Luc de Clapiers Vauvenargues
We should expect the best and the worst from mankind,
as from the weather.
  Reflections and Maxims

Voltaire [François Marie Arouet]
Animals have these advantages over man: they never hear
the clock strike, they die without any idea of death, they
have no theologians to instruct them, their last moments
are not disturbed by unwelcome and unpleasant ceremo-
nies, their funerals cost them nothing, and no one starts
lawsuits over their wills.
   Letter, 1769

William Wordsworth
The still, sad music of humanity
   Tintern Abbey

LIFE

Hans Christian Andersen
Every man's life is a fairy-tale written by God's
fingers.
  Works, Preface

P(hilip) J(ames) Bailey
It matters not how long we live, but how.
  Festus: Wood and Water

The Bible
For what is your life? It is even a vapour, that appeareth
for a little time, and then vanisheth away.
  James 4

Samuel Butler
Is life worth living? This is a question for an embryo, not
for a man.
To live is like love, all reason is against it, and all healthy
instinct for it.
  Notebooks

Nicolas Chamfort
Living is a sickness from which sleep provides relief
every sixteen hours. It's a palliative. The remedy is death.

Abraham Cowley
Life is an incurable Disease.
   Pindarique Odes

George Crabbe
Life is not measured by the time we live.
   The Village

Dinah Maria Mulock Craik
The secret of life is not to do what one likes, but to try to like that which one has to do.

Emily Dickinson
I took one draught of life,
I'll tell you what I paid,
Precisely an existence—
The market-price, they said.
   Further Poems

Guy Carleton Drewry
Ah, life could be so beautiful, Yet never is.
   Father and Son

Ralph Waldo Emerson
Life is good only when it is magical and musical, a perfect timing and consent, and when we do not anatomize it.
   Society and Solitude: Works and Days

Life is a festival only to the wise. Seen from the nook and chimney-side of prudence, it wears a ragged and dangerous front.
   Essays, First Series: Heroism

Donald Evans

Born with a monocle he stares at life,
And sends his soul on pensive promenades.
  En Monocle

Sir William Schwenck Gilbert

Life's a pudding full of plums,
Care's a canker that benumbs,
  Wherefore waste our elocution
  On impossible solution?
  Life's a pleasant institution,
Let us take it as it comes!
  The Gondoliers 1

Thomas Hardy

For life I've never cared greatly,
As worth a man's while.
  For Life I Had Never Cared Greatly

William Hazlitt

The most rational cure after all for the inordinate fear of
death is to set a just value on life.
  Table Talk

Katharine Hepburn

Life's what's important. Walking, houses, family. Birth
and pain and joy.

Thomas Hobbes

The life of man, solitary, poor, nasty, brutish, and short.
  Leviathan: Of Man

Elbert Hubbard

Life is simply one damn thing after another.
  Attributed

Dr Samuel Johnson
Life must be filled up, and the man who is not capable of intellectual pleasures must content himself with such as his senses can afford.
Mrs Piozzi's Johnsoniana

That kind of life is most happy which affords us the most opportunities of gaining our own esteem.
Works

Harriet Eleanor King
Measure thy life by loss instead of gain;
Not by the wine drunk, but by the wine poured forth.
The Disciples

Fran Lebowitz
Life is something to do when you can't get to sleep.
The Observer, 21 Jan. 1979

Jean de La Bruyère
There are only three events in a man's life; birth, life, and death; he is not conscious of being born, he dies in pain, and he forgets to live.
Caracteres

Edgar Lee Masters
It takes life to love Life.
Lucinda Matlock

Herman Melville
Life's a voyage that's homeward bound.
Cournos' *Modern Plutarch*

H(enry) L(ouis) Mencken
The basic fact about human existence is not that it is a tragedy, but that it is a bore.
Prejudices

Edna St Vincent Millay
It is not true that life is one damn thing after another—it's one damn thing over and over.
Letters of Edna St Vincent Millay

Wilson Mizner
Life's a tough proposition, and the first hundred years are the hardest.

Michel Eyquem de Montaigne
Mon métier et mon art, c'est vivre.
My business and my art is to live.
Essays

Were I to live my life over again, I should live it just as I have done. I neither complain of the past, nor fear the future.
Ibid

Ovid [Publius Ovidius Naso]
Vive pius; moriere pius.
Live righteously; you shall die righteously.
Amores

Stephen Phillips
How good it is to live, even the worst!
Christ in Hades

Arthur Schopenhauer

Each day is a little life; every walking and rising a little birth, every fresh morning a little youth, every going to rest and sleep a little death.

Our Relation to Ourselves

Seneca

Quemadmodum vivas, quamdiu vivas.

As long as you live, keep learning how to live.

Epistulæ ad Lucilium

Cotidie cum vita paria faciamus.

Let us balance life's account avery day.

Ibid

William Shakespeare

All the world's a stage,
And all the men and women merely players:
They have their exits and their entrances;
And one man in his time plays many parts,
Its acts being seven ages.

As You Like It 2

Life's but a walking shadow, a poor player
That struts and frets his hour upon the stage,
And then is heard no more; it is a tale
Told by an idiot, full of sound and fury
Signifying nothing.

Macbeth 5

Life is as tedious as a twice-told tale,
Vexing the dull ear of a drowsy man.

King John 3

George Bernard Shaw
Life is a disease; and the only difference between one
man and another is the stage of the disease at which he
lives.
Back to Methuselah

There are two tragedies in life. One is not to get your
heart's desire. The other is to get it.
Man and Superman

(Lloyd) Logan Pearsall Smith
There are two things to aim at in life: first, to get what
you want; and, after that, to enjoy it. Only the wisest of
mankind achieve the second.
Afterthoughts

Henry David Thoreau
I love a life whose plot is simple,
And does not thicken with every pimple.
Conscience

Virgil [Publius Vergilius Maro]
Pone aurem vellens, "vivite," ait, "venio"
Set forth the wine and the dice, and perish who thinks of
tomorrow!
Here's Death twitching my ear, "Live," says he, "for I'm
coming!"
Copa

Israel Zangwill
Oh, for the simple life,
For tents and starry skies!
Aspirations

AUTHOR INDEX

A

Acheson, Dean 367
Acton, Baron 260, 441
Adams, Franklin P. 224
Adams, Henry 215, 330, 427
Adams, John Quincy 252
Addison, Joseph 241, 345, 386, 433, 454
Aeschylus 245
Albery, James 375
Alcott, Bronson 310, 401, 433
Alexander the Great 241
Alfonso the Wise 270
Alfred, Lord Tennyson 399
Allen, Fred 260
Allen, Woody 228, 260, 296, 471
Ames, Fisher 446
Amiel, Henri Frédéric 215, 260
Amis, Kingsley 228, 354
Anacreon 265, 315
Anaxandrides 228
Andersen, Hans Christian 501
Anderson, Maxwell 296
Andrewes, Lancelot 477
Anouilh, Jean 414
Anthelme, Brillat-Savarin 363

Anthony, Susan B. 302,
Antiphanes, Macedonia of 427
Aristophanes 215, 302, 441
Aristotle 252, 330, 381, 446, 492
Armistead, Lewis Addison 338
Armstrong, Neil 492
Arnold, Matthew 394
Attlee, Clement Richard 446
Auden, W. H. 414
Augustine, St 270, 296, 454, 477
Austen, Jane 209, 245, 282, 302, 310, 386, 401

B

Bach, Alvan L. 362
Bacon, Francis 228, 252, 260, 265, 274, 302, 310, 321, 325, 330, 345, 401, 433, 441, 463, 467, 471
Bagehot, Walter 253, 270, 427, 477
Bailey, P J 501
Balzac, Honoré de 303, 477
Barère de Vieuzac, Bertrand 454
Baretti, Giuseppe 325
Barham, R. H. 354

C

D

E

I

J

M

S

Y

Z